PREFIGURING POSTBLACKNESS

PREFIGURING POSTBLACKNESS

Cultural Memory, Drama, and the African American Freedom Struggle of the 1960s

Carol Bunch Davis

University Press of Mississippi *Jackson*

www.upress.state.ms.us

Published with licensing and editorial support from the
Texas A & M at Galveston Department of Liberal Studies

The University Press of Mississippi is a member
of the Association of American University Presses.

Copyright © 2015 by University Press of Mississippi
All rights reserved
Manufactured in the United States of America

First printing 2015
∞
Library of Congress Cataloging-in-Publication Data

Bunch Davis, Carol.
 Prefiguring postblackness : cultural memory, drama, and the African American freedom struggle of the 1960s / Carol Bunch Davis.
   pages cm
 Includes bibliographical references and index.
 ISBN 978-1-4968-0298-9 (hardback) — ISBN 978-1-4968-0299-6 (ebook) 1. American drama—African American authors—History and criticism. 2. American drama—20th century—History and criticism. 3. African Americans—Race identity. 4. African Americans in literature. 5. African American theater. I. Title.
 PS338.N4B86 2015
 812'.5409896073—dc23
                        2015009869

British Library Cataloging-in-Publication Data available

FOR JIMMIE AND BETTIE BUNCH WITH LOVE AND GRATITUDE

CONTENTS

Acknowledgments ix

Introduction
The Postblack Ethos in "Texts Out of Time": Rosa Parks and the African American Freedom Struggle in Cultural Memory 3

Chapter One
"One for Whom Bread—Food—Is Not Enough": Beneatha Younger, Uplift Ideology, and Intellectual Freedom 22

Chapter Two
"A Ghost of the Future": Racial (Mis)perception and Black Subjectivity in LeRoi Jones's *Dutchman* 57

Chapter Three
"Ghost(s) in the House!": Black Subjectivity and Howard Sackler's *The Great White Hope* 81

Chapter Four
Gathering Black Subjectivities and Cultural Memory in Alice Childress's *Wine in the Wilderness* 104

Chapter Five
Prefiguring Postblackness in Charles Gordone's *No Place to Be Somebody: A Black Black Comedy in Three Acts* 129

Coda
Postblackness's Ancestors and Relatives or "The Past Pushing Us into the Present" 156

Notes 161

Bibliography 190

Index 200

ACKNOWLEDGMENTS

I thank James Kincaid, David Román, and George Sanchez who provided their guidance during this project's earliest stages. I am especially grateful to David for his generosity and support.

I also thank Kimberly N. Brown, Koritha Mitchell, Andrew Sofer, and Daniel S. Traber, who offered insights on and asked important questions about various segments of the project at different stages in its development.

The Texas A&M System Program to Enhance Scholarly and Creative Activities awarded me two grants that provided research support at the Schomburg Center for Research in Black Culture at the New York Public Library and the Harry Ransom Humanities Research Center at the University of Texas at Austin. The Popular Culture Association/American Culture Association's Marshall Fishwick Travel Award provided travel funding for research at the Schomburg Center. I also thank my department chair, JoAnn DiGeorgio-Lutz, for providing subvention support.

I owe a debt of gratitude to Paula Court, Rashid Johnson, and Lorna Simpson for permitting reproduction of their work, as well as Allison Pekel and Lynn Mason at WGBH-TV Boston, who helped track down still images from its production of Alice Childress's *Wine in the Wilderness* and secured permission for their use. I also thank Steven Fullwood and the staff at the Schomburg Center's Manuscripts, Archives, and Rare Books Division for their assistance in locating play manuscripts.

I thank Walter Biggins, formerly acquisitions editor at UPM, for his interest in the project and for guiding it in the early stages of the process, as well as Vijay Shah, UPM's current acquisitions editor, who saw it through to completion. I am also grateful to Katie Keene and the editorial staff for their guidance. Special thanks go to the manuscript's anonymous reader, to June Gilliam for her indexing help, and to Micheal Levine for his astute copyediting.

A version of Chapter Three: "Ghost(s) in the House!": Black Subjectivity and Howard Sackler's *The Great White Hope* appeared in *MELUS* in 2012, and I thank former editor Martha Cutter and the essay's anonymous readers for their thoughtful comments.

I also want to express my gratitude to a small group of friends and family which has sustained me over the long haul leading to this book. Conry Davidson, Shakira Holt, David Mitchell, Arnita Woods, and Ed and Terry Paul provided distractions, laughter and pep talks when I needed them most. Mrs. Shirley Gordon Jackson, Charles Gordone's sister, provided articles about his work, reflections on their childhood, and her enthusiastic encouragement throughout the last three years. Thanks also go to my extended Bunch and Brown families for always offering their love and support.

What my parents, Jimmie and Bettie Bunch, have provided, not just throughout this project's completion, but my entire life, goes so far beyond support. Every idea I hold about African American identity's complexities stems from watching them quietly, but skillfully navigate its terrain. They shape each page here, and I am so grateful to have them as my parents and as my friends.

Finally, I offer my love and gratitude to Peter Davis and Kai Davis for their endless sacrifices and support. Thank you both for all the love and joy you bring to my life.

PREFIGURING POSTBLACKNESS

INTRODUCTION

The Postblack Ethos in "Texts Out of Time": Rosa Parks and the African American Freedom Struggle in Cultural Memory

I wasn't surprised when my seven-year-old daughter told me in February that she had learned about Rosa Parks in her first grade class. When I asked her to tell me more, she replied, "Rosa Parks said no" and dutifully recited the outcome of her refusal: "After she said no when they tried to be unfair to her, it helped other people say no too and then everyone could be treated the same." Though she draws her version of Parks's narrative with very broad strokes, it reflects the story many of us recite about her refusal to accept the terms of Jim Crow segregation in Montgomery, Alabama, on December 1, 1955. As the story usually goes, as she was heading home at the end of a long day of work at her job as a seamstress at the Montgomery Fair department store, an exhausted Parks found a seat on Bus 2875 during rush hour traffic. After the first ten seats reserved for white passengers filled, Parks and three other black passengers were told by the bus driver to relinquish their seats. The other riders reluctantly did so, but the forty-two-year-old Parks refused to give hers up to the waiting white male passenger because, according to the narrative, the quiet seamstress was too tired to move. The bus driver, James Blake, summoned police officers and then pressed charges against her for a violation of Chapter 6, Section 100 of the Montgomery city code. Parks was arrested and held in the Montgomery jail. Her arrest prompted Dr. Martin Luther King's leadership of the Montgomery Bus Boycott, gave birth to the Civil Rights Movement's "heroic era" that reached a crescendo with the 1963 March on Washington, and culminated with President Lyndon Johnson's signing of the Voting Rights Act of 1965, which Parks watched him sign.

This narrative—or what historian Jeanne Theoharis has called an "inspirational fable"—identifying Parks's refusal as the start of the Civil Rights

Movement dominates US cultural memory.[1] But it serves as more than a chronological marker of the movement's beginning. This narrative accurately outlines the defeat of racial segregation and consequently, in the view of many, marks the end of racial inequality. It also drives cultural memory of the era, or the media, institutions, and practices that construct a collective past for the nation by transforming Parks's rejection of racial injustice into a moment of national triumph.[2] The victory over racial inequality ultimately enables a stronger nation precisely because cultural memory situates racial injustice safely in the past and frames it as a moral aberration that the nation has overcome through a variety of means, including legal, legislative, and social protest actions; media representations; and cultural production.[3] Parks's stand is usually framed as the first direct action protest that helped instigate subsequent direct action protests, as well as legal and legislative actions which followed. In short, the narrative situates her refusal as the spark that ignited the Civil Rights Movement's fire.

The representational figure of Parks, then, serves several purposes in US cultural memory of the civil rights era and the notion of a collective national past in multiple ways. First, cultural memory frames her as the narrative's sympathetic protagonist, very often as the "mother of the Civil Rights Movement," and situates images of her and her stand as a symbol of the nation's long-ago resolved problems with racial inequality. This reading of Parks informs her invocation in the current historical moment and is deployed to demonstrate the nation's progress in eradicating racial inequality. In other words, since segregation has ended and African Americans can vote due to the struggle in which Parks was engaged, all of the nation's citizens now enjoy equal access to life opportunities and concerns about racial inequality can be put aside. Second, and perhaps more significant than Parks as a symbol of a nation's resolved racial problems, are the various ways in which she and her stand are deployed to substantiate this end. Most often, cultural memory positions Parks's refusal as the impetus for national reflection on racial injustices in the South that resulted in a collective shift in national consciousness marked by social change and political progress on such issues.[4] She symbolizes both the means of resolving racial injustice as well as its result. Her multivalent cultural work is best illustrated in two events: the national mourning of her death in 2005 and the postage stamp and statue dedicated in her honor in 2013. The significance of national reflection and racial progress in the Parks civil rights narrative is evident in the national mourning of her death when she became the first woman and the second African American to lie in honor in the Capitol Rotunda. However, her key role in the nation's redemption narrative comes at the cost of a one-dimensional view of Parks and the life she lived. As Theoharis observes, the memorial services held for her in Birmingham, Detroit, and Washington, DC, memorialized the reserved seamstress and omitted a more complicated perspective on her activism in order to serve a more pressing national need: an opportunity "for the nation to lay to rest a national heroine *and* its own history of racism."[5]

Nearly ten years after her death, on what would have been her one hundredth birthday, the US Postal Service issued a stamp bearing her likeness, and just three weeks later, a statue of Parks was unveiled and dedicated in the National Statuary Hall of the US Capitol. The unveiling of a statue in her honor in ceremonies presided over by the nation's first African American president offers seemingly irrefutable evidence of racial progress in the United States and remarks by the event's speakers echo that notion. At the dedication ceremony, President Obama and two of his most vocal critics, Senator Mitch McConnell and Representative John Boehner, set aside partisan rancor and shared the dais with the president engaging the inspirational fable's rhetoric, as well as showcasing the nation's eagerness to appropriate Parks and her stand against Jim Crow segregation as part of a triumphant national narrative presumably marking the end of racial injustice. Continuing the cultural memory work of Parks's 2005 memorial services, the occasion of the statue's dedication provided the opportunity for Parks to occupy what President Obama called "her rightful place among those who shaped this nation's course."[6] While he suggests that Parks has earned a position within the nation's pantheon of important historical figures, his colleagues' interpretation of what that position might be reinscribes the rhetoric of the "inspirational fable," particularly the trope of national redemption. Representative Boehner observed that Parks's likeness stands "right in the gaze" of a statue of Confederate president Jefferson Davis, figuratively offering a permanent rebuttal to a history of race-based inequality in the United States that has now been put to rest.[7]

Moreover, Senator McConnell spoke of Parks in language reminiscent of the "spiritual bellhop," or a figure who in his or her suffering becomes a carrier of experiences from which others can benefit, describing her stand as "a spur to reflection and self-examination, and the reconciliation of cherished ideals of freedom, democracy and constitutional rights with the reality of life as others lived it."[8] Emphasizing a notion of racial progress that requires white reflection upon how the nation's basic tenets failed black "others," Senator McConnell frames Parks's stand as an opportunity for whites to ponder the incongruity between the presence of freedom and full citizenship in their own lives and its absence in the daily lived experience of African Americans. Finally, as he identifies the national introspection Parks initiated,

Senator McConnell offers in the statue's unveiling an official pardon of the nation's denial of full citizenship for African Americans as her stand's most significant outcome because it allows us to move beyond identifying and discussing racial injustice in the current moment. Senator McConnell leaves no doubt about her centrality in a national redemption narrative that frames racial injustice as an anachronism by asserting that her stand resulted in a country where "segregated buses only exist in museums . . . where children of every race are free to fulfill their God-given potential . . . where [a] simple carpenter's daughter from Tuskegee is honored as a national hero. What a story. What a legacy. What a country."[9] If the 2005 public memorials framed her as "a self-sacrificing mother figure for a nation that would use her death for a ritual of national redemption," then the 2013 unveiling of the stamp and the statue to a repentant American public extends her role as a mother figure *and* the nation's redemption in perpetuity.[10] Almost sixty years after the Montgomery Bus Boycott, cultural memory attributes her refusal to nothing more than physical fatigue, and her lifelong advocacy for social justice is expunged from its narrative. Yet she was part of a network of civil rights workers and activists in Montgomery and had also been trained in nonviolent resistance and civil disobedience at Tennessee's Highlander Folk School, so while Parks's impromptu refusal to adhere to Jim Crow segregation might be understood as the impulse of an "everywoman" who was both physically and psychically tired of second class citizenship's daily indignities, she understood exactly what her refusal meant and what its implications were. She was not a naïve Civil Rights Movement ingénue, as cultural memory suggests, but was instead a seasoned campaigner whose history of activism long preceded her bus refusal. She joined the Montgomery NAACP in 1943 and served as its secretary until 1957. In addition, her involvement in Montgomery's civic life demonstrates that she saw the value of collective action.[11]

Despite this, cultural memory's image of the reserved, bespectacled seamstress who inspired a nation to reflect upon and then set racial injustice right mobilizes the narrative most of us know. The dedication's sweeping rhetoric as well as the memorial stamp and statue themselves not only confirm racial injustice's end, but perhaps more importantly, mark the nation's progress. Yet both the dedication and the memorial markers only heighten the incongruity between cultural memory's linear narrative about the Civil Rights Movement that is built upon a selective construction of Parks; the facts of her lived experience trouble that simplistic narrative.

Furthermore, in framing the current historical moment's racial landscape as one that no longer requires the acts of resistance in which Parks engaged, the stamp and the statue not only confirm cultural memory's linear narrative of the Civil Rights Movement's genesis with the singular act of a one-dimensional Parks; they also enable the nation to reflect upon and see evidence of the resolution of the racial injustices from 1955 that supposedly have no implications today. Yet, on the same day of the statue's unveiling, the US Supreme Court heard oral arguments in a challenge to a key provision of the Voting Rights Act of 1965, legislation that Mrs. Parks watched President Lyndon Johnson sign on the Capitol Rotunda and that came into being as a result of the commitments and long-term activism in which she and many other people engaged before but also after her stand on December 1, 1955. Four months later, in June 2013, the court struck down Section 4 of the 1965 Voting Rights Act requiring that the federal government approve any changes in election laws in nine mostly southern states, including Parks's home state of Alabama. In Shelby County, Alabama, which initiated the lawsuit resulting in the Court's ruling, some African American voters were culled from voting rolls after a clerk improperly removed their names based on local utility records.[12]

The irony is hard to miss in Parks's national enshrinement on the same day that the US Supreme Court eliminated the very legislation she played a significant role in establishing with her ongoing civil rights advocacy alongside thousands of other activists. It is one example in a series of contradictions about race and racial inequality in the United States that might be understood as a defining characteristic of the nation's race discourse. But the institutional irony in the Supreme Court's decision put alongside her ongoing enshrinement as a national icon also shows the significant role that images and representations of the Freedom Struggle era play in a range of arguments that at different turns undermine and support some of the broader goals of the Freedom Struggle itself. In this instance, Parks's enshrinement helps to justify the Court's observation that voter discrimination no longer warrants federal oversight or intervention. Though the Court acknowledged that such discrimination continues, Justice John Roberts argued that congressional inaction since the act's last renewal forced the Court's decision, writing in the majority opinion that "our country has changed, and while any racial discrimination in voting is too much, Congress must ensure that the legislation it passes to remedy that problem speaks to current conditions."[13] The nation's simultaneous memorialization of Parks and dismantling of the 1965 Voting Rights Act illustrates how cultural memory's inspirational narrative of Parks, specifically, and the Civil Rights Movement, broadly, serves to unravel the progress made against racial injustice that she and many others struggled to secure. By reinterpreting and repackaging the people and the events comprising the Civil Rights Movement and the Black Arts Movement—collectively the African American Freedom Struggle—cultural memory constructs a narrative of the era that serves a multitude of ends in the current moment.

Cultural memory's consolidating power to forge these narratives is driven largely by our consumption of them. They are deeply informed by our collective unwillingness to embrace what Rebecca Wanzo has called "narrative messiness" in telling the story of the Civil Rights Movement.[14] Cultural memory's framing of the Freedom Struggle's leaders, its rank-and-file participants, its cultural products and producers, its influences, and its chronologies depends on an easily digested, simplistic narrative enacted by two-dimensional figures resulting in the "Santa Clausification" of figures such as Reverend Martin Luther King and Rosa Parks.[15] Too often, we reject complicated, fallible, and therefore, undeniably human protagonists, opting instead for morally unimpeachable heroes and immoral villains in a story of good overcoming evil—a narrative strategy that continued into the Black Power/Arts era and helped established a master narrative of the African American Freedom Struggle of the 1960s. By necessity, then, cultural memory's framing of Parks in the current moment omits many aspects of her life and activism because the narrative's broad strokes cannot simultaneously accommodate the Freedom Struggle's narrative messiness and continue to advance the narrative's overriding theme of redemption.[16] To do so would undermine the narrative's purpose to render racial inequality a part of the nation's past and would necessarily reveal the complexities, pitfalls, and promises of the Freedom Struggle era that might not always support a linear narrative of national redemption.

Yet such omissions obscure the richness and texture of our understanding of the Freedom Struggle era and its participants.[17] Even if we recognize the events and relationships that might complicate cultural memory's framing of Parks, perhaps it is even more important to understand that cultural memory's narrow representation of Parks that underwrites the narrative of the Civil Rights Movement sharply contrasts with how she defined herself. One compelling example of this is while she supported and deeply admired Dr. King and his leadership in the Southern Christian Leadership Conference and the bus boycott, she identified Malcolm X as her hero and role model, which defies many aspects of cultural memory's standard Civil Rights Movement narrative we have all come to accept as unimpeachable truth.[18] Further, at the invitation of the Nation of Islam's Louis Farrakhan, Parks addressed thousands gathered on the National Mall for the Million Man March, jointly organized by the National African American Leadership Summit, a broad range of local NAACP organizations, and the Nation of Islam in October 1995. She also opposed US engagement in the Vietnam War. These and other departures from the linear narrative complicate the way we understand Parks and the Civil Rights Movement and interrupt the "inspirational fable" that has been created about her and her act of resistance. Still, it is this fable or linear master narrative about the civil rights era that the stamp and the statue commemorate far more than it celebrates Parks's lifelong activism and her work for racial justice specifically and social justice broadly. But Parks isn't exceptional in this regard. Nearly all of the figures of the era have been pressed into the service of cultural memory's one-dimensional narrative, which contributes to its longevity as well as to a narrow understanding of both the Freedom Struggle and its implications in the current moment.

Although the events and figures like Parks are most commonly put in the service of this resilient narrative, the era's cultural products have played a significant role in its development as well. Their analysis has been limited in comparison to that of figures like Parks; however, culture and cultural production significantly informs how we understand and discuss the era. Scholars including Joe Street and Brian Ward have called for further study of the era's cultural products and point to their importance during the Freedom Struggle era as well as their continuing significance in the current moment. Street emphasizes the role that they played in spurring direct action, arguing that the "cultural organizing" of Freedom Struggle era participants "made an explicit attempt to use cultural forms or expressions as an integral . . . part of the political struggle."[19] He further suggests that gaining a better understanding of those efforts can help us to "come to terms with the massive impact and legacy of the civil rights movement."[20] Similarly, Ward contends that too often African American Freedom Struggle histories pose cultural production as "posterior, ancillary or alternatives to the real political nitty and economic gritty" of the struggle and asserts that reconsidering the era's "interlocking worlds of media and culture, art and entertainment" will afford us "insight into postwar American race relations, black and white racial consciousness, and the struggle for racial justice."[21] In short, culture and cultural expression produced in the Freedom Struggle era helped to mobilize Freedom Struggle participants and continued exploration of the era's culture can illuminate race discourse in the current moment.

Mindful of these calls for further exploration of the cultural products of the Freedom Struggle era, *Prefiguring Postblackness* intervenes in a narrative of declension that limits the representation of African American identity within the Civil Rights Movement to Martin Luther King's nonviolent protest leadership in the segregated South and casts Malcolm X's advocacy of black nationalism and the ensuing Black Power/Arts Movement as undermining civil rights advances. Through its five case studies of African American identity staged in plays between 1959 and 1969, it instead offers representations that engage, critique, and revise racial uplift ideology and Black Arts' cultural nationalism—the two primary ideologies underwriting African American representations within cultural memory of that era.

Cultural memory of the African American Freedom Struggle era hinges on a master narrative that focuses on the "heroic period" of the Civil Rights Movement. Beginning with the *Brown v. Board of Education* Supreme Court decision in 1954, followed by Mrs. Parks' stand and the Montgomery Bus Boycott in 1955, this master narrative marks the passage of the Voting Rights Act of 1965 as the era's apex and characterizes the emergence of Black Power politics and Black Arts cultural production in 1966, alongside Student Nonviolent Coordinating Committee (SNCC) activist Stokely Carmichael's calls for Black Power the same year, as evidence of the Civil Rights Movement's decline. *Prefiguring Postblackness* argues that the plays subvert cultural memory's master narrative by strategically revising the rhetoric, representations, ideologies, and iconography informing the African American Freedom Struggle. This revision necessarily critiques racial uplift ideology's tenets of civic and moral virtue as a condition of African American inclusion in the American plurality appearing in the Civil Rights Movement's nonviolent direct action protests, as well as reimagines the Black Arts Movement's sometimes proscriptive notions of black authenticity as a condition of black identity and cultural production. In so doing, the representations put forward in the plays construct a counternarrative to cultural memory of the African American Freedom Struggle in the midst of that era.

Prefiguring Postblackness offers close textual analysis of African American identity in the plays and posits a postblack ethos as the means by which these representations construct their counternarratives to cultural memory and to broaden narrow constructions of African American identity shaping racial discourse in the US public sphere of the 1960s. The phrase *postblack ethos* marks a temporal distinction between the exploration of black identity present in the plays discussed here and those of late 1980s postblack discourse. Consequently, these prescient representations prefigure late 1980s postblack discourse's narrative tropes and representational strategies that embody contradicting perceptions of black identity and reject, embrace, satirize, magnify, and revise African American identity's cultural codes.

Put alongside textual analysis of the plays' representations are close readings of the plays' theater reviews published in both the mainstream and the African American press, which enable a reading of cultural memory's master narrative of the era in the midst of the era. Pointing to the significant influence theater critics held in interpreting representations of African American identity for a broad audience, *Prefiguring Postblackness* calls attention to how their print media reviews of the plays frequently turned to the politics of the then-current moment, as well as to earlier historical moments, simultaneously constructing and drawing upon cultural memory to translate and contextualize the representations on stage for a national audience.[22] This study contends that their work shapes our collective imagination of the 1960s, outlines how their framing of the era informs their discussion of these six plays, and details how it situates them in cultural memory. Most often, theater critics turn to the past to interpret the representations on stage, where it serves as "a point of comparison, an opportunity for analogy, an invitation to nostalgia, a redress to earlier events."[23] Considering reviews of the plays under study as an archive of cultural memory, *Prefiguring Postblackness* emphasizes how African American identity is constructed and transmitted through cultural memory and foregrounds the ways in which the representations it studies seek to complicate that identity in ways that "prefigure" postblackness and our current discussions of postblack identity.

My rationale for the postblack ethos in the 1960s derives from literary critic Marianne DeKoven's mapping of the postmodern. Contending that 1960s radical politics and counterculture enabled the shift from the modern to the postmodern, she points to the Freedom Struggle's specific contribution to that move, arguing that the "development of an 'identity politics' based on race and the simultaneous location of that development in the liberatory humanist universalism of modernity and the local, particularist subject politics of postmodernity" as the African American Freedom Struggle's most significant role in the shift from modern to postmodern.[24] In other words, the Freedom Struggle's collective political, legal, social, and cultural challenges to race-based oppression enabled it to intervene in and disrupt universality's meanings through its deconstruction of white hegemony. The Freedom Struggle fused these aspects of the modern and the postmodern, and in so doing, serves as a pivot from modern to postmodern cultural production in the 1960s. Following DeKoven, I locate postblack identity's emergence in the long 1960s—that is, the late 1950s until the early 1970s. Though vestiges of modernist universalism surface in different degrees in the plays that are home to these early gestures toward postblack identity, they retain two significant postblack sensibilities: a critique of essentialism that enables an "affirm[ation] of multiple black identities [and] varied black experience[s]" and a refusal to engage in a "nostalgic allegiance to the past" or the nascent Freedom Struggle's then-current moment.[25]

But not only do they bask in its possibilities, they also critique and reimagine how the Freedom Struggle itself frames identity by drawing upon the key sensibilities attributed to postblack representations. Critic Bertram Ashe allows that while there are always "texts out of time" that buck the conventions of every literary period, the primary distinction between the texts of previous periods and the post-soul era's is that the latter do not "conform in lockstep ... to a quest for black freedom."[26] *Prefiguring Postblackness* contends that the texts it studies refuse this lockstep formation as well. They envision black identity beyond the quest for black freedom and shift their attention to a critique of the ways in which the Freedom Struggle has narrowed the scope of that identity. Refusing to yield to the politics of respectability and civility that were central to the Civil Rights Movement's successes, the representations anticipate postblack discourse in two ways. First, the representations of blackness in the plays reject the white supremacist premise underwriting Jim Crow segregation. Segregation's basic premise was rooted in the notion that it was "essential to defend[ing] American civilization from black contamination."[27] As a result, much of the Freedom Struggle's rhetoric and direct action took aim at dismantling and disproving that premise by demonstrating civic and moral fitness for full citizenship. I argue that the representations of black identity which *Prefiguring Postblackness* studies reject the impulse to disprove that premise and instead offer iterations of black identity that flout those premises, opting instead to shape their own notions of black identity. Further, the expansion of rights on the horizon for African Americans during that era helped to mobilize the refusal of civility and respectability, but most importantly, empowered them to imagine identities beyond a quest for black freedom. In effect, these playwrights' representations envision what black identity might look like when it is not bound to securing collective freedom.

Finally, Ashe's allowance for "texts out of time" resonates with his and other critics' observations about the existence of what might be called "quasi-post-black" texts appearing prior to the post-soul era. In both instances, the artists and their texts are situated as literary eccentricities that do not represent a "school" or a broader literary movement. Yet I contend that while the plays under consideration may not themselves constitute a movement or a school in the same way that we understand the Harlem Renaissance/New Negro Movement, they can be understood as part of what cultural critic Raymond Williams has called a "structure of feeling." Describing a particular community of experience that is distinct from our notions of culture in its broadest meaning, as it names an emerging culture that is "in part unconscious ... [and] is described with great deal of difficulty by new literature and art," it resonates with emergent postblack identities in the 1960s. Though the texts that *Prefiguring Postblackness* studies are not temporally of the postblack era, they gesture toward the emergence of postblack identity.

If the post-soul text's and, by extension, postblack identity's signal move is, to leave "many 'traditional' tropes of blackness dated and even meaningless," to "trouble blackness, . . . [to] stir it up, touch it, feel it out, and hold it up for examination," or to be "rooted in, but not restricted by [b]lackness," then the representations of African American identity in *A Raisin in the Sun* (1959), *Dutchman* (1964), *Wine in the Wilderness* (1969), *The Great White Hope* (1969), and *No Place to Be Somebody* (1969) make the same moves within their then-contemporary historical moment.[28] In short, while the timing of the plays under study might appear to make the emergence of postblack identity in the 1960s a temporal impossibility, rethinking concepts of the contemporary, framing the African American Freedom Struggle as a pivot from the modern to the postmodern, and considering these works as contributions to a "structure of feeling" of that era enables postblack identity's emergence in the long 1960s.

These sensibilities inform the work of critics engaging and formulating the post-soul era, including Mark Anthony Neal, Trey Ellis, Nelson George, Lisa Jones, Bertram Ashe, and Greg Tate, among others who frame postblack identity as a product of the post-soul aesthetic. Neal defines it as "an aesthetic center within contemporary black popular culture that at various moments considers . . . the general commodification of black life and culture, and the proliferation of black 'meta-identities,' while continuously collapsing on modern concepts of blackness."[29] All of these critics establish the post-soul era as following the end of the Freedom Struggle era, and the earliest citation of its start is Neal's observation that *Regents of the University of California v. Bakke* challenged affirmative action in 1978.[30] While the periodization of the post-soul era requires a "what now?" moment that the Freedom Struggle era's end seemingly mobilizes, I maintain that in reading the long 1960s as a pivot from modern to postmodern, such periodization does not preclude postblack identity's advent before the end of the Freedom Struggle era. Even as *Prefiguring Postblackness* recognizes the necessity of a "what now?" moment that enabled the fully bloomed post-soul era to surface, it argues for the importance of a "what if?" moment in the long 1960s that privileges the texts it studies as contemporary within that historical moment. In effect, acknowledging texts within the long 1960s as anticipating the fully flowered texts of the post-soul era in the long 1980s does not undermine the value of either sort of reflective moment within African American expressive culture. What it illustrates is that these impulses continued to be relevant and worthy of discussion and deployment for cultural producers across fifty years of African American cultural production.

Theatre and performance critic David Román's theorizing of the contemporary further illuminates my argument for postblack identity's emergence in the Freedom Struggle era. He describes the contemporary as "a fluid and nearly suspended temporal condition . . . a moment not yet in the past and not yet in the future, yet a period we imagine as having some power to shape our relation to both history and futurity."[31] Likewise, I understand the representations of black identity in these plays within the then-contemporary moment. Speaking to de jure and de facto segregation's waning influence on how African Americans constructed identity precisely because of the Freedom Struggle's successes, they demonstrate their power to shape relation to both history and futurity through the representations of black identity they offer. With freedom imminent due to the movement's progress and in a "nearly suspended temporal condition," these playwrights creatively imagine black subjects who delight in the Freedom Struggle's possibilities for identity during a range of moments within that social movement.[32]

Further, the reviews aid in confirming Román's perspective on the term *contemporary* that refutes it as "presentist" or "as if the contemporary could only be understood as antagonistic to the past, or in a mutually exclusive relationship to it." In further disputing claims around "presentism," he argues that "contemporary performance is itself already embedded in a historical archive of past performances that help contextualize the work in history. In this way, the contemporary participates in an ongoing dialogue with previously contemporary works now relegated to literary history, the theatrical past, or cultural memory."[33] The reviews published in both the mainstream and African American press at the time of each play's production make visible the archive of previous performances that impinge upon subsequent performances. Román's notion of the relationship between contemporary works and "previously contemporary" that binds them in an ongoing dialogue has three important implications for this project. First, the "previously contemporary" works considered here have been consistently produced in venues across the country and in Europe in the more than forty years since their initial production. What this enduring production history suggests is that though they have been relegated to "literary history, the theatrical past or cultural memory," these plays and their representations still resonate with the cultural workers who stage them and potentially for the audiences who view them.[34] In a sense, they remain contemporary, in the here and now, because they have been summoned from the past to speak to and in the present moment. Accessing and analyzing the reviews can provide an entry into discovering what resonates and why it does so in the current historical moment.

Second, the review archive throws into relief the specters of previous representations of black identity. Even if the plays themselves do not always resurrect or allude to previous representations of "blackness" on stage, though they often do, the critics reviewing the plays consistently draw upon preceding representations of "blackness" in an effort to make sense of the representation being staged. Accessing the review archives illuminates how such representations are put in the service of unraveling the current representations the critics interpret and helps to determine what tools they have at their disposal to read them. Often, for the critics of the plays considered in *Prefiguring Postblackness*, these tools are the ghosts of previous representations, performances, and historical events occurring in that current moment.

Finally, the pivotal role critics play in how the representations on stage are interpreted by audiences across the country is significant. I turn once more to Román, who in emphasizing theater critics' influence in the twentieth century, suggests that a cadre of critics who began writing for daily and weekly publication in the mid-1920s held considerable sway over audiences because their work was "readily found in newspapers and magazines [and they] helped educate an audience of readers on the merits of theater."[35] Moreover, by the start of the long 1960s, when the plays considered here were produced, this upper echelon of theater critics had firmly established themselves as effective readers of theater and drama. In short, how they interpreted the works they reviewed mattered to their readership and was taken seriously by them. Consequently, drawing upon the review archive reveals the ways in which theater critics drew upon the contemporary moment to interpret the works under consideration and how those assessments shape cultural memory of the era.

I want to address terminology used throughout the text. Critics such as Lisa Jones, Trey Ellis, Greg Tate, and others writing in the late 1980s initially called the aesthetic they saw in the work of artists and writers the New Black Aesthetic (NBA). In the mid-1990s, other critics, including Mark Anthony Neal and Bertram Ashe, referenced it as the Post-Soul Aesthetic (PSA). I will use postblack to collectively reference both the New Black Aesthetic and the Post-Soul Aesthetic. The NBA/PSA reflects the two different names attached to and preferred by some scholars to reference what are closely related notions of cultural production after the end of the long 1960s and cultural producers born after the Civil Rights Movement. Though I will make reference to the NBA/PSA in the subsequent chapters, I will use postblack identity and postblack cultural production to indicate an acknowledgment of both schools in an attempt to discuss them collectively rather than singling out one or the other. While for some, postblack might suggest a retreat from or a disavowal of blackness in terms of racial struggle and the realities of race in the United States, that is not the meaning I want to convey in its usage here.

I argue instead that postblack signals an engagement with and, ultimately, a critique of monolithic notions of black subjectivity offered in US cultural production. The postblackness that the plays under consideration prefigure explores and investigates black subjectivity in an effort to broaden the scope and range of black subjectivity's representation.

The first chapter, "'One for whom bread—food—is not enough': Beneatha Younger, Uplift Ideology, and Intellectual Freedom," argues that while Lorraine Hansberry's 1959 play *A Raisin in the Sun* foregrounds the necessity for racial uplift ideology in the Younger family's pursuit of the American Dream, culminating in the occupancy of their new home in the all-white enclave of Clybourne Park, it also sketches the postblack ethos in its representation of Beneatha Younger, the younger sister of the play's protagonist, Walter Lee Younger. Beneatha disrupts her family's commitment to racial uplift ideology through her interrogation of patriarchal family structure, religious ideology, motherhood, African liberation struggles, and class mobility. Through the exchanges between Beneatha and her mother, Lena, her sister-in-law, Ruth, and her suitors, George Murchison and Joseph Asagai, Hansberry poses, but leaves unanswered, questions about the efficacy of ideologies shaping the range of African American identities presented in *A Raisin in the Sun*.

One example of Beneatha's pursuit of intellectual freedom comes in a scene that was deleted from the original playscript but restored to its American Playhouse broadcast in 1989 and to the Random House publication of the play. After she snubs the family's meddlesome and envious neighbor, Mrs. Johnson, who invokes Booker T. Washington's notion that "education has spoiled many a good plow hand" in her critique of Beneatha's college education as well as the Younger's impending move to Clybourne Park, Beneatha alludes to intraracial debates about the false opposition between intellectual and corporeal freedom. Though Lena criticizes Beneatha's behavior toward Mrs. Johnson, Beneatha defends herself, telling her mother "there are two things we, as a people have got to overcome, one is the Ku Klux Klan—and the other is Mrs. Johnson."[36] In this and other scenes, Beneatha's recognition of intraracial conflict about the pursuit of both intellectual and corporeal freedom contributes significantly to the play's ideological import and continually disrupts the play's action. Even as she stands witness to her brother's climactic rejection of an offer to buy the Youngers' home at a profit to them to maintain a segregated neighborhood, she contests Walter Lee's "coming into manhood," as her mother would have it. As they depart the South Side apartment, Walter Lee and Beneatha return to their debate about her ambition to become a doctor, her possible move to Nigeria, and her potential marriage to Asagai. Ultimately, in her interrogation of racial uplift ideology and the patriarchy that often underwrites it, she offers an alternative mode of self-representation built upon the pursuit of intellectual freedom.

Yet theater critics reviewing the play in the African American and mainstream press frame the Youngers' eminent desegregation of Clybourne Park as well as Walter Lee's ascent to manhood as signaling the continued viability of racial uplift ideology as a means of achieving full citizenship within the broader African American Freedom Struggle, leaving Beneatha's pursuit of intellectual freedom unexplored. Most importantly, this chapter posits that the questions raised by Beneatha's ideological inquiry and their link to African American subjectivity are examined in subsequent representations of African American identity in the remaining four plays under consideration.

Amiri Baraka, one of the most important architects and practitioners of the Black Arts Aesthetic, the cultural component of the Black Power Movement, advanced what are described by some critics as didactic and restrictive aesthetic codes for African American literary production in the 1960s that postblack cultural producers in the current moment are forced to subvert. According to Nita Kumar and other critics, Baraka and other Aestheticians outlined a proscriptive artistic program that substituted neo-African essentialism and a fixed notion of black identity for Western essentialism.[37] Yet as the Black Aesthetic's spiritual leader, Larry Neal, suggests, its artistic program also addressed "the necessity for black people to define the world in their own terms" in addition to making legible the notion that "there are in fact and spirit two Americas—one black, one white" in the literary culture its advocates produce.[38]

The second chapter, "'A Ghost of the Future': Racial (Mis)perception and Black Subjectivity in LeRoi Jones's *Dutchman*," contends that Amiri Baraka's play, *Dutchman* (1964), employs race icons to engage with white liberal response to racial uplift ideology and its implications for African American subjectivity. During a subway ride "heaped in modern myth," the dialogue between the play's "fake middle-class black man" Clay and the bohemian Lula reveals the failures of racial perception. Countering claims that the play relies upon essentialized blackness and the degradation of white femininity in order to prop up Clay's identity, this chapter instead argues that it disputes the static representations of racial identity essential to uplift ideology and espoused by Lula and some prominent writers and critics, including Philip Roth, as well. Through Clay, *Dutchman* critiques white liberal investment in uplift ideology by employing a variety of cultural genealogies and practices to sketch identity that range from Charles Baudelaire to Bessie Smith, as well as his insistence upon "blackness" as performance that hinges on what he makes visible and available to spectators. While Clay successfully exposes the vulnerabilities of 1960s era racial common sense underwriting Lula's attempts to fix his identity, his enactment of the postblack ethos results in his murder at Lula's hands. Yet this chapter reads *Dutchman* as illuminating the dire consequences of troubling racial uplift ideology as well as amplifying the possibilities for African American subjectivity in the appearance at the play's end of the train's conductor and a twenty-year-old passenger and refutes theater critics' contention that the rage depicted in the play diminishes its significance and casts doubt on its artistic merit.

Though Howard Sackler drew *The Great White Hope*'s protagonist, Jack Jefferson, from events in the life of the nation's first African American heavyweight champion, Jack Johnson, whose reign from 1908 to 1915 sparked racially motivated violence throughout the United States, he consistently argued for the universality of the play's characters and themes, insisting that it was "a metaphor of struggle between man and the outside world." Despite this claim, Jefferson's racial identity and the nation's racial turmoil framed theater critics' discussion of the play in both the mainstream and African American press.

This critical impasse between Sackler and theater critics drives the analysis in Chapter Three, "'Ghost(s) in the House!': Black Subjectivity and Howard Sackler's *The Great White Hope*." Reading the play's representation of Jack Jefferson as both a critique of Progressive Era racial common sense and the continuing significance of racial uplift ideology in the then-current moment, this chapter asserts that Jefferson offers a mode of black identity that emphasizes interiority as an alternative to the dissemination of appropriate racial representations intended to counter the stereotypical images of African Americans circulating in the public sphere and subverts such representational tactics. His signifying rhetoric engages the discourse of race with the press corps covering his title fight, the civic leaders who seek to prosecute him through the Mann Act of 1910, and the spectators invested in the outcome of the title fight. Jefferson's signifying engagement with the public sphere endows him with a means of escape from the representational binary imposed upon him as well as refutes the racial hierarchy underwriting uplift ideology. As he interrogates the logic of uplift and reveals that adherence to its representational strategies holds no guarantee of full citizenship, he points to, but does not fully reveal, his interior self. By repudiating the public sphere discourse of racial common sense and its attempts to regulate black identity, Jefferson gestures toward the post-soul aesthetics' "cultural mulattos," who refuse to "deny or suppress any part of [their] complicated and sometimes contradictory cultural baggage to please either white people or black."[39]

Yet while many of the theater critics reviewing the play turned to the spectral presences of both Johnson and Ali to interpret it, critics themselves did not redact what one critic called the play's tragedy or its consequences in that historical moment, and they are silent on what is at stake in the interplay between *The Great White Hope*'s Jack Jefferson and the specters of both Johnson and Ali whom they summon. In demonstrating regret for historical wrongs against Johnson and linking them to Ali in the then-current moment, *The Great White Hope*'s reviews served as a racial repentance that ultimately elided the complexities of African American subjectivity as they are staged in the play.

Chapter Four, "Gathering Black Subjectivities and Cultural Memory in Alice Childress's *Wine in the Wilderness*," turns to Alice Childress's 1969 meditation on black identity within the black public sphere. Originally written as a screenplay and produced for Boston Public Television station WGBH-TV, it was broadcast in September 1969 and aired as the first installment of a ten-week National Educational Television (NET) series titled *On Being Black*. Not coincidentally, it addresses at least one concern of the February 1968 Kerner Commission Report when it calls upon the national media to seek to "develop programming which integrates Negroes into all aspects of presentations."[40] However, critics largely ignored the play's initial broadcast, electing instead to focus their attention on other new NET programs. Yet while the report critiqued the national media, it also took to task calls for black consciousness and solidarity—key tenets of the Black Power/Arts Movements. In a survey of those who took part in the disturbances, the commission found that they held "strong feelings of racial pride, if not superiority" and interpreted those sentiments as evidence of the "frustrations of powerlessness" and a longing for inclusion in the American plurality.[41]

Refuting these claims in its counternarrative, *Wine in the Wilderness* offers an exploration of the intersections of class, race, and gender in the play's representations, situating the Harlem riot during which the play takes place as a site enabling productive reflection on and reconsideration of the rhetorical and representational strategies underwriting some Black Arts cultural expression and, by extension, African American identity. The play's protagonist, Tommy, an eighth grade dropout and factory worker who loses her home in the riot, reveals the instability of a range of class markers that the college-educated Bill, Cynthia, and Sonny-Man employ in their attempt to literally and figuratively situate her as the iconic representation of the community's "lost woman" in the triptych Bill paints during the riot for public display. In contrast to the framing of riots as a site of interracial conflict, *Wine in the Wilderness*'s counternarrative foregrounds an intraracial discussion of some iterations of Black Arts expression's insistence on gender hierarchies for its success and critiques the efficacy of those rhetorical and representational strategies. And despite the Kerner Report's findings, it does so through a call for black consciousness and unity that does not envision inclusion in mainstream American society as its ultimate goal. Instead, the play's counternarrative constitutes black solidarity and black consciousness through its critique of the sometimes reductive gender and class ideologies underwriting certain strains of Black Arts cultural production alongside an alternate history of black protest led by African American fraternal organizations, whose role in the African American Freedom Struggle is often neglected. Ultimately, *Wine in the Wilderness* interrogates both cultural memory's master narrative of riots and the role such a master narrative suggests the Black Power/Black Arts Movements play within those riots.

Charles Gordone's Pulitzer Prize–winning play, *No Place to Be Somebody: A Black Black Comedy* (1969), also questions cultural memory's master narrative of the African American Freedom Struggle. Chapter Five, "Prefiguring Postblackness in *No Place to Be Somebody: A Black Black Comedy*," reads its protagonist, Gabe Gabriel, as both playwright and "a solo black performer within the context of the play," but situates his four solo performances within the play's onstage action as counternarratives to heroic era accounts of both the March on Washington of 1963 for Jobs and Freedom and the residential desegregation of the era.⁴² Gabriel's four solo performances question the efficacy of racial uplift ideology visible in the moderate philosophies of civil rights organizations such as the NAACP and also trouble the depiction of urban riots as detailed in the Kerner Commission Report as well as the strategies employed by activist organizations such as Us advocating for black nationhood. Ultimately, his solo performances frame both the uplift ideologies of traditional civil rights organizations such as the Southern Christian Leadership Conference (SCLC) and the cultural and political nationalism deployed by groups like the Black Panther Party as untenable foundations for the development of black subjectivity. Offering "a new life" for black subjectivity in his final solo performance as a woman in mourning, he refuses black identity's monolithic representation offered in both direct action protest and black cultural nationalism, and through his performances he laments the passing of African American subjectivity defined through "the struggle, the dehumanization, the degradation [blacks] suffered. Or allowed themselves to suffer perhaps."⁴³ While many, if not most, critics in both the African American and mainstream press applauded the play, one segment of the African American press approached it with trepidation. Prominent Black Aestheticians not only took issue with the play and its representations, but also with Gordone's own flirtation with "race treason" in identifying himself as an "American writer" whose primary goal while developing *No Place to Be Somebody* was "to write about the human and spiritual isolation of both black and white."[44] Yet Gordone's participation in the Committee for the Employment of Negro Performers during the 1960s, which sought to increase representation on theater stages of African Americans, and his work with Cell Block Theater, an inmate rehabilitation program at the Bordentown (New Jersey) Youth Correctional Facility, demonstrate his commitment to racial and social justice, which belie charges of race treason and might help us to engage Gordone and his play as anticipating writer and critic Trey Ellis's figuring of "cultural mulattos," who, he wrote in 1989, "refuse to deny or suppress any part of their complicated and sometimes contradictory cultural baggage to please either white people or black."[45] Gordone and Gabriel instead offer black subjectivity as neither rooted in nor limited to cultural memory's binary opposition between civil rights heroism and Black Nationalist villainy.

Prefiguring Postblackness concludes with a coda, "Postblackness's Ancestors and Relatives or 'The Past Pushing Us into the Present,'" which turns to recent revivals of the plays under consideration. It argues that theater critics continue to limit the ways in which the representations signify in the current historical moment, noting the ways that their discussions serve cultural memory's dominant narrative of the Freedom Struggle era. In light of cultural memory's dialectic of remembering and forgetting in service that narrative, the coda urges a reconsideration of postblackness's literary genealogies.

CHAPTER ONE

"One for Whom Bread—Food—Is Not Enough": Beneatha Younger, Uplift Ideology, and Intellectual Freedom

> *BENEATHA:* Well sometimes it seems like Mama and Walter and Ruth and even Travis—well, they are all sort of rushing through life working hard for the right to be like everybody else. Do you know what I mean?— And do you know what I want George, what I really want—? All I want is the right to be different from everybody else—and yet —be a part too.
> —Lorraine Hansberry, *A Raisin in the Sun*,
> Original Playscript with Annotations (1957)[1]

Twenty-seven years after Beneatha's assertions about black subjectivity in Hansberry's original play script, writer Lisa Jones offered parallel observations about her participation in the Rodeo Caldonia High-Fidelity Performance Theater, a black feminist performance collective. Jones composed *Carmella & King Kong* and *Combination Skin*, the two performances the group staged between 1986 and 1988, and proclaimed that the ensemble's twelve African American women were "in [their] twenties and giddy with [their] own possibilities."[2] Reflecting on their work, Jones posed their representations as a departure from those of previous eras—they were not "career girls or call girls or Bess or Beulah" but instead were black women "breathing intelligence, mischievousness, and triumph."[3] Finally, Jones points to the significance of the Rodeo's intervention in black female representations, as she asserted that "this was a brand new image. Had young black women been presented this way before in the mainstream? Apparently not."[4]

Jones's description of the Rodeo's representations seemingly responded to Beneatha Younger's call for the right to shape identity that is simultaneously distinct from, yet reflective of, "everybody else." Yet Beneatha could have easily been one of the women of the Rodeo who breathe intelligence, mischievousness, and triumph as her desire throughout the play to "experiment with different forms of expression" as she puts it, or to "flit so from one thing to another" in her mother's words, would seem to align her both ideologically and expressively with the Rodeo collective.[5] Jones suggested that the ensemble's take on black female representations where "Diana Ross' whine matters as much as Mary McLeod Bethune's institution building" were not present in mainstream representations before the Rodeo began performing in 1986.[6] However, Beneatha's representation in Hansberry's 1959 play has not been viewed as the innovation that it was because cultural memory too often frames the play as a singular response to the euphemistic Negro Question and the nascent African American Freedom Struggle of the 1960s. She was hidden in plain view, contained in a text that many onlookers believed took up nothing beyond the pressing issues propelling the Freedom Struggle, including voting rights and fair housing and employment access, among many others. The notion that the Freedom Struggle would seek to create something beyond attaining those tangible legislative goals might appear to be secondary, less important concerns in the pursuit of civil rights legislation that would then enable access to life opportunities. Yet the yearning for a discursive space where the subtle shadings of an interior life concerned with exploring questions about identity can be discerned in Freedom Struggle era texts such as *A Raisin in the Sun*. Embedded in the early steps into the Freedom Struggle era was a desire to explore questions of African American identity. Hansberry, like other writers and their texts during that era, championed political and social issues, but in the interstices of her play she also addressed the subtleties of African American identity just beginning to become apparent in the mainstream public sphere and that had been hinted at in the black public sphere.

Too often, Beneatha Younger is viewed as the play's "overintellectualized daughter," "the giddy adolescent," or in one instance, the "spoiled" sister, but rereading her with an eye toward her engagement with her immediate family's and her suitor's ideologies shows us that she is far more complicated than such simplistic characterizations would have her be.[7] In Beneatha, Hansberry demonstrates that representing both the broader Freedom Struggle's pursuit of full citizenship for African Americans and black female identity's complexities are not mutually exclusive, and in so doing she reveals that such exploration is not exclusive to postblack cultural production. Hansberry and

A Raisin in the Sun can be considered a part of a loosely affiliated group of writers and texts within the Freedom Struggle era that address those so-called secondary concerns within the civil rights era.[8] Although Hansberry temporally situates her character's observations "sometime between World War II and the present," Beneatha's representation anticipates the Rodeo Caldonia's innovative representation and exploration of black feminine identity. Accordingly, this chapter contends that Lorraine Hansberry was one among several writers during the Freedom Struggle era that understood and demonstrated the complex representation of African American identity in ways that predicted postblack discourse of the mid-1980s to the mid-1990s and further argues that *A Raisin in the Sun*'s Beneatha Younger anticipates narrative tropes that inform postblack identity. As Beneatha navigates the social constraints and expectations imposed by her family and her suitors, she offers a compelling prelude to the postblack feminine identity that Jones and the Rodeo Caldonia would sketch.

Before detailing how Beneatha Younger's representation in *A Raisin in the Sun* prefigures the postblack move, an exploration of the ideological tenets that shape the NBA/PSA will help to clarify the tensions and the continuities between the cultural production of the Freedom Struggle era and the New Black Aesthetic/Post-Soul Aesthetic's cultural products. The Rodeo performed *Carmella & King Kong* and *Combination Skin* and also developed a poetry review, *Welcome to the Black Aesthetic*, which was never staged. However, this group and its performances or what Jones called "rites of self-discovery staged in supper-club basements, church sanctuaries, and bars" gave rise to the upstart New Black Aesthetic (NBA), sometimes called the Post-Soul Aesthetic (PSA), taking shape in the mid-1980s.[9] Acknowledging the growing interest in "a new way of looking at the world by young black artists," Jones not only argued for the significance of the NBA/PSA taking root during this period, but asserted that Rodeo Caldonia and its representations ushered in the new wave of inventive cultural production occurring during that era when she wrote, "It's clear to me that our take on blackness and femaleness did trumpet the cultural explosion that followed."[10] What seemingly propelled the cultural explosion and what the artists and the art they produced shared was their willingness to critique, lampoon, and otherwise utilize events, figures, and ideologies from the Freedom Struggle era often viewed as beyond reproach for discussion and exploration. Participating in the NBA as both an author and critic, writer Trey Ellis argues that it is ultimately an "anti-aesthetic that defies definition" and an "attitude of liberalism rather than a restrictive code."[11] While there is clearly an attitude of liberalism or what Ellis further explains is the NBA's ability to be "more honest and critical of ourselves than ever before," there also exists within the NBA/PSA discourse since the mid-1980s three recurring themes that can help to track its overriding concerns. As is the case with other artists of the NBA/PSA, the Rodeo sought to cast off threadbare representations of a fixed and collective black identity deeply informed by, or perhaps even burdened by, a convention that was retooled and repackaged in the Freedom Struggle era: racial uplift ideology. In a broad swath of NBA/PSA texts, unpacking racial uplift ideology is a central concern.

Racial uplift ideology describes a social and political strategy employed in the era of de jure segregation during the late nineteenth and early twentieth centuries that charged black middle-class spokespeople and leaders with refuting the pervasive stereotypical representations of African Americans widely circulating in US culture. Presenting themselves as living rebuttals to such stereotypes, this select group of African Americans cultivated images of civility and respectability that depended on class stratification among African Americans as well as a narrative of upward mobility that would aid in "reforming the character and managing the behavior of the black masses"—of families like the Youngers—steadily streaming into northern industrial cities from the South during the Great Migration.[12] But this strategy was not limited to the Progressive Era. Uplift ideology's focus on representing black homes and family life within the parameters of respectability and civility continued through the Freedom Struggle era where the images of civility and respectability played a key role in the mass protests of the period. Traces of uplift's agenda are visible in the actions of participants who demonstrated respectability and civility in their manner of speaking, their dress, and their attitudes toward the angry mobs they might, and in many instances did, encounter in civil rights era demonstrations.[13] As previously noted, uplift ideology likewise informed the selection of Rosa Parks instead of Claudette Colvin to become the face of the challenge to segregation in public transportation in Montgomery in 1955. Yet its basic premise, which contends that through the black middle-class's leadership, the black masses can be "rehabilitated" and can then usefully contribute to proving that all of black America is fit for full citizenship, is a notion that the NBA/PSA rejects wholesale. For example, in framing how uplift's influence has prohibited a discussion of what might be considered problematic representations of black identity, critic Mark Anthony Neal has warned that "efforts to create the most 'positive' historical read of the black experience and its various icons have often denied a full exploration of the humanity of black folks."[14] In short, a key element of the new world view proffered by the NBA/PSA seeks to end "efforts to sanitize black life and culture" by prohibiting \cultural producers from "teas[ing] out radical political and social sensibilities in existing and often problematic (stereotypical) caricatures of black identity."[15] Perhaps the most visible rejection of uplift ideology in the work of Jones and other NBA/PSA artists is their refusal to accept its premise that adhering to its conventions results in freedom for all African Americans. In all of its iterations, the NBA/PSA proposes that freedom, however the artist in question defines it, cannot be achieved through uplift ideology because in seeking to dispute or respond to stereotypical representations there is an implicit acceptance of them. Moreover, these artists have refused the individual autonomy versus collective freedom dichotomy which proposes that "race" men and women are meant to stand in for and represent the collective—the broader black community. Instead, they have argued for more complexly drawn representations that reject the position, held by W. E. B. Du Bois and other race men and women in the early twentieth century, that black art should serve to counter racist propaganda. This is clear in Jones's declaration about the Rodeo's representational agenda as she wrote, "Our need was to get out in public and act up; to toss off the expectations laid by our genitals, our melanin count, and our college degrees. Rodeo heralded our arrival: young, gifted, black and weird (so we thought), and in search of like souls."[16] In this assertion and others like it, the Rodeo's rejection of racial uplift ideology echoes the rejection of racial uplift ideology visible in other iterations of the NBA/PSA's products. This rejection of collective identity as well as the notion of race men and women who represent the race shape every trope endemic to a wide swath of NBA/PSA texts.

But uplift ideology's remainders are not the only convention identified by the NBA/PSA as suppressing fuller explorations of black identity. The representational politics of the Black Arts Movement in particular are referenced throughout postblack discourse as both enabling and restricting post-soul representations. As an example, Trey Ellis wrote in "The New Black Aesthetic" (1989) of the NBA's willingness to parody Black Arts Aesthetics and to "flout publicly the official, positivist black party line" but reiterates the NBA's indebtedness to the Black Arts Movement.[17] Similarly, curator Thelma Golden argued in the introduction to the 2001 *Freestyle* catalogue that she "holds a certain degree of nostalgia for the passion and energy that created the nationalist/aesthetic dogma of the 1970s Black Arts Movement," yet she is compelled to exhibit the work of artists whose work speaks to "the quest to define ongoing changes in the evolution of African American art and ultimately to ongoing redefinition of blackness in contemporary culture."[18] This turn away from what is often described as the proscriptive aesthetic agenda of the Black Arts Movement of the 1960s, which in some iterations mandated what Ellis called "a propagandistic positivism" in its representations, marks a key element of postblack cultural production and criticism.

Aside from the rejection of racial uplift ideology and a critique of the Black Arts Aesthetic is the final defining feature of the NBA/PSA—the varied cultural genealogies it claims in producing its art.[19] Critic Greg Tate has argued that the NBA reflects "a maturation of a postnationalist black arts movement, one more Afrocentric and cosmopolitan than anything that has come before" and further that it is peopled by artists "for whom 'black culture' signifies a multicultural tradition of expressive practices."[20] Ellis echoed Tate in the former's essay, "The New Black Aesthetic," as he identified himself and his NBA peers as "cultural mulattos . . . educated by a multi-racial mix of cultures" and who are committed to creating what philosopher Arthur Danto has called "Disturbatory Art."[21] Moving beyond such imposed boundaries on how black identity can be represented, the NBA/PSA emphasizes an "elastic" notion of black identity that embraces a wide range of cultural influences and genealogies that stands as the distinguishing aspect of its cultural production.

Shifting from these discussions of the NBA/PSA in the mid-1980s to the mid-1990s, these three tenets can be found in Thelma Golden's and visual artist Glenn Ligon's discussion of postblackness in the early 2000s. Golden, director and chief curator at the Studio Museum in Harlem, was responsible for the influential 2001 *Freestyle* exhibition there. Emerging from conversations with Ligon, her take on postblackness is significant because she posited that the difference between the *Freestyle* show artists and the black artists preceding them was that the newer generation of artists did not feel they had to address questions of what makes "black art" or black aesthetic practices, yet all the while maintaining that they created black art. She offers that she and Ligon used the word "postblack" as a kind of shorthand for their own dialogues about black cultural production, but suggested that it can also describe artists whose work speaks to "the quest to define ongoing changes in the evolution of African American art and ultimately to ongoing redefinition of blackness in contemporary culture."[22] Echoing the elastic notion of African American identity that both Tate and Ellis discuss, Golden argued that postblack is a way to name black cultural production that broadens the scope of blackness and frees it from a proscriptive and didactic mode of practice. Noting the artists whose work was included in the *Freestyle* exhibition felt no need to deliver a treatise about their stance on "black art," she asserted that

> we were now willing to exist at a place where we could talk about the complexity of Black creation and the politics behind it through multiple voices and

through multiple strands. And that this embrace was a stance. It wasn't a kind of art, it wasn't a particular way of making work. It was a stance, an attitude, a vibe, a feeling, and that would be post-black . . . at its essential core, it was a way to create a space to talk about things outside of the existing paradigms that had existed for even me as a curator.[23]

It becomes clear then that whatever name endures, the NBA/PSA hinges almost entirely on circumventing static definitions of African American cultural production and representations of African American identity.

Despite resistance among some critics of African American culture to the notion that the NBA/PSA was something entirely new, its existence as cultural formation has generally been accepted.[24] Nearly twenty-five years after its first notices, literary critic Bertram Ashe's theorizing of the post-soul aesthetic has established a clear critical framework for the study of post-soul artists and texts and has outlined the "post-soul matrix" as a hallmark of both.[25] In refining the workings of post-soul texts, he included three key features of the matrix: the "cultural mulatto archetype"—artists or characters who cross traditional racial lines in the development of identity; the use of "blaxporation," which "troubles blackness"; and the "allusion-disruption strategy," which summons and signifies on previous eras of African American history as well as the ideologies and representations linked to those historical moments.[26] As he read both Tate's and Ellis's essays as "self-generated, black-on-black emancipation proclamations," which declare their freedom from W. E. B. Du Bois's "sense of looking at one's self through the eyes of others . . . two warring ideals in one dark body," Ashe defined the post-soul writer's concept of freedom as one that embraces both black consciousness and artistic freedom as interdependent—part of a dialectic.[27] But Ashe argued while many texts preceding the post-soul era might on the surface seem to trouble blackness in the ways outlined above, the historical context in which post-soul artists and texts are embedded is the determining factor in the post-soul aesthetic's distinction from other African American literary periods. While he accepts that "there are always exceptions to the prevailing literary conventions of the day," Ashe locates the key difference between post-soul texts and their predecessors in the post-soul artist's "relationship to the idea of freedom," because the post-soul text refuses the opposition between collective struggle and artistic freedom. Put differently, in earlier periods the struggle for collective freedom necessitated limits on artistic freedom that the post-soul artist feels no obligation to observe. In short, the absence of an organized struggle for collective freedom in the post-soul era shifted freedom's emphasis in earlier periods from a fixed, collective black identity to the post-soul period's explorations of such constructions. How, then, can Lorraine Hansberry's Beneatha Younger exemplify a postblack aesthetic when the text in which she is embedded is bound to the Freedom Struggle era and in cultural memory often stands in for the Civil Rights Movement's goals and aspirations?

It is because the presence of an organized, or in the case of this play, an emerging struggle for freedom does not prevent her from repudiating the opposition between collective struggle and artistic freedom. As illustrated in the chapter's epigraph, Beneatha rebuffs the opposition between collective struggle and artistic freedom and her interactions with other characters highlight her efforts to question this opposition. Yet most often, the positions she takes puts her at ideological odds with the rest of her family, and her assertions are met with derision and hostility because she dares to give them voice. Drawing on literary critic Marianne DeKoven's work on postmodernism and its emergence in nonfiction of the 1960s, the perspectives of Beneatha's family approximate modernity's "meta-or master narratives—universal syntheses premised on hierarchical self-other dualisms," while her worldview emphasizes "the diffuse, antihierarchical, antidualistic, local, particular, partial, temporary."[28] Moreover, while there are clear distinctions between the modern and the postmodern, elements of continuity can also be located in "pivot texts" which demonstrate elements of both the modern and the postmodern, and I argue that *A Raisin in the Sun* also enables the continuities from the modern to the postmodern. Since it shuttles between these characteristics of the modern and the postmodern, the play enables a reading of Beneatha Younger's representation as one that anticipates formations of black identity present in the postblack era's cultural production. Cultural memory of the play emphasizes its universal appeal, and in particular, the dualistic and hierarchical relationship between Walter and his mother Lena, yet the relationships between the Youngers family members, and in particular, how the cultural politics of uplift ideology inform those relationships, are often left unexplored.

However, those relationships serve Beneatha's enactment of the dialectic that Ashe and others have maintained is central to post-soul cultural products. George Wolfe's 1986 play, *The Colored Museum*, is a series eleven exhibits that are basically short satirical performances in the play. One of them satirizes Hansberry's play in its "Last Mama on the Couch Play" exhibit, which alleviates any doubts about its enduring cultural influence as well as how it has been framed in cultural memory. Speaking to the play's continual staging during Black History Month at regional theaters around the country when those institutions invariably "discover black people," Wolfe

A Raisin in the Sun. 2014 Ethel Barrymore Theater Playbill. Collection of the author.

argued that his play clears space for new representations of black identity and removes "dead, stale, empty icons blocking [him] from [his] own truth."[29] Yet Beneatha's representation participates in a parallel project that seeks to remove ideological obstacles that stand in the way of her development of black female subjectivity. Her relationship to the idea of freedom is not one in lockstep formation with the broader freedom struggle. Instead, both Hansberry and Beneatha imagine black female identity around the figurative corner of civil rights era freedom with a representation of it that challenges racial uplift ideology's orthodoxy.

The domestic drama's action occurs entirely in the Younger family's apartment and focuses on the family's aspirations but is particularly attentive to siblings Walter Lee and Beneatha and their attempts to realize their aspirations. However, conflict arises over which dreams are worthy of the windfall

A Raisin in the Sun. 1959 Ethel Barrymore Theater Playbill. Collection of the author.

that arrives in the wake of their father's death. The arrival of the check from his $10,000 life insurance policy offers an opportunity for the Youngers to change their life circumstances and possibilities. Walter Lee, who works as a chauffeur, seeks self-determination through belief in the basic premise of the American Dream—or the idea that "an individual holds the possibility of unlimited riches."[30] He hopes to persuade his mother, Lena, to invest the insurance money in a liquor store that would enable entrepreneurship and the opportunity to gain access to the markers of wealth and social status that inundate him in his work. Already a college student, Beneatha also pursues self-determination, setting her sights on continuing to medical school to become a doctor. However, Beneatha, Lena, and Walter's wife Ruth, all express misgivings about Walter's ambitions, and those doubts give way to outright rejection, which fuels both anger and desperation in him. While they pursue different means to their ends, both Walter's and Beneatha's drive for self-determination shares the same origins—the waning influence of racial uplift ideology on their notions of identity—which I will address shortly. But for now, I want to focus on Beneatha's pursuit of self-determination because it troubles static concepts of black female identity in a number of ways: first, in her debates with her immediate family members, which frequently critique the cultural politics of uplift ideology that continued to inform questions around African American identity, and second, in her discussions of intellectual freedom with her suitors, which also address questions of uplift ideology's significance. If postblack aesthetics are generally concerned with "the problem of identity . . . [and] the question of who we are, *now*, dominates the thematics" of its representative artists and critics, then *A Raisin in the Sun* poses parallel questions in Beneatha's pursuit of self-determination in 1959.[31] After all, it is Beneatha who tells Joseph Asagai, her Nigerian suitor, that she is looking for her identity, and it is through her discourse on African American identity with other characters in the play that we see the play's interrogation of black identity—its postblack ethos.

Her first appearance on stage immediately follows Walter Lee's argument with Ruth about encouraging his mother to invest the insurance money in his plan to open a liquor store with two other men. After observing that he is "tied to a race of women with small minds," Beneatha appears on stage as a rebuttal to that claim.[32] Hansberry's text works hard to dispel Walter Lee's contentions about black women. To cue Beneatha's distinctions from both Lena and Ruth, the stage direction describes her "almost intellectual" face; her speech a "mixture of many things" reflecting a range of geographical and cultural genealogies—Chicago's Southside, the Midwest, the South, and her education—which have "permeated her sense of English."[33] Even her name serves similar ends as Hansberry selected it to signify on minstrel representations showcasing "the hopeless 'earthy' charm of a 'childlike' people" by giving a folksy name to a character "who speaks the stuff of truth" in the play.[34]

Some of the postblack expansion of black female identity's boundaries comes in her contrasts with Ruth and Lena as detailed in the stage direction. The stage direction at the play's outset is devoted to a detailed description of the Youngers' Southside apartment. Lena and her husband took the apartment when they initially migrated to Chicago from an unnamed location in the South, and though it has adequately accommodated the second generation of the Younger family in Chicago, "weariness has won [the] room."[35] What would otherwise be a comfortable living room holds "a number of indestructible contradictions," and while the stage direction finds many of them in the home's décor, the Younger women reflect parallel contradictions. Though Beneatha is marked by the intersection of cultural influences and genealogies, "disappointment has already begun to hang" in Ruth's face and the stage direction predicts that in a few years, she "will be known among her people as a 'settled woman.'"[36] Ruth's emerging status as a settled woman suggests limited possibilities for transformation in her life, and the fact that her life is described as disappointing and "little that she expected" speaks also to the Youngers' tired and physically and psychically confining home.[37] Like the apartment itself, Ruth embodies weariness and limited possibilities for change.

However, Lena Younger does not physically bear weariness as Ruth does. She is described as a strong woman "who has adjusted to many things in life and overcome many more" and who wears her beauty and grace "unobstrusively" so much so that it "takes a while to notice it."[38] In situating both Ruth and Lena as black female identity's standard in the African American Freedom Struggle era, they represent the figurative paradigm of black womanhood with which Beneatha engages in crafting her own identity. In particular, she defies their allegiance to uplift ideology in their emphasis on the significance of the home, family, and Christian respectability and the importance of demonstrating that allegiance to those outside of their family. Moreover, both Lena and Ruth have experienced marriage and motherhood, which evolves into a continual source of conflict between Beneatha and nearly every character in the play because she has not experienced either and demonstrates skepticism toward both, marking a rejection of black women's traditional roles within uplift ideology.

Unlike her mother and sister-in-law, Beneatha is not concerned with cleaning the house nor does she link the apartment's appearance to her own sense of identity as Ruth and Lena do throughout the play. Further, in her range of interests—horseback riding, photography, guitar lessons, and acting—she seeks a mode of self-expression that goes beyond that of the domestic space that is central to both Lena and Ruth's notion of identity. In effect, it is the absence of these experiences that bonds Lena and Ruth and separates Beneatha from them. Both women repeatedly encourage Beneatha to hew more closely to their modes of representing black femininity throughout the play. In their attempts—including both physical aggression and derision—to coerce Beneatha's compliance with uplift ideology, they discourage her meanderings away from the paths of black womanhood they have trod. Further,

her access to education, a standard mode of enacting social mobility and a key tenet of uplift ideology, both extends the distance between them and yet never completely alienates her from that milieu.

It is within and against these singular, unified, black female figures of weariness and strength that Beneatha sketches postblack identity. But this work of expanding the boundaries of black identity in ways that anticipate the post-soul aesthetic through Beneatha's representation goes beyond the play's stage direction. It is embedded in her dialogue and informs each of her appearances on stage. Propelled by her debates with both her mother, Lena Younger, and her sister-in-law, Ruth Younger, her gestures toward postblack identity are also discernible in her arguments with Walter Lee. But the bulk of her post-soul interventions are carried on her discussions with the men she dates—Joseph Asagai and George Murchison.

Beneatha embeds in each of these interactions what performance studies critic José Esteban Muñoz calls "disidentification" and what literary critic Bertram Ashe calls "allusion-disruption" ideology in post-soul cultural production.[39] Though they are deployed in different contexts, these critical theories work in very similar ways for people of color and the cultural products they develop because they help account for the often paradoxical relationships within and across different subject positions held by those within communities of color. Disidentification marks identification with and against another subject position in the development of identity.[40] Allusion-disruption ideology showcases a reference to iconography, images, events, and figures of the earlier eras of African American history, particularly the civil rights era, but in the allusion to that historical moment, the text simultaneously intervenes in the standard ideas associated with it and signifies on it, creating a new meaning. Drawing upon both disidentification and allusion-disruption, Beneatha limns her post-soul iteration of black female identity. While she does not reject wholesale her family's ideas of black female identity, she does mediate between their concepts, those of her suitors, and her own. Very much like her language, which has been permeated by a range of influences, Beneatha links a range of cultural genealogies to craft identity. But while racial uplift ideology continues to sway her family, its effect on Beneatha wanes.

Comprised of many strains and contradictions, racial uplift ideology can be broadly described as a strategy taken up by the black middle class during the late nineteenth century and continued through the mid-twentieth and still influencing black cultural production and notions of identity in the current historical moment. Historian Kevin Gaines has argued that representing the "struggle for a positive black identity in a deeply racist society," racial uplift ideology combines racial solidarity across class lines, self-help, and a bourgeois morality focusing on demonstrating respectability, thrift, social purity, and chastity within the patriarchal family in a cultural politics that, if embraced fully, could then demonstrate African Americans' fitness for full citizenship and their ability to be assimilated into the American body politic.[41] Yet it also hinged on a pernicious contradiction that often colluded with the very race and class hierarchies it attempted to overturn, and in its deployment "many black elites sought status, moral authority, and recognition of their humanity by distinguishing themselves, as bourgeois agents of civilization from the presumably undeveloped black majority."[42] Uplift ideology underwrites the daily lived experiences of the characters in *A Raisin in the Sun* and stands at the crux of the conflicts between them that are ultimately concerned with which iteration of its cultural politics will guide the family's decisions. However teasing and congenial the conflicts sometimes are, Beneatha's turn away from defining herself entirely within the constraints of uplift ideology, unlike her family, poses a threat to its continuing influence, and in that sense it anticipates the narrative conventions of the postblack text.

Gaines has further observed that respectability within uplift ideology "often meant denouncing nonconformity to patriarchal gender conventions and bourgeois morality."[43] Since Christianity shapes both the play's adherence to gender conventions and its notions of morality, nowhere is the generational divide between the Younger women clearer than in Beneatha's confrontation with her mother over the existence of God. While George C. Wolfe's "The Last Mama on the Couch Play" exhibit satirizes Lena's matriarchal control over the family with its echoes of so-called black pathology in households headed by women, a subtler critique of Lena's ideologies and power exists in *A Raisin in the Sun*, and it is pivotal in understanding Beneatha's difficult relationship with a central tenet of racial uplift ideology.

After discussing her plans for medical school, she tells her mother and Ruth that God doesn't have anything to do with her ability to become a doctor. Vigilant in her commitment to the cultural politics of uplift, Lena tells Beneatha that it doesn't "sound nice for a young girl to say things like that" and reminds her that she "wasn't brought up that way."[44] In a scene that moves from a discussion of her "experimentation" with forms of expression and her wealthy suitor George Murchison, all significant factors in her crafting of identity, Beneatha tells her mother that she doesn't understand that "it's all a matter of ideas" and challenges the utility of her parents getting her and Walter to church every Sunday by asserting that "there simply is no blasted God—there is only man and it is he who makes miracles!"[45] Her defiance of uplift warrants a violent response from Lena, who "*absorbs this speech, studies her daughter . . . and slaps her powerfully across the face.*"[46] While Ruth chides Beneatha, telling her "what you did was childish—so you got treated like a child," Beneatha's response speaks to her commitment to her own sense of her identity that moves beyond the narrow boundaries enforced by her mother and Ruth, who both subscribe to uplift's cultural politics.[47] Not only does she indict her mother's animosity and the rest of the family for their complicity with it by telling Ruth, "everybody thinks it's all right for Mama to be a tyrant"; she also points out the futility of her mother's insistence, saying "all the tyranny in the world will never put a God in the heavens!"[48] Despite what can only be called humiliation at the hands of her mother and sister-in-law, Beneatha remains steadfast in her commitment to her own worldview, rather than notions of uplift ideology shaped by Christianity that are representative of her mother's and Ruth's generations. This exchange also marks the start of her insolence toward racial uplift throughout the play.

But beyond Beneatha's rejection of bourgeois morality, Lena's anxieties about Walter and Beneatha and her inability to control their perspectives reveal the waning influence of uplift ideology and points to a shift to a new worldview that refuses the significance of uplift ideology on shaping African American identity. She laments to Ruth, "There's something come down between me and [my children] that don't let us understand each other and I don't know what it is. One done almost lost his mind thinking 'bout money all the time and the other done commence to talk about things I can't seem to understand in no form or fashion. What is it that's changing, Ruth?"[49] While Ruth avoids a direct response to the question by suggesting that she is taking the discord between herself and her children "too seriously," later, in Act II, Lena may answer her own question in an exchange with Walter after he tells her that money is "life." Her response maps the trajectory of African American migration from the South to the North before World War II and embedded in the migrant experience in the North are the politics of uplift ideology. In a monologue worth quoting, Lena tells Walter that

> something has changed. You something new, boy. In my time we was worried about not being lynched and getting to the North if we could and how to stay alive and still have a pinch of dignity too. . . . Now here come you and Beneatha—talking 'bout things we ain't never even thought about hardly, me and your daddy. You ain't satisfied or proud of nothing we done. I mean that you had a home; that we kept you out of trouble till you was grown; that you don't have to ride to work on the back of nobody's streetcar—You my children—but how different we done become.[50]

By Lena's account, she and her husband's most urgent concerns were to leave the South's Jim Crow segregation alive and to then make a life in Chicago, among the thousands of other black migrants who left the South seeking job opportunities there. As is well documented, many of those migrants faced discrimination in employment and housing, so much so that some migrants chose to return to the South. Others, like the Youngers, remained, but found it exceedingly difficult to move beyond the run-down, overcrowded neighborhoods and financial circumstances they found themselves in upon their arrival in Chicago. In short, the notion of pull yourself up by the bootstraps–style class mobility was not readily accessible to most southern migrants, nor was it available to most Americans—black or white. Yet racial uplift's elite progenitors argued that, on one hand, southern migrants could be assimilated through uplift's cultural politics, but at the same time, some deployed minstrel imagery and stereotypes about black laziness and immorality in their rejection of southern migrants because it threatened their own elite status in northern urban areas.[51]

Racial uplift ideology's ambivalence about southern migrants illuminates Lena's interactions with both Walter and Beneatha. Lena's description of her transition from South to North underscores the contingency of both uplift ideology and her status as a migrant within it, but it also points to the ways in which the move is only successful if the next generation sustains the previous generation's progress. In other words, when she points out that her children are neither proud nor satisfied with an upbringing shaped by the politics of uplift, and further that they embrace ideas that challenge uplift's parameters, the question of uplift's success, of its ability to remain relevant to the next generation and thus to succeed, is vulnerable. Both Walter and Beneatha want to explore African American identity in ways that push beyond the boundaries outlined by uplift ideology, and in that regard they suggest a postblack concept of identity. While Walter wants to move from working class to black elite status, Beneatha has no interest in the acquisition of goods and class mobility; she is in search of an alternative to racial uplift ideology in crafting black subjectivity.

Lena and Big Walter's move from South to North represents a deep desire for and persistence in securing a better life for their families and ultimately, as Gaines observed, "the magnitude of this social transformation and its effect on popular black aspirations cannot be overemphasized."[52] In sum, simply making and surviving the journey, no matter what ultimately happened to the family in the final destination, was an incredible accomplishment, and many welcomed its inherent risks because it offered the possibility of better jobs and access to education. Still, many migrants working in service jobs like Ruth, a domestic, and Walter, a chauffeur, found themselves struggling financially and facing discrimination that left them in search of the "pinch of dignity" that Lena describes.

While pursuing those aspirations came at a cost as they likely contributed to her husband's premature death, they also deeply inform Lena's identity and often stand in for it. In effect, Walter's pursuit of wealth and power and Beneatha's notion that God is nothing more than an idea unsettles uplift ideology's foundations of Christian faith and morality. For Lena, there can be no viable black identity without those qualities, and Walter and Beneatha's ideas represent an affront to her own worldview, which turns on uplift ideology's emphasis on normative family gender roles, morality, and Christian faith. More importantly, their refusal to tow the uplift ideology line undermines Lena's belief in its presumed outcome, since uplift ideology gauges linear race progress in terms of African Americans' conformity with patriarchal gender roles, thrift, chastity, and social purity that substantiates the broader argument for African American humanity and full citizenship. As Lena points out, she and her husband complied with those dictates by providing their children with a home, keeping them out of trouble, and shielding them from experiencing the sting of Jim Crow segregation; therefore, Walter and Beneatha's refusal to accept uplift ideology's cultural politics marks a fissure in its continuing influence that she believes a new home can potentially staunch. She tries to compel Walter's acceptance of the patriarchal legacy his father's death bestows upon him within the logic of uplift by challenging him: "I'm waiting to hear how you be your father's son. . . . I'm waiting to hear you talk like him and say we a people who give children life, not who destroys them." Walter refuses and leaves the apartment.[53] Put alongside Beneatha's assertion about God that in Lena's view pushed the Youngers "backwards 'stead of forwards," these negations prompt the offstage search for a new home, and she strategically reveals the down payment she has made on a home to her grandson Travis to prevent the family from "falling apart . . . falling to pieces in front of [her] eyes."[54] What Lena sets out to confirm here is uplift ideology's power in salvaging the family as well as Walter's ascent to patriarchal leadership or what Lena calls later in the play "coming into his manhood." While on one hand, her down payment on the Clybourne Park home reflects the family's resistance to segregation's logic and, in particular, what critic Michelle Gordon has called the Youngers' "right to refute the economic exploitation of Chicago segregation," at the same time, the down payment marks the significance of the patriarchal family structure within a proper home that is pivotal to every iteration of uplift ideology.[55] Put differently, the impulse to assert the Youngers' right to reject economic exploitation is propelled by Lena's commitment to the cultural politics of uplift and likewise reflects the ideological conflicts around uplift within the play. With the down payment on the home in the all-white Clybourne Park neighborhood, Lena calls for her children's compliance, but their efforts to circumvent uplift in achieving their aspirations of social mobility warrant Lena's actions.

Much of the first act and scene of the play focuses on the discord among the Youngers and Lena's attempts to remedy it through uplift ideology, but it also introduces George Murchison, a vanguard of the black elite, who is Beneatha's classmate and one of her two boyfriends. The son of a wealthy black businessman, Murchison embodies the imagined possibilities and potential outcome of racial uplift ideology in his family's social and economic progress and bears the accoutrements of his social status. While he serves as a harbinger for the future that Walter's entrepreneurial aspirations might hold, more significant is George's parroting of racial uplift ideology, particularly its patriarchal underpinnings, and Beneatha's defiance of them.

Within the earlier discussion between Beneatha, Ruth, and Lena about her future and the likelihood of her marriage, Beneatha makes it clear that George's family, in keeping with the dictates of uplift ideology, would not be pleased with a Younger-Murchison marriage because of the class differences between the two families. The Youngers are too close to their migrant origins, and the weary Southside apartment is a clear marker of that status; therefore, the Murchisons must steer clear of them in order to maintain their status. But Beneatha clarifies what makes the Murchisons different from other black families committed to the cultural politics of uplift, explaining that they are "honest-to-God-real-*live*-rich colored people, and the only people in the world who are more snobbish than rich white people are rich colored people."[56] Hansberry's italicized emphasis on "real *live*" here is important because it alludes to and underscores a disconnect within uplift ideology between African Americans' economic status and their social status within the black community, which demonstrates that middle-class status was more often an ambition than a lived experience. As Kevin Gaines observed, "The material conditions of many blacks within these aspirations was often indistinguishable from those of impoverished people of any color," and they were not middle class "in any truly material or economic sense."[57] Ultimately, the black middle class, including families like the Youngers, usually did not have middle-class financial resources, but their adherence to the cultural politics of uplift stood in for what they lacked in their material conditions. But the Murchisons demonstrate the rewards of adhering to uplift's "moral economy," and George in particular embodies its endgame in *A Raisin in the Sun*. He is the culmination of race progress, of hewing to the uplift ideology party line, and in that sense he models that lived experience for the Younger family.

Yet uplift's limits on black identity come into focus when Beneatha's interactions with George Murchison are juxtaposed to her discussions with her Nigerian boyfriend, Joseph Asagai. It is within and against the ideologies embodied by Joseph and George and her discussions with both that Beneatha develops her sense of identity and gains permission to pursue intellectual freedom unencumbered by uplift ideology.

George Murchison offers a perspective on African American identity that follows uplift ideology to its logical close, which is the end of black cultural differences' significance in shaping identity. Ultimately, uplift's logic maintains that African American identity can and should be assimilated into a universally "American" identity, and Murchison embodies the superficial success to be gained by such a perspective. During his brief but pivotal appearance on stage in Act II, he denies any links to an African American or African history and their possible implications for identity that other characters attempt to draw. Further, and most importantly, he advocates instead for a patriarchal family model that is crucial in achieving uplift's goals. Specifically, his interactions with Ruth, Walter, and Beneatha illustrate uplift ideology's inherent contradiction, which reinscribes the racist, classist, and sexist practices it presumably sought to overturn.

He immediately begins this work by questioning Walter and Beneatha's reconfiguring of uplift's tendency toward representing the entire race as a family. While Beneatha and Walter imaginatively reenact a homecoming for Walter as an African warrior accompanied by the traditional Nigerian music Beneatha has received as a gift from Asagai, Murchison enters their apartment, and Walter, caught up in the emotions of the moment, greets George as "Black Brother," extending "his hand for the fraternal clasp."[58] Rejecting both the figurative connection between them as members of the same racial family well as any link to African history or anti-colonial movements in countries across the continent, George refuses Walter's hand and replies "Black brother, hell!," marking an early indication of his disregard for any cultural genealogies deriving from African or African American history as well as his disdain for Walter.[59]

His rejection of those genealogies finds a target in Beneatha's embrace of them as well. George's visit to the Younger home explores uplift ideology's cultural politics and reveals the tensions between black elites and the black masses that are demonstrated in his interactions with them. Continuing with his critique of Walter and Beneatha's play acting, George reprimands Beneatha: "Look honey, we're going *to* the theater, were not going to be *in* it ... so go change, huh?"[60] In a scene omitted from the play's debut staging but restored to the 1994 Vintage Books edition—which Hansberry's literary executor, Robert Nemiroff, called the most complete ever published—George's dig prompts her to reveal to both George and Ruth that she has cut off all of her chemically straightened hair and wears what remains in an Afro. Nemiroff, who was married to Hansberry from 1953 until 1962 and who served as her literary executor from 1965 until his death in 1991, explained that the actress Diana Sands's haircut was "not contoured to suit her: her particular facial structure required a fuller Afro of the sort she adopted in later years. . . . Rather than vitiate the playwright's point—the beauty of black hair—the scene was dropped."[61] In the late 1950s and early 1960s, this style had not yet made the transition to the iconic status it would hold in the late 1960s at the height of the Black Power/Black Arts Movements. Still, during that earlier period, natural hair was worn among black women artists and intellectuals, including Odetta, Abbey Lincoln, and Nina Simone and was also popular among South African women.[62] Historian Robin Kelley suggests that while the style was viewed by both black and white elites as exotic, and its appearance often grew from a desire to "achieve healthier hair and express solidarity with newly independent African nations, [it] entered public consciousness as a mod fashion statement that was not only palatable to bourgeois whites, but in some circles celebrated."[63] Yet it is Ruth, not George, who reacts to Beneatha's haircut with shock and, possibly, shame. In keeping with uplift's representational politics and already "embarrassed for the family" because of Walter and Beneatha's impromptu performance, Ruth admonishes her, saying "Girl, you done lost your natural mind?!"[64] Significantly, Ruth frames Beneatha's change of hairstyle as an affront to George and uplift's cultural politics when she asks her, "You expect this boy to go out with you with your head all nappy like that?"[65] Laying claim to notions of respectability within uplift ideology that compelled women in particular to conform to patriarchal gender conventions, Ruth's anxiety about the family's adherence to uplift prompts her later efforts to "demonstrate the civilization of the family" to George.[66] Beneatha's haircut instigates additional discussions about African American history and maintaining uplift's cultural politics. When Beneatha challenges George by asserting that he will go out with her if he isn't "ashamed of his heritage," George angrily tells her not to be "proud of herself just because [she] look[s] eccentric" and advises that "being eccentric means—being natural. Get dressed."[67] Once again showing his condescension toward the Youngers, his admonishment of Beneatha is instructive because it suggests that being unnatural or *not* being eccentric is a state of being that must be continually maintained and in that regard, is very much like the upkeep and representational vigilance required to sustain racial uplift ideology. By cutting her hair, Beneatha not only refuses to conform to gender and behavior conventions attached to uplift's cultural politics, but she rejects uplift ideology itself.

She continues her dismissal of uplift and consequently reveals George's indebtedness to it after she calls George an assimilationist, or as she defines it, "someone who is willing to give up his own culture and submerge himself in the completely dominant, and in this case, oppressive culture."[68] Explaining to Ruth that Beneatha's definition constitutes "a college girl's way of calling people Uncle Toms," George retorts that the black heritage she references is "nothing but a bunch of raggedy-assed spirituals and some grass huts!"[69] His assertions echo both the civilizing missionary rhetoric used in discussions of African Americans' relationship to Africa within some iterations of uplift ideology as well as appropriations of spirituals derived from minstrelsy; Beneatha promptly and angrily refutes his rhetoric and in the process claims a cultural genealogy that his version of uplift rejects.

Ultimately, George's commitment to uplift's gender politics prompts Beneatha's dismissal of him as a "fool" and underscores her allegiance to an alternate path toward subjectivity. After they return from another night out, she tries to engage him in conversation as he moves in to kiss her. Annoyed by her refusal, he tells her, "You're a nice looking girl . . . all over. That's all you need, honey, forget the atmosphere. Guys aren't going to go for the atmosphere—they're going to go for what they see. Be glad for that."[70] He continues that he doesn't go out with her "to discuss the nature of 'quiet desperation' or to hear all about [her] thoughts—because the world will go on thinking what it's thinking regardless."[71] When she asks why they should pursue education, he impatiently replies, "to learn facts—to get grades—to pass the course—to get a degree. That's all—it has nothing to do with thoughts."[72]

George reads Beneatha through uplift's emphasis on the patriarchal family and her potential role within it as his wife, which is crucial to establishing and sustaining black respectability. His advice that she focus on male perceptions of her identity and, more importantly, how it might serve freedom and security within the family speaks to the threat she poses—Beneatha's "atmosphere" undermines the woman's role within the patriarchal black family. His indifference to her intellectual reflections points to not only black women's limited role within uplift, but also to the emptiness of its pursuit. For all of his financial wealth and the privilege it provides him, Murchison lives an impoverished life in pursuit of wealth and goods for the sake of owning them. Beneatha represents for him a marker of his status, and her compliance with his notion of the patriarchal family would sustain his status. She is a commodity that is assessed and collected or cast off according to her value. He clearly appreciates Beneatha's physical beauty and implies that if she drops "the moody stuff," she would become more valuable to him and anyone else committed to uplift's cultural politics. Yet he scorns and devalues her ambition and her intellectual curiosity. In short, Beneatha is a potential trophy wife to George who aids him in fulfilling uplift ideology's prophecies, and she rejects his vision for her.

His behavior toward both Ruth and Walter Lee demonstrates a parallel dismissal. When Walter Lee attempts to engage him in conversation about his father's business, Murchison is aloof, highlighting the class tensions within uplift ideology. What he fails to recognize, however, is that Walter Lee is perceptive and insightful enough to understand his indifference and his need to set himself apart from the Youngers through both his class status and his cultural literacy. As George leaves the Youngers' home, he tells Walter, "Good night, Prometheus," referencing the Greek mythological figure representing human striving at the risk of unintended consequences.[73] The reference signals his education, which values knowledge of the western classical tradition, and George mocks Walter's inability to access or interpret that knowledge. He uses his education and elite status to sustain the divide between the black elite, or "real-*live*-rich colored people," and the black masses, the "very plain people" as Walter later describes them, like the Youngers.[74]

However, Beneatha's critiques go beyond the black elite; she also takes on Mrs. Johnson, the family's meddlesome and envious neighbor and focuses particularly on the way that she attempts to limit black identity's scope. In a scene omitted at the play's debut but restored to PBS's 1989 American Playhouse film and the 1994 Vintage edition, Mrs. Johnson facetiously congratulates the Youngers on their move to Clybourne Park, and she makes sure to show them a recent newspaper story about a black family whose home has been bombed for attempting to integrate an all-white enclave. She then greets Beneatha, who has entered to go to the bathroom, and receives a cool response, prompting Mrs. Johnson to announce that Beneatha "act[s] like she ain't got time to pass the time of day with nobody [who] ain't been to college."[75] Indignant, Mrs. Johnson then invokes Booker T. Washington's warning against African Americans prioritizing higher educational over industrial education in his autobiography, *Up From Slavery*, that "education has spoiled many a good plow hand" in her critique of Beneatha.[76] When Lena refutes Mrs. Johnson's claim that Washington was "one of our great men" by calling him a fool, she leaves. Still, Lena chastises her daughter for being rude to her, but Beneatha defends herself, telling her mother "there are two things we, as a people have got to overcome, one is the Ku Klux Klan—and the other is Mrs. Johnson."[77] As is often the case with Beneatha's dialogue, the humor mobilizes her critique and functions similarly to the post-soul aesthetic's allusion-disruption strategy. She suggests here that while the KKK's institutionalized program of white supremacy exerts considerable power over the lives of African Americans, Mrs. Johnson's mode of limiting black subjectivity in her allusion to Washington's institutionalized and often condemned program of black deference to white supremacy is equally damaging. The stage direction makes this clear as it reveals that Mrs. Johnson lies about her willingness to integrate white neighborhoods, telling Lena that while some black families "don't go where they ain't wanted and all that—but not me, honey!"[78] Then just a few lines later in a contradiction of this claim, she advises Lena that she'll be praying that the Youngers are not bombed in Clybourne Park as the move marks their refusal to accept white supremacy's basic premise. Rather than engage in such a refusal, she advises Lena and the family that "you have to think of life like it is—and these here Chicago peckerwoods are some bad peckerwoods."[79] Mrs. Johnson's warning describes how she imagines white supremacy's power over her lived experience; it necessitates thinking of "life like it is," dictated by segregation, rather than imagining life's possibilities beyond white supremacy's limits. Conversely, the Youngers do envision possibilities beyond residential segregation and seek to push beyond such imposed boundaries in their move to Clybourne Park. It is not only black acceptance of white supremacy's power, then, that Beneatha's assertion about Mrs. Johnson addresses. She also speaks to the significance of imagining black subjectivity beyond the spatial and ideological limits that residential segregation, enforced by Chicago's real estate covenant, seeks to impose. But if Beneatha's assertion acknowledges black identity shaped outside of the paradigms dictated by white supremacy, her relationship with Joseph Asagai widens its possibilities.

Beneatha's relationship with George Murchison illustrates her disidentification with racial uplift ideology and its implications for African American identity, particularly in its narrative of race progress and black assimilation into American culture, but her relationship with Nigerian student Joseph Asagai offers a compelling alternative to racial uplift ideology and its cultural politics. Drawing on allusion-disruption strategy, which summons and signifies on previous eras of African American history as well as the ideologies and representations linked to those historical moments in his discussions with Beneatha, Asagai offers both levity and discernment concerning her identity work. Though Asagai's preoccupation with marriage seemingly resonates with uplift's normative gender roles and its emphasis on the family, his representation points to a partnership and an intellectual engagement with Beneatha that is absent in her relationship with Murchison. Simply put,

Asagai interacts with Beneatha as a peer rather than attempting to use her as a prop to serve uplift ideology's ends, as Murchison does.

While Asagai teases her about her earnestness, it is done in the service of expanding her concept of identity, particularly how beauty standards inform that concept. The era after World War II not only marked a transition in how African Americans referenced themselves, moving from colored or Negro to black, but also how African American women began to challenge white standards of beauty in the public sphere through their hairstyles. Driven by both the burgeoning African American Freedom Struggle in the United States and the rising tide of African countries seeking independence from colonial power, this shift gained momentum in the postwar period and came to its apex during the Black Arts Movement. Beneatha's decision to cut her hair speaks directly to this shift. Within the confines of uplift ideology, such an expression of identity warrants admonishment from Ruth, Murchison, and Walter. However, the series of questions Asagai poses about her hair does not reflect either uplift's anxiety over any divergence from an assimilated black identity that mimicked white standards of beauty, nor does it reflect the compulsory natural hair that marked alliance with an "authentically" black cultural politics of the Black Power/Black Arts Movements. Instead, he gently pushes her to examine her perceptions of her hair and to link those perceptions to her quest for identity. In their allusion to the power that the cultural politics of uplift hold over black women's self-representation of their hair, Asagai's questions provide an opportunity for Beneatha's critical reflection on the standard of beauty that she has followed and enable her to explore identity from new vantages.

After Beneatha opens the gift of Nigerian records and robes that Asagai has given her, he helps her try them on in front of a mirror. He observes, "You wear it well . . . very well . . . mutilated hair and all."[80] When she asks what's wrong with her hair, rather than confirming or denying there is anything "wrong" with it, he poses another question: "Were you born with it like that?"[81] As Beneatha responds "no . . . of course not," the stage direction indicates she begins her ruminations by "reaching up to touch" her hair and in the same moment, "she looks back to the mirror, disturbed."[82] Their exchange continues:

ASAGAI: *(Smiling)*: How then?
BENEATHA: You know perfectly well how . . . as crinkly as yours . . . that's how.
ASAGAI: And is it ugly to you that way?

BENEATHA *(Quickly)*: Oh, no—not ugly. . . . *(More slowly, apologetically)* But it's so hard to manage when it's, well—raw.
ASAGAI: And so to accommodate that—you mutilate it every week?
BENEATHA: It's not mutilation!
ASAGAI: *(Laughing aloud at her seriousness)*: Oh . . . please! I am only teasing you because you are so very serious about these things. (*He stands back from her and folds his arms across his chest as he watches her pulling at her hair and frowning in the mirror.*) Do you remember the first time you met me at school? . . . (*He laughs.*) You came up to me and you said—I thought you were the most serious little thing I had ever seen—you said: (*He imitates her*) "Mr. Asagai—I want very much to talk with you. About Africa. You see, Mr. Asagai, I am looking for my identity!"
(*He laughs.*)
BENEATHA: *(Turning to him, not laughing)* Yes—
(*Her face is quizzical, profoundly disturbed.*)[83]

Though Beneatha has demonstrated in both interactions with her family and George Murchison her keen intellect and curiosity, her discussion with Asagai reveals blind spots in her exploration of identity. Increasingly unsettled both literally and figuratively by what she sees in the mirror, Beneatha's discomfort derives from the realization that she has not critically evaluated the cultural politics of her hair and, as Asagai points out, she naïvely locates the start of her search for identity to the African continent. In short, Asagai questions why her search for identity begins in another continent rather than within her own cultural practices at home. While he does not foreclose the possibility that the continent's culture might productively inform her pursuit, his probing about identity posits that she might usefully think globally and act locally about black female subjectivity. In so doing, Asagai frames the challenges of Beneatha's searching as the careful navigation of multiple cultural genealogies. He suggests as much as he comforts, but once again gently challenges her, in the midst of her critical reflection:

ASAGAI: (*Still teasing and reaching out and taking her face in his hands and turning her profile to him*) Well . . . it is true that this is not so much a profile of a Hollywood queen as perhaps a queen of the Nile—(*a mock dismissal of the importance of the question*). But what does it matter? Assimilationism is so popular in your country.
BENEATHA: (*Wheeling, passionately, sharply*) I am not an assimilationist!
ASAGAI: (*The protest hangs in the room for a moment and* ASAGAI *studies her, his laughter fading.*) Such a serious one. (*There is a pause.*) So—you like

the robes? You must take excellent care of them—they are from my sister's wardrobe.
BENEATHA: (*with incredulity*) You—you sent all the way home—for me?
ASAGAI: (*with charm*) For you—I would do much more.... Well, that is what I came for. I must go.[84]

Fashioning a "post-soulesque" allusion-disruption that hinges on the qualifying phrases "not so much" and "as perhaps," Asagai summons the representation of both a movie star and an African queen and situates Beneatha between the two, which highlights her contingent relationship with them. Through his linkage, he does not subvert one image to the other, but instead offers representational space for Beneatha that enables her to lay claim to the cultural genealogies attached to both representations. Yet even as Asagai points to this representational space, he takes up a potential obstacle to Beneatha's access to that space, racial uplift ideology and one of its goals, assimilation. Significantly, the stage direction draws attention to how Asagai mitigates this issue by inflecting his observations with humor. His "mock dismissal" of the representational space's significance when juxtaposed to the alternative of assimilation emphasizes its necessity to Beneatha's search for identity. Through his mock dismissal, he proposes securing a representational space for her on a continuum between the Hollywood queen and the queen of the Nile that resonates with, but is not bound to, either representation. Beneatha's impassioned rejection of assimilation as a means of developing identity confirms the legitimacy of Asagai's proposition because compliance with assimilation's conditions, its compulsory immersion in white mainstream culture's values and standards, inhibit the representational possibilities that can embrace elements of dominant, African American, and African cultures. In facilitating this discussion of hair and its relationship to black female identity, Asagai broadens Beneatha's reflection upon the representational space she occupies within her family and beyond its boundaries. Their debate enables Beneatha to legitimize "what the New World hath finally wrought" as she incorporates aspects of each of these cultural genealogies in crafting identity yet refuses any of them as a singular mode of shaping identity.[85]

Asagai further enables Beneatha's experimentation with identity in the third act, after the Youngers learn that Walter has lost the insurance money in a failed attempt to open a liquor store. He visits their home to help them pack for the move, unaware of what has occurred, and finds Beneatha and Walter in an apartment "full of the empty sound of profound disappointment."[86] Beneatha shares Walter's botched business plans and the loss of her medical school tuition with Asagai, but rather than offering consolation, he challenges her to critically reflect on her reactions to the turn of events and to reinterpret their implications for crafting subjectivity, particularly how they inform her own aspirations. In a discussion that frames Asagai's efforts toward Nigerian independence and Walter's failed attempt at entrepreneurship as analogous, Beneatha initially questions her desire to become a doctor because it "it doesn't seem deep enough, close enough to what ails mankind."[87] Relentless in her despair, she tells Asagai that he cannot answer the question of what good is struggle or why people should bother to have dreams and finally asserts that "there isn't any real progress . . . there is only one large circle we march, in around and around . . . each of us with our own little picture . . . that we think is the future."[88] In a pointed personal critique of Asagai's idealistic commitment to African independence, she asks, "What about all the crooks and petty thieves and just plain idiots who will come into power to steal and plunder the same as before—only now they will be black and do it in the name of new independence—You cannot answer that."[89] Positioning himself as part of a larger historical continuum, he shouts over her "I live the answer!" and continues with his plans to make an impact when he returns to Nigeria: "I will teach and work and things will happen, slowly and swiftly. At times it will seem that nothing changes at all . . . and then again . . . the sudden dramatic events which make history leap into the future."[90] Yet he also recognizes the inherent contingency of those plans and the regenerative possibilities of his own death as he tells Beneatha, "Perhaps the things I believe now for my country will be wrong and outmoded. . . . Don't you see that there will be young men and women . . . to step out of the shadows and slit my then useless throat? . . . and that such a thing as my own death will be an advance?"[91] Through the lens of postcolonialism and the struggle for freedom in Nigeria, Asagai offers Beneatha an alternate perspective on the family's loss that frames it as regenerative. As a foil to George Murchison, Asagai envisions himself both as engaged with a broader African cultural genealogy and the progression of history that he describes as "a long line that reaches into infinity."[92] Ultimately, as he acknowledges his role in affecting change in his home country—which is to simply live there, to connect with the community members in his village, and to share his knowledge and life with them—he positions himself as an agent of historical progress rather than an object of it and encourages Beneatha to view herself, her family, and her current situation in the same light.

Asagai's notion of loss as regeneration has implications for Walter as well. Significantly, the stage direction makes clear that Walter Lee eavesdrops on Beneatha and Asagai's conversation and that he "visibly respond[s] to the words of his sister and Asagai" and is subsequently inspired to act by what he has heard.⁹³ Although his initial move following Asagai's departure is to accept the Clybourne Park Improvement Association's offer to buy the home from the family at a profit to keep them from moving in, he cannot follow through on that action precisely because he imagines himself as an agent rather than an object of history. As he tells Karl Lindner, the association's chairman, that his father earned the home for them "brick by brick," his refusal to accept the offer marks a renewed commitment to both his cultural genealogy and to the long line of history before him—namely his father—and that which will follow him—his son, Travis. Walter Lee's ascent to "living the answer" is revealed in his rejection of the offer, which necessarily entails his willingness to take responsibility for the family's setback. But at the same time, in accounting for his lapse in judgment, he clears the way for committing to being an agent of history rather than becoming an object of it. In much the same way that Asagai describes the effort to hold on to his power in his home country as one that could cause his own death, Walter Lee's implicit admission of fault also results in his and his family's replenishment in terms of affirming their cultural pride and rejecting white supremacy's logic by moving into their new home, despite the danger it may ultimately pose to them.⁹⁴

In the end, Asagai foregrounds the ways in which she and her family fall prey to despair after Walter's failed investment in the liquor store and initiates their push beyond despondency and into renewal. Beneatha's debate with Asagai provides the impetus for the Youngers' efforts toward living the answer to questions of why one continues on in the face of adversity. Living the answer means contending with and walking through the possibilities for both change and regression in Asagai's long line of progress. The play's final scene not only speaks to the long line of history's implications for Walter as he rejects the association's offer, but also for Beneatha and her pursuit of black subjectivity beyond uplift ideology's confines. As she shares the news of Asagai's marriage proposal with her family, she and Walter end the play as they began it—arguing about how she defines herself and whether she should marry Asagai. He tells her to marry "a man with some loot" and she angrily asks, "What have you got to do with who I marry?"⁹⁵ Beneatha's struggle for subjectivity continues through the play's end, but her work parallels the family's broader struggle as they move to Clybourne Park to contend with and walk through the possibilities for both change and regression. By the play's end, Beneatha locates black identity, or her "right to be different from everybody else-and yet-be a part too" in the interstice between racial uplift ideology and intellectual freedom.

While Beneatha skillfully navigates African American identity's contested landscape in *A Raisin in the Sun* and draws upon a range of cultural genealogies to shape her iteration of black identity, there is virtually no discussion of her in theater critics' reviews of the play at its debut. Instead, the reviews emphasized Lena's and Walter's characterizations and the ways in which they contribute to the ostensible paradox between the play's universality and particularity. As critic Robin Bernstein explained, the universal and the particular are categories that intersect and are mutually permeable—they are part of a dialectic.[96] Yet "the appearance of a paradox depends on the assumption that universality and particularity are static."[97] Thus, while *A Raisin in the Sun* demonstrates the fluidity between universality and particularity, maintaining a false paradox between them in the reviews enabled critics to ignore the ways in which it troubled those boundaries. Often the reviews put Lena and Walter's representation in the service of maintaining that paradox, but they rarely discuss Beneatha because she more readily troubles that paradox. As a result, critics circumscribe her contributions within the narrative to representing either an "overintellectualized daughter" or a "giddy adolescent" that better serves the paradox's maintenance.[98]

Limning the boundaries between the universal and the particular, Brooks Atkinson noted in the *New York Times* that the play is "about human beings who want, on the one hand, to preserve their family and pride and, on the other hand, to break out of the poverty that seems to be their fate. Not having any axe to grind, Miss Hansberry has a wide variety of topics to write about—some of them hilarious, some of them painful in the extreme."[99] Echoing Atkinson, the *New York World-Telegram*'s Frank Aston asserts the play "has no axe to grind. It is honest drama, catching up real people. It may rip you to shreds. It will make you proud of human beings."[100] Suggesting here that the particularity of the Youngers' African American identity does not impede the play's universal implications, these critics framed *A Raisin in the Sun* as a play that is simply about racially unmarked "human beings." Yet embedded in both assessments is the assertion that it has no axe to grind, or that the play does not critique white supremacy and is therefore not a propaganda play that would obscure its universal implications. Further, in emphasizing that the play's realism—its "honest drama"—portrays African American identity with a fidelity that falls in line with these critics own notions of "blackness," they give the work universal implications and erase its engagement with African American identity politics and a critique of the larger cultural sphere.

Hansberry, however, rejected such assessments, and the omission of the impact of racial identity in the critical evaluations of the play became increasingly problematic for her. Defending the significance of racial oppression in the play, she asserted, "The fact of racial oppression, unspoken and unalluded to, other than the fact of how they live, is through the play. It's inescapable. The reason these people are in a ghetto is because they are Negroes. They are discriminated against brutally and horribly . . . so in that sense it is always distinctly there."[101] Even as the author's intention—a representation of black identity imbued by the lived reality of racial oppression and a critique of that oppression—was recast by critics as universal, it was also figured as an "honest" play with "vigor as well as veracity."[102] This erasure of race-based oppression in the critical assessments suggests a reticence to read Hansberry's representation of blackness as a lived experience and instead imposes a rubric of universality on the representations that skirts the issue. In effect, the cultural negotiations around representations of blackness as reflected in the critical evaluations fail to fully engage the issue at the core of Hansberry's representation—race-based oppression and how it impacts concerns of equal housing access, economic enfranchisement, and African American identity politics.

Still, many reviews not only willfully overlook black identity and white supremacy's implications in the play's representations but also reveal fissures in the false opposition of universality and particularity; Beneatha's representation presents those fractures. One example appears in Brooks Atkinson's favorable review of the play, which observes that while Claudia McNeil's Lena and Sidney Poitier's Walter "have solid footing in the script," the playwright missteps with the representations of Beneatha and her suitors: "The belligerent racism of the daughter who is attending college, her provincial ignorance of Africa, her confusion of Liberia and Nigeria, the amused maturity of a college student who comes from Africa, the sophomoric sophistication of an American college student—these are pungent notes by the way set down by Miss Hansberry out of experience, observation and a sense of comedy."[103] He goes on to attribute Lena's confusion about Nigeria and Liberia to Beneatha, who actually corrects Lena's misunderstanding in the play. Nonetheless, Atkinson frames Beneatha as a necessary comedic intrusion in the play's otherwise wholly aracial "practical accounting of a life of a family."[104] By narrowly framing the ways in which her representation complicates the simplistic notions of black identity that undergird many critical assessments of the play, while at the same time emphasizing Lena and Walter's authenticity, Atkinson broadens the divide between the universal and the particular. He situates Beneatha's "belligerent racism" as necessary comic relief, but it remains an intrusion of the black particular upon the presumably white universal. Atkinson's framing resonates with Hansberry's contentions about audiences' difficulties in confronting black characters who clearly departed from one-dimensional representations of black identity or "the image of the simple, glandular, loveable Negro" that populated US cultural productions.

Writing in the *Village Voice*, Hansberry argues that such representations are not intended to slander African Americans, but instead offer "a mental haven for readers and audiences who could bask in unleashed passions of those 'lucky ones' for whom abandonment was apparently permissible."[105] In effect, critical assessments of such representations reinforced hegemonic whiteness and critics' assessments of Beneatha served the same ends. Bearing in mind Hansberry's contentions, Atkinson's assertion that despite the "acrimonious daughter," the play is ultimately "a lively and illuminating drama about people of great emotional vitality" demonstrates critics' refusal to engage any representation that contradicts the "simple glandular Negro." Yet the mainstream press is not alone in its simplistic discussions of Beneatha. Al Monroe's favorable review of the play in the *Chicago Daily Defender* applauded Diana Sands's portrayal of "the giddy adolescent" as "mischievously adorable."[106] Similarly, Darcy Demille's *Los Angeles Sentinel* review reduced her to "the spirited, know-it-all college girl" and devotes more column inches to Ivan Dixon's portrayal of Asagai than to Beneatha, though she is in nearly every scene in the play.[107] In short, critics refuse to meaningfully engage Beneatha's representation and the complications it offers to enduring images of women broadly, and black women in particular. Instead, they emphasize the more familiar representations of African American women offered in the play, particularly Lena, who for many critics represented the familiar, stereotypical mammy, despite the stage direction and dialogue that suggests otherwise.

Moreover, critics repeatedly discuss the play's sentimentality and the opportunity for emotional catharsis it presents to its audiences, as well as the occasion it offers for a racially integrated theater experience. Their emphasis on the play's sentimentality demonstrates a slightly altered version of Hansberry's "mental haven" that only reinscribes what critics identified as the play's universal implications. In one example, Walter Kerr suggested that the moments of catharsis are essential to the play, proposing that Walter's refusal to take the Clybourne Park Improvement Association buyout offer marks "a cumulative swell of emotion [that] reaches back over the evening to surround, and bind up, an honest, intelligible, and moving experience."[108] Likewise, theater critic Frank Aston locates the significance of the play in its appeal to emotions, suggesting that "the number of tears shed by presumably worldly first nighters must have set a new record at the Ethel Barrymore last evening" and adds that "the major weeping comes in two waves," one at the end of the second act, the other in Walter's refusal scene near the play's end.[109] For other critics in the mainstream press, *A Raisin in the Sun*'s sentimentality facilitated desegregation and, presumably, the play's universal implications by emphasizing its transcendence of racial categories. Critic Tom F. Driver asserted that its sentiment offers "theatrical magic in which the usual barriers between audience and stage disappears; the people up there are living among us, and we down here are mixing with those up there of easy terms."[110] Similarly, John McClain addressed the historical significance of the play in the *New York Journal-American*: "A small hunk of history was made last night. A play by a Negro about Negroes with an almost all Negro cast opened on Broadway and was a stupendous unsegregated hit. It proved to me at least, that when these people create and participate in something for themselves, they can make the rest of us look silly."[111] McClain's declarations crystallize the tensions within the so-called universal and particular paradox. On the heels of declaring *A Raisin in the Sun*'s universality as an "unsegregated hit," he recovered black particularity by situating the play as evidence that African American cultural production can only speak to the experience of African Americans. In effect, it offers an opportunity for white audiences to access an authentically "Negro" experience in a desegregated theater without troubling the static categories of the universal or the particular. By emphasizing both the false division between the universal and particular as well as the play's emotional impact, critics not only echoed Hansberry's notion of a "mental haven" that enables audiences' entry to emotions that only the racially othered "lucky ones" can access, but it also resonates with antislavery fiction's cultural work in the nineteenth century.

Critic Karen Sánchez-Eppler argued that sentimental antislavery fiction's popularity derived in part from white readers' fascination with reading the lurid details of the "the abuses they ostensibly oppose" and that further, they were tales in which the "tears of the reader" were "pledged as a means of rescuing the bodies of slaves."[112] Finally, in the emotional responses to the narratives, Sánchez-Eppler has argued that the "physicality of the reading experience radically contracts the distance between narrated events and the moment of their reading as the feelings in the story are made tangibly present in the flesh of the reader."[113] While antislavery fiction's nineteenth-century historical context greatly differs from the twentieth-century, post–World War II historical context of critics reviewing *A Raisin in the Sun*, what sustains through those eras is racial identity's continuing impact on African Americans' living conditions and access to life opportunities, and as Bernstein argues, the play seemingly made those conditions "appear understandable and consumable by white audiences."[114] As a result, while critics and audiences at the play's debut may have opposed the real estate covenants informing the Youngers' move to Clybourne Park as well as the historical conditions that produced the Southside ghetto, critics reviewing *A Raisin in the Sun* focused on making the Youngers' experience legible through their own and audiences' ability to access and display sympathy for them.

Further, the reviews reduced the distance between the events on stage and the moment of their viewing. Parallel to the success of antislavery fiction, which Sánchez-Eppler noted depends in part on "its ability to translate words into pulse beats and sobs," both critics' and audiences' emotional reaction to the events detailed in the play rather than critics' interpretation of those events become the focus of the reviews.[115] By drawing attention to the play's sentiment and emotional impact, critics pledged their own and audiences' responses as a means of identifying with the Youngers' experiences, but did so at the expense of interpreting how the Youngers embody African Americans' always-contested pursuit of class mobility, as well as their struggles with the ideologies underwriting it. As critic Dean Peerman discerned, the play's reviews demonstrated that "Americans seemed to be embracing the play without fully understanding it—or perhaps wanting to understand it."[116] Instead, the reviews revealed the lengths to which critics would go to avoid addressing the specific terms of the Youngers' experience. While Driver's otherwise favorable review offered a critique of the play's craft, it also proposed a reason for its popularity that supported Peerman's contention:

> If *A Raisin in the Sun* had been written by a white
> instead of colored woman and if it had been written about a
> white family it would have done well to recover its
> investment. As a piece of dramatic writing it is old fashioned.
> As something near to the conscious of a nation troubled by
> injustice to Negroes it is emotionally powerful. Much of its
> success is due to our sentimentality over the "Negro
> Question."[117]

Even after applauding the play's ability to perform "theatrical magic" that eliminates racial barriers and consequently demonstrates its universality, Driver revisited the universal/particular paradox, but in this return, he not only revealed how the play affords an opportunity for the nation to show its sympathy toward African Americans struggling against race-based oppression, he also unwittingly pointed to how the universal emerges from the particular.

The problem is that critics reduced the particular to the euphemistic "Negro Question" rather than framing the particular as a "thorough probing of the individual within the specifics of culture, ethnicity and gender."[118] As a result, critics' readings of the universal and the particular, as well as their emphasis on emotion and sentimentality in *A Raisin in the Sun*, reveals mainstream American culture's anxiety—or perhaps guilt—about race-based oppression, but very little about the African American cultural specificity that engineers the universality that all the critics applaud. Insisting upon narrow interpretations of the play's representations that invariably return to maintaining the universal/particular paradox, critics missed the opportunity that *A Raisin in the Sun* offers to span the historical and cultural gaps between African Americans and whites by failing to critically engage the play's representations and, in particular, its black female representations. Yet after Hansberry's death, actor, activist, and playwright Ossie Davis addressed those critical oversights. In "The Significance of Lorraine Hansberry," originally published in *Freedomways* in 1965, Davis argued that sentimental and uncritical assumptions about race and representation owing to "our mythic conviction that, underneath, all of us Americans, *color-ain't-got-nothing-to-do-with-it*, are pretty much alike," denied both Hansberry and the play more serious consideration and analysis.[119]

Similarly, critic Margaret Wilkerson observed, the play's dialectic between the particular and the universal resides in its representations, which are shaped by Hansberry's refusal "to diminish the pain, suffering or truths of any one group to benefit another, a factor which makes her plays particularly rich and her characters thoroughly complex."[120]

Beneatha embodies that dialectic. Writer and critic Amiri Baraka's critical reassessment of the play in 1989 identified it as the "essence of black people's striving and the will to defeat segregation, discrimination and national oppression," yet Beneatha refuses to be defined by those strivings alone.[121] As she disidentifies with the politics of racial uplift ideology, she rejects its conscription of black female subjectivity but retains its commitment to defeating white supremacy and race-based oppression. In so doing, she not only bridges the ideological gaps between her family members, but also the historical and cultural gaps that critics embedded in their assessments of the play. Though they ignored her significance to the play's interpretation as well as to unraveling the false paradox they constructed between the universal and the particular, she embodies one important facet of a black particular that feeds *A Raisin in the Sun*'s universality.

Beneatha navigates black female subjectivity's tightrope within a mid-twentieth-century historical context that insisted upon a narrow range of representations of black female subjectivity, and Hansberry wrote her specifically to address that lack, asserting that Beneatha presents "the kind of character that people had never seen before, a Negro girl with intellectual pretensions of any sort, [is] just unknown to the theater."[122] Yet by crafting a representation of black female identity that not only challenges critics' and audiences' notions of black female identity, but also draws upon a range of cultural genealogies in asserting it, Beneatha sits squarely on postblackness's cusp.

CHAPTER TWO

"A Ghost of the Future": Racial (Mis)perception and Black Subjectivity in LeRoi Jones's *Dutchman*

Conceptual artist Rashid Johnson is a key practitioner of and contributor to postblack identity discourse. One of the twenty-eight up-and-coming artists featured in the Studio Museum in Harlem's *Freestyle* exhibition in 2001, Johnson's work explores the African American Freedom Struggle's relationship to black identity or, as the writer Touré observes, his work both recognizes African Americans' achievement in that era and enables us to "see their limitations, the places where they'd fallen short."[1] In his solo exhibitions, including 2008's *The Dead Lecturer: Laboratory, Dojo and Performance Space* and 2002's *Chickenbones and Watermelon Seeds: The African American Experience as Abstract Art*, Johnson has summoned the fraught history around stereotypical images of African Americans, but deploys them in ways that intervene in the standard meanings attached to them.

While his work "sasses" an earlier generation of cultural producers and products in its refusal either to honor racial uplift ideology's cultural politics or to tow the blacker-than-thou black aesthetic party line, Johnson's *The Dead Lecturer* exhibition simultaneously referenced the era in its allusion to LeRoi Jones's *The Dead Lecturer*. Published in 1964, the same year as *Dutchman*'s debut, *The Dead Lecturer* is a collection of poems published during what is often referenced as Jones's transitional period before he left Greenwich Village's avant garde milieu for Harlem and changed his name to Amiri Baraka to mark his solidarity with black cultural nationalism and the Black Arts Movement.[2] As theater critic Harry Elam has observed, the retrospective gesture that Johnson and other postblack artists enact is not only endemic to postblack cultural production; it also enables postblack products' cultural work of accommodating the fluid and shifting meanings of blackness within the current historical moment. Elam has written, "It is this working through and against the past that allows its practitioners and audiences to contemplate the present."[3]

Within that context, then, Johnson's restaging of Baraka's 1964 play, *Dutchman*, for Performa 13, the New York performance art biennial, might be understood as another instance of a postblack cultural producer working through and against the past in order to grapple with black identity in the current moment. Yet beyond the location of its staging—the Russian & Turkish Baths in New York's East Village—Johnson refused to change any aspect of the play, saying that it more readily spoke to the current historical moment than the one of its debut staging because "the way that we imagine the struggle of the hero or anti-hero character is more married [than it would have been then] to our understanding of the Civil Rights Movement, meaning things like the March on Washington."[4] Johnson crystallized here the idea that cultural memory of the Freedom Struggle era in the current historical moment frames that era's cultural products as irretrievably bound to the direct action protest of the period, and in his restaging of the play, he looked toward intervening in such a simple association by proposing that the Freedom Struggle is as much about African American identity as it is African American voting rights.

The one-act play is a dialogue between Clay, a twenty-year-old African American man on his way to a party, and Lula, a thirty-year-old white woman, which occurs during a chance meeting on a subway train "heaped in modern myth." Over two scenes and in an increasingly contentious encounter that addresses interracial sex, US history, and black identity, *Dutchman* lends itself to such an intervention in the current moment because the play's protagonist, Clay, situates his iteration of African American identity within the tension between his articulation of black male subjectivity and white dominant culture's efforts formulate it. In his suggestion that the play "feels like it lives really appropriately today, as opposed to the way we would have [experienced] it in '64," Johnson framed *Dutchman* as "a text out of time" analogous to other postblack texts' exploration of black subjectivity. Similarly, this chapter argues that *Dutchman* unpacks whiteness's investment in uplift ideology by employing a variety of cultural genealogies and practices to sketch identity and, in so doing, exposes the vulnerabilities of Freedom Struggle era iterations of uplift ideology.

Racial uplift ideology was enacted and disseminated in a range of venues, and an important one was the magazines of the era. Probably the best-known black lifestyle magazine is *Ebony*, published by Chicago-based Johnson Publishing Company, in addition to three other black lifestyle magazines. A full-

Rashid Johnson's *Dutchman*, a Performa commission. Photograph © Paula Court, courtesy of Performa.

Rashid Johnson's *Dutchman*, a Performa commission. Photograph © Paula Court, courtesy of Performa.

size picture monthly "dedicated to telling the story of the life of Negro America," *Ebony* strategically presented images of African Americans to its readers emphasizing their lives as "ordinary mortal human being[s]—not a freak or a stereotype, not a debate or a resolution."[5] In the same month as *Dutchman*'s debut, a March 1964 *Ebony* photo-editorial declared that while the collective future for African Americans had been delayed because of racial segregation, the combined effects of legislative actions and direct action protests put the future within sight. Celebrating these new possibilities, the editorial

Rashid Johnson's *Dutchman*, a Performa commission. Photograph © Paula Court, courtesy of Performa.

exclaimed, "It's great to be a Negro and live through the excitement of that period when the future is coming to pass."[6] It continues, speaking directly to their implications for black representations and particularly the burden to represent the race in ways that defy white supremacist stereotypes, maintaining that a by-product of the Freedom Struggle is the casting off of such burdens:

> This is a new kind of dignity. Not the dignity of the field hand who refused to knuckle under or the white collar worker who refused to tom. . . . It is a dignity that is expressed in going back time after time to register to vote. . . . It is a dignity that would allow the darkest Negro in New York to actually enjoy watermelon for dessert in the best dining room of the Waldorf-Astoria. It is a dignity that comes when one is able to say, let the stereotypes be damned! I am my own man![7]

Ebony's editorial proposes that the direct action protests meant to initiate legislative actions that would enable full citizenship for African Americans had an equally important impact on African Americans' self-concepts. Those protests also facilitate the rejection of uplift ideology's cultural politics and demand that such stereotypes be refuted. But more importantly, they reject the white representations of black identity that warrant uplift ideology. Not quite a year after the March on Washington and roughly a year prior to the passage of the 1965 Voting Rights Act, the *Ebony* editorial identified a shift in African Americans' self-concepts of identity unfettered by concerns with substantiating African American humanity.

Another more subtle, yet equally important outcome of the "new dignity" is the rejection of W. E. B. DuBois's veil and double consciousness, or the idea that African Americans viewed themselves and other blacks through white constructions of black identity. While uplift ideology is a series of cultural practices offering evidence of black humanity in an effort to gain full citizenship, it also held the possibility of assuaging double consciousness's conditions—alienation from self and the nation—among African Americans. However, the editorial's new dignity circumvented both uplift and double consciousness. In allowing the stereotypes to be damned, or the declaration of a singular selfhood and situating the new dignity as more than both the elite and working class black's refusal to "tom," *Ebony*'s editorial traces a mode of representation and self-concept liberated from white supremacist notions of blackness, as well as black alienation from self and the nation. Echoing what Bertram Ashe has identified in the work of post-soul generation writers as "transcend[ing] double consciousness," the editorial's assertions gestured toward a parallel move. Likewise, Rashid Johnson's assertion that his restaging of *Dutchman* creates an opportunity to find identity somewhere between "the narrative of struggle and the narrative of Negro Exceptionalism" resonates in LeRoi Jones's[8] contention that the struggle is as much about "the right to choose."[9] Ultimately, Jones's play offers an iteration of African American identity and situates it on the continuum between narratives of struggle and exceptionalism. In his turn away from the politics of uplift and double consciousness, *Dutchman*'s Clay proclaims black male identity's fluidity, declines its service as proxy for the status of the race, and exposes the nation's incapacity to abide such assertions, which leaves the question of full citizenship unanswered. Yet even in revealing that incapacity, *Dutchman* gestures toward the historical conditions that give rise to postblack representations by framing a representational space that allows for the inherent contradictions of living while black.

One way that it accomplishes this is through its exploration of citizenship and its relationship to the nation. Amiri Baraka invoked the nation in his own assessments of *Dutchman*, arguing at its debut that it was about "the difficulty of becoming a man in America," and forty-three years later, at its 2007 revival, he asserted that Lula, the play's white female protagonist, was "a metaphor for America" who represented "temptation and seduction, but also death, if not of the flesh then of the spirit."[10] Similarly, Rashid Johnson's Performa13 staging of *Dutchman* was one of the 2013 season's three performances whose theme is a broad examination citizenship's meaning. *Dutchman*'s Clay not only unpacks the psychic costs of African Americans' mitigating the pursuit of full citizenship through a range of strategies including racial uplift ideology, but significantly, traces his retreat from those strategies. Through his conversation with Lula on a subway "heaped in modern myth," he demonstrates that the nation's perceptions of African American identity that would enable full citizenship cannot be reconciled with the broad range of African Americans' self-concepts. Clay's contentions about African American identity's complexities fall on the deaf ears of a nation that refuses narrative dissonance in its project of assimilating African Americans; he refuses to stick to the nation's scripting of black identity that would enable his full citizenship. Yet the play moves beyond exposing a conundrum of black efforts toward freedom thwarted by the nation's refusal to embrace those efforts because Clay offers narrative dissonance as a representational necessity for African Americans. As "a ghost of the future," Clay points to the multiplicity of black identities that move beyond the monolithic representations that Lula presses him to authenticate and actualize and, in so doing, rejects assimilation and its conditions. Resisting Lula's tendency to privilege the visible and to apprehend black identity as a transparent object, Clay exposes "the changing discursive processes by which identities are ascribed, resisted, or embraced and which processes themselves are unremarked and indeed achieve their effect because they are not noticed."[11] In the end, it is his refusal to limit identity by submitting to assimilation as Lula defines it, and, by extension, citizenship's conditions, that results in his death. Still, his death offers representational possibilities for African American identity in the interstices between limited and full citizenship, as well as between "Negro exceptionalism" and black struggle.

Clay displaces Lula's perceptions of blackness as the prevailing narrative of black identity's scope by the play's end, but at the outset, he rarely questions the significance or accuracy of her racial perceptions, and when he attempts to examine her insights, she thwarts those efforts by redirecting the conversation. In these early exchanges, Clay's simultaneous impulse to dispel Lula's assertions and to explore them illustrates his desire to assimilate and conform with uplift ideology's cultural politics. Throughout the play's first scene, he is willing to hear her out and to consider that her observations about who he is might be accurate or of value. One example of this occurs shortly after Lula boards the train and tells Clay that he's dull. Taken aback, he says that he "wasn't prepared for party talk"; she agrees and then asks what he is prepared for. Attempting to confront her challenges and shift the conversation, the stage direction points out that Clay "takes her conversation as pure sex talk" and asserts, "I'm prepared for anything. How about you?" Lula ridicules him by "laughing loudly" at his question and opines that Clay wants to "take [her] somewhere and screw [her]." He asks if that is how he really looks and she replies,

> LULA: You look like you been trying to grow a beard. That's exactly what you look like. You look like you live in New Jersey with your parents and are trying to grow a beard. That's what. You look like you've been reading Chinese poetry and drinking lukewarm sugarless tea.
> *[Laughs, uncrossing and recrossing her legs]*
> You look like death eating a soda cracker.
> CLAY: *[Cocking his head from one side to the other, embarrassed and trying to make some comeback, but also intrigued by what the woman is saying . . . even the sharp city coarseness of her voice, which is still a kind of gentle sidewalk throb]*
> Really? I look like all that?
> LULA. Not all of it.
> *[She feints a seriousness to cover an actual somber tone.]*
> I lie a lot.
> *[Smiling]*
> It helps me control the world.
> CLAY. *[Relieved and laughing louder than the humor]*
> Yeah, I bet.[12]

Outlining the rhetorical strategy she follows throughout the play as well as the rules of engagement for their encounter, Lula frames her fictionalized perception of Clay as authoritative, which is essential in maintaining her power in directing the conversation. Here she shifts from his presumed sexual desire for her to mocking the signposts of 1960s era bohemian subculture—reading Chinese poetry, growing a beard, drinking lukewarm tea—and in so doing, Lula traces the limits of identity for Clay that become more racially specific and charged throughout the play. More importantly, this tableau, along with others in the play's first scene, reveal how Clay grapples with double consciousness and its "continual struggle against an *intellectual* dependence on dominant ideologies of whiteness and white constructions of blackness" demonstrated in his ambivalence about what Lula claims to see in him.[13] He is at once embarrassed and intrigued by her assertions and struggles to refute them with a comeback, yet he is also relieved by the revelation that she lies about them but tries to offset how unsettled he is by her disclosure that she manipulates her perceptions with overwrought laughter.

In short, it describes Clay's position within double consciousness's conundrum—his reactions demonstrate that he "feels his twoness—an American, a Negro; two souls, two thoughts, two unreconciled strivings; two warring ideals in one dark body."[14] Similar to the Flying Dutchman, he is forever doomed to navigate the choppy seas of white constructions of black identity, shuttling between competing impulses to refute the claims she makes about his identity and to examine them, to feel relief about her admission that she lies about her perceptions and to laugh uneasily at her power to manipulate them. As a stand-in for the nation and its ambivalence about African American citizenship, their exchange illustrates Lula's power in constructing black identity. By framing it in ways that prohibit representations of blackness outside of the scope of her own concepts of it, Lula restricts representation of black identity's full range and consequently limits the representation of black humanity, which warrants uplift ideology's project of removing such restrictions blocking black citizenship.

While the play's first scene shows double consciousness's significance in Clay's interactions with Lula, just as important to Clay's eventual retreat from double consciousness and uplift's cultural politics is the play's exploration of white identity and how it informs the nation and citizenship. Specifically, *Dutchman* addresses the fraught relationship between white liberals and African Americans, using its tensions to animate Clay's assertion of identity. *Ebony* magazine devoted its entire August 1965 issue to what it named "The White Problem in America." In its compilation of essays from journalists, activists, artists, and scholars, including Whitney Young, Carl T. Rowan, and Kenneth B. Clark, the special issue critically reads white identity from a range of perspectives, including analysis of white hate groups, the economic impact of discrimination, and white liberals. The issue insists, as managing editor Lerone Bennett Jr. writes in his essay, that there is "no Negro problem in America" but instead that the "white American created, *invented* the race problem, and his fears and frailties are responsible for the urgency of the problem."[15] Within that context, journalist Louis Lomax explores the figure of the white liberal, or what he calls the country's new power elite. Asserting that this segment of society faces continual attack from the New Left, Old Right, and from African Americans, Lomax painstakingly emphasizes that the white liberal comes from all walks of life and religions—Jewish, Catholic, and Anglo-Saxon Protestant—"marching along the road from Selma while [their] eyes dart furtively to the rising Negro crime rate."[16] Yet Lomax asserts that ambivalence about African Americans' full citizenship and African American identity within this range of white liberal experiences unites them:

> He is the clergyman torn between the new gospel he must now preach and the conservatism of the flock he must feed and which feeds him as well; he is the

businessman quite willing to accept change so long as things remain the same; he is the parent welcoming the new Negro neighbor and praying God that his daughter will marry one of her own kind; he is the academician peppering his lectures with liberalism and mumbling over why there are not more qualified minority students in his classes; . . . he is the common laborer sitting at a bar and mumbling over his beer, "I don't hate nobody; but I don't know what to do about it."[17]

By Lomax's account, the irony of the white liberal in all of its registers outlined here—at once committed to African American equality on a broad scale and ambivalent about extending those commitments to daily lived experience—resonate in *Dutchman*'s representation of Lula. She stands in for the white liberal power elite that supports and even advocates for African American autonomy yet, as Lomax observes, whose relationship with African Americans is "flecked with condescension."[18] Lula's interaction with Clay reveals that while white liberals experience guilt and remorse for racism in America, ultimately, there is no moment of conscience about the distribution of power—even in the struggle over the ways that African Americans seek to define themselves.

Moreover, Lomax's glossing of the white liberal intersects historian William Chafe's discussion of "the progressive mystique" in his study of race relations in Greensboro, North Carolina, over thirty years. It is a series of implicit assumptions, nuances, and modes of interacting with and relating to African Americans used by white liberals that are a masterful weapon of social control because progress is achieved only when direct conflict is avoided and the parties involved must voluntarily agree on an appropriate course of action. While he focused on Greensboro, Chafe contended that his study "speaks to larger issues at work in our society and culture" and it addresses "the underlying issues of justice, self-determination, and autonomy . . . the story of America."[19] In *Dutchman*, the progressive mystique informs Lula's representation, and her mode of relating to Clay illustrates the position of power it creates for her, not unlike what Chafe described in the interactions between African Americans and whites in Greensboro. One particularly powerful mode of relating to Clay becomes apparent in her self-representations.

The stage direction describes her as a thirty-year-old tall, slender, beautiful white woman with long red hair wearing sunglasses, summer clothes, and sandals.[20] During the course of the play, she positions herself in a multitude of ways to Clay: that they share a mutual friend—Warren Enright—making them contemporaries; in a nod to the African American vernacular tradition of "playing the dozens" that she's a former lover to his sister; that she's older than she appears; that she's a poet; that she's an actress; that she's a liar; that she's politically astute; that she's sexually available to him; that she's "nothing"; and finally, that she knows Clay "like the palm of her hand" and based on that knowledge that he is a "well-known type."[21] Armed with authoritative knowledge of Clay and his type, Lula occupies a range of subject positions, yet she casts doubt on Clay's own assertions of knowledge and his perceptions. After propositioning him with "would you like to get involved with me" and garnering his response of "I'd be a fool not to," she replies,

> LULA: And I bet you're sure you know what you're talking about.
> [*Taking him a little roughly by the wrist, so he cannot eat the apple, then shaking the wrist*]
> I bet you're sure of almost everything anybody ever asked you about . . . right?
> [*Shakes his wrist harder*]
> Right?[22]

Rather than continuing with the discussion of her initial sexual proposition, Lula takes up the failures of Clay's perceptions and knowledge, a strategy she employs throughout both scenes in the play. As Lula questions the veracity of Clay's perceptions and knowledge, she outlines her efforts to control and define not only the nature and tone of their conversation, but his role in it. Reiterating this notion in her literal staging of a performance within the play's performance, she proclaims herself as "Lena the Hyena, the famous woman poet" and once again broaches the issue of Warren Enright's party, imploring Clay to invite her to it:

> LULA:
> [*Starts laughing again*]
> Now you say to me, "Lula, Lula, why don't you go to this party with me tonight?" It's your turn, and let those be your lines.
> CLAY: Lula, why don't you go to this party with me tonight, Huh?
> LULA: Say my name twice before you ask, and no huh's.
> CLAY: Lula, Lula, why don't you go to this party with me tonight?
> LULA: I'd like to go Clay, but how can you ask me to go when you barely know me?
> CLAY: That is strange, isn't it?
> LULA: What kind of reaction is that? You're supposed to say, "Aw, come on, we'll get to know each other better at the party."[23]

Lula's strategies of self-representation, coupled with her staging of a play—or what Clay later calls a "pageant"—point to white liberal agency within the progressive mystique. Her fluid identity continually shifts at her own accord, while Clay's identity is fixed, a known quantity and accessible to everyone *but* Clay. He does not "know" his "lines" and cannot access the power she wields in order to create his own script. Following the progressive mystique, she consistently avoids direct confrontation with Clay while utilizing a series of implicit assumptions and nuances about his identity that becomes a means of social control. Ultimately, even as Lula implicitly critiques categorization and fixed identities in her self-representations, she invokes them in her interactions with, reactions to, and misperceptions of Clay.

Another aspect of the progressive mystique at work in *Dutchman* is civility, or "a way of dealing with people and problems that made good manners more important than substantial action."[24] For African Americans, the cultural politics of uplift called for deference to whites in order to maintain economic stability and offered little room for self-assertion and independence. Further, it suppressed honesty and protest when African Americans were in direct contact with whites. Chafe suggests that while African Americans shuttled between two social spheres, one public that involved contact with whites and one private African American social sphere, the need and desire to resist the social control of the progressive mystique and the function of civility within it was ongoing. He contends that they reflected "an incipient rebellion no less powerful for not being able to find open expression."[25] Clay's interactions with Lula demonstrate how civility functions within their struggle over African American identity and its relationship to her concepts of both citizenship and the nation.

Clay's reactions to Lula and her many assertions about him illustrate this notion of civility. He "idly" looks at her through the subway window, he "laughs louder than the humor" to smooth over a potentially uncomfortable social moment, he "leans back hard against the back of the seat . . . still trying to look amused," and tries to "be as flippant as Lula" in response to her sexual innuendos. In short, Clay evades each instance of a potential confrontation and strategically maintains a stance of civility toward Lula's assertions. Yet even as he pushes civility's limits by presenting a self-concept that might unsettle her reading of him as a "well-known type," Lula responds by framing Clay's self-presentation as a transgression against the nation's narrow concept of its history that consequently circumscribes African Americans' citizenship. She asks, "Did your people ever burn witches or start revolutions over the price of tea? Boy, those narrow-shoulder clothes come from a tradition you ought to feel oppressed by. . . . What right do you have to be wearing a three-button suit and striped tie? Your grandfather was a slave, he didn't go to Harvard."[26] Alluding to the Salem witch trials, the Revolutionary War, and an elite institution of higher education as markers of national identity, Lula maps criteria for citizenship that exclude the descendants of slaves. From her vantage, his three-button suit and striped tie mark an attempt to "pass" as a citizen and her assertion that he is a descendant of slaves thwarts that effort. Not only does she limn citizenship's contours with the sanitized and simplistic history she provides, thereby outlining who can and cannot lay claim to citizenship, but significantly, she rejects any autonomy he holds in aligning himself with the nation's history, however problematic it might be. Clay's response to her questions and their ensuing dialogue underscore the comingling of power and ambivalence that both Lomax and Chafe have described as central to white liberalism's efforts to define African American identity:

> CLAY: My grandfather was a night watchman.
> LULA: And you went to a colored college where everybody thought they were Averell Harriman.
> CLAY: All except me.
> LULA: And who did you think you were? Who do you think you are now?
> CLAY: Well, in college I thought I was Baudelaire. But I've slowed down some since.
> LULA: I bet you never once thought you were a black nigger. [*Mock serious, then she howls with laughter.* CLAY *is stunned but after initial reaction, he quickly tries to appreciate the humor.* LULA *almost shrieks.*] A black Baudelaire.

Once more Lula limits the cultural genealogies to which Clay can lay claim in developing his identity. As she condescendingly and incorrectly assumes that Clay and his peers aspired to become wealthy entrepreneurs, politicians, and diplomats in the mold of Harriman, an assertion that Clay refutes, she simultaneously ridicules his ambition to emulate a nineteenth-century French symbolist poet who rejected wealth and acclaim to pursue expressive culture. For Lula, and by extension the nation, Clay's "black bohemian" representation of a young black man wearing a suit while also aspiring to rival Baudelaire is an oxymoron. Consequently, his self-presentation to Lula necessitates the ultimate racialized and pejorative debasement that not only denies his self-representation but maintains her command of black identity's discourse.

Clay and Lula's final lines in the first scene foreshadow the second scene's violence and point to the continuing impact of Clay's self-representation on her. Reflecting on his appeal to black bohemianism, she declares, "The Black Baudelaire! Yes! [*and with knifelike cynicism*] My Christ. My Christ," and issues a warning to Clay about his pursuit of black male identity beyond what she sees as its extant boundaries: "May the people accept you as a ghost of the future. And love you that you might not kill them when you can." She concludes her meditation on Clay and his identity with an accusation, "You're a murderer Clay, and you know it," and closes the scene with a final proclamation:

> LULA: And we'll pretend the people cannot see you. That is, the citizens. And that you are free of your own history. And I am free of my history. We'll pretend that we are both anonymous beauties smashing along through the city's entrails.
> [*She yells as loud as she can*]
> GROOVE!   Black[27]

By likening Clay to "a ghost of the future," or a harbinger what will come in terms of black identity's contingency and instability, Lula not only suggests that he anticipates more complex renderings of blackness, but also that he is a temporal anomaly. In effect, within her historical framework, there is no accounting for the complexities in black identity he offers within the then-current historical moment. Clay is an anachronism. Moreover, she makes legible the intersection of race, visibility, citizenship, and history by calling attention to the absolute necessity of his invisibility in sustaining her proposed narrative that situates black identity as determined. To put it another way, Lula's insistence that they must pretend that he cannot be seen by other citizens and that they are both disentangled from their histories denies knowledge of the contingent mode of black identity that Clay proposes. The invisibility she demands would allow them to travel as racially unmarked and ahistorical subjects. In effect, Lula offers here a second evasion of Clay's iteration of black identity. The first framed her vision of him as a direct apprehension of his identity, this second move poses invisibility as a viable means of contending with the narrative disorder he presents to the knowledge she purports to have about his identity, his history, and, therefore, his suitability for citizenship. Yet the play's second scene treats the impossibility of either option as it marks the entry of the "citizens"—passengers boarding the train—who witness Lula and Clay's encounter. Their appearance is significant not only because of their complicity with the end that Clay ultimately meets, but also because they bear witness to Clay's counternarrative of black identity—a monologue—which challenges the boundaries of it that Lula attempts to impose.

If the play's first scene produces a discourse of black identity guided by Lula's truncated notions of both the nation's history and citizenship, Clay's monologue in the final scene at once historicizes and contextualizes black subjectivity's discourse. In his counternarrative, which fully realizes the ways in which Clay undermines Lula's attempts at establishing a stable black identity outside of the history she recounts,, he offers black subjectivity as contingent and imbricated in that very history. As the subway car fills with passengers, the monologue comes on the heels of her racial epithet-laced song and dance, encouraging Clay to "rub bellies" with her and referring to him as "Uncle Thomas Woolly Head."[28] Embarrassed, he tells her to sit down as other passengers begin to join in the singing and laugh at her impromptu performance. Clay grabs her arm and drags her to the seat, telling her to shut up when she replies, "You're afraid of white people. And your father was. Uncle Tom Big Lip!"[29]

The unraveling of their encounter hinges on Lula's performance, and it initiates his retreat from civility and the cultural politics of uplift that sets off precisely the kind of confrontation the progressive mystique seeks to avoid. During their confrontation, Clay exposes black identity's multiple cultural genealogies by outlining both the internal mechanics of his self-representation as well as the external pressures that collectively forge his subjectivity. After intervening in her performance, Clay transgresses uplift's ideals in his admission that he could murder Lula and the white onlookers "even if they *expected* it . . . as skinny and middle class as [he is]"[30] (emphasis added). Yet even as he contextualizes himself as part of the black middle class seeking to establish ideological common ground with white liberals, he allows that he could murder them, fulfilling white expectations of black criminality that uplift seeks to avoid. In effect, he bridges the gap between these identity categories—these well-known types—in order to carve out subjectivity that acknowledges those social constraints but does not reside entirely in either category.

Navigating this minefield of identity, he tells Lula and the others in the car, "Let me be who I feel like being. Uncle Tom. Thomas. Whoever. It's none of your business. You don't know anything except what's there for you to see. An act. Lies. Device. Not the pure heart, the pumping black heart. You don't ever know that."[31] Responding to Lula's earlier contentions that visibility equates transparency in reading black subjects, Clay rejects her notion that "seeing is the origin of knowing."[32] He argues that what she—and the nation—sees is strategically deployed dissemblance that created "the appearance of disclosure or openness . . . while actually remaining an enigma to whites."[33] But it is also important to remember that dissemblance, as historian Kevin Gaines has argued, "must also be understood as part of the majority American culture's silence, evasion, or outright distortion on matters of race."[34] As a result, Clay's revelation proposes that the majority culture shares responsibility for dissemblance's deployment. In detailing her vision's failures by both disclosing dissemblance's tactics and by his refusal to argue for or against Lula's charge that he is an Uncle Tom, Clay reveals the inherent agency in that refusal because it shifts the power dynamics in shaping subjectivity. As Kimberly N. Brown argues, Clay's "unmasking," or his retreat from dissemblance, both reveals "a self that is unfettered—one that is not governed by the anticipated reactions of white people" that can be equated with the notion of gaining voice" and frames "certain truth-claims as fallacies or myths created in the interest of the status quo."[35] In other words, his disclosure frees black identity from double consciousness's conundrum and uplift ideology's social tactics. By proposing that he can be Uncle Tom or Thomas and further that he manipulates her visibility and consequently her access to knowledge through the device of race, Clay argues for the contingency and construction of black identity by historicizing and contextualizing it within dissemblance and that strategy's origins.

Turning to another black cultural genealogy, he draws on Bessie Smith and Charlie Parker to further illustrate vision's failure to contain black identity, as well as how black cultural production critiques seeing as the origin of knowing. He asserts that while audiences claim to love Smith's music, they fail to understand that she is saying "kiss my black unruly ass" and that while they applaud Parker's "tortured genius," he would not have played a note of music if he had "walked up to East Sixty-Seventh Street and killed the first ten white people he saw."[36] Situating black cultural production as both an intervention in the impulse to equate visibility with knowledge, as well as a means of escape from double consciousness's conundrum, Clay proposes murder—the elimination of white impingement on black identity—as an alternative to cultural production that would put an immediate end to black identity's continual skirmishes with both.

Equating cultural production with insanity and murder with sanity, but becoming weary, Clay reflects, "Ahhh. Shit. But who needs it? I'd rather be a fool. Insane. Safe with my words, and no deaths, and clean, hard thoughts, urging me to new conquests. My people's madness. Hah! That's a laugh. My people. They don't need me to claim them. They got legs and arms of their own. Personal insanities. Mirrors. They don't need all those words. They don't need any defense."³⁷ Reclaiming his status as a poet, despite Lula's contentions, Clay rejects murder as a substitute for cultural production. Further, he refuses to replicate Lula's and the nation's misreading of black subjectivity as he corrects his own assertions about the scope and the quality of his "people's madness." He proposes that he cannot speak for "his people" because their iterations of black identity are as contingent and constructed as his own. Finally, in these rhetorical moves, Clay further marks his retreat from the cultural politics of uplift and double consciousness's conundrum. He refuses violence not because such a refusal serves uplift ideology's purposes, but because it doesn't serve his needs to put writing in the service of his own vision of black subjectivity. Rather than electing to represent "the race," he follows through on his own contentions in the monologue—black subjectivity is contingent and constructed and further, that black subjects can and do articulate and construct black identities using the resources available to them.

As the play ends, Lula tells Clay that she's "heard enough," and as he moves to exit the train, she stabs him twice in the chest, enlisting the help of the other passengers to remove his body from the train and instructing them to leave at the next stop. After they throw Clay's body from the train, another twenty-year-old black man with books under his arm enters the coach and takes a seat; however, in contrast to Clay, who consistently turned away from Lula's gaze, the young man drops his books in his lap to return her "long slow look."³⁸ As the same time, "an old Negro conductor" enters the car "doing a sort of restrained soft shoe, and half mumbling the words of some song."³⁹ He greets the younger man, "Hey, brother!" and continues down the aisle where Lula "turns to stare at him and follows his movements down the aisle."⁴⁰ The conductor tips his hat to Lula and continues his soft shoe out of the car as the curtain falls.⁴¹

In light of Clay's monologue, the entry of both the young man and the conductor redoubles black subjectivity's contingency and construction and underscores the instability of seeing as the origin of knowing. The young man's returned gaze and Lula's efforts to track the conductor's movements both point to how seeing failed her with Clay and how the potential for failure remains in the way she sees these two new characters who behave in ways that both diverge from and align with the iteration of black identity that Clay outlined. Clay's death then can be read as regenerative in that it enables representative possibilities for black identity that were unavailable before his monologue and his murder. The conductor's misleadingly deferential soft shoe dance and mumbled song put alongside the young man's returned gaze begs the questions of where in the spectrum of representational possibilities for black identity do they fall and whether Lula can make a resolute determination about where they situate themselves. Ultimately, she cannot and the play leaves that question unresolved. But in so doing, *Dutchman* creates conceptual space for the representation of black identity's multiple iterations and enables agency in self-representation. Returning to conceptual artist Rashid Johnson's contentions about the play, *Dutchman*'s historicizing and contextualizing of black male subjectivity offers "the opportunity to consider locating yourself between the narrative of struggle and the narrative of Negro Exceptionalism" both in 1964 and perhaps again in 2013.

Embedded in Rashid Johnson's observation that "the way that we imagine the struggle of the hero or anti-hero character is more married [than it would have been then] to our understanding of the civil rights movement, meaning things like the March on Washington" are two notions of cultural memory. One addresses cultural memory in the current historical moment and the influence of images and events like the 1963 March on Washington that have come to stand in for the meaning of the era. The other speaks to the unfolding of cultural memory about a historical moment that was still in progress. In other words, it suggests that there were no events or images to stand in for what we now call the African American Freedom Struggle, and it, therefore, posed a range of possibilities for its interpretation. The Freedom Struggle itself was ongoing; it lacked temporal designations and a master narrative detailing its successes and failures to frame it as a historical moment worthy of critical reflection. Johnson suggested, then, that the play's reception in 1964 would not carry as much of cultural memory's freight of the Freedom Struggle era as it does in the current moment.

Nevertheless, the play's reviews point in a decidedly different direction. Despite the possibilities such a representation offered, critics reviewing *Dutchman* framed it as yet another representation of the always-already present Negro Problem or Negro Question. Echoing the critical reception of Hansberry's *A Raisin in the Sun*, *Dutchman*'s reviews at its March 1964 Off-Broadway premiere at the Cherry Lane Theater returned to the apparent paradox between the universal and the particular in its representation of both Clay and Lula. In her discussion of this tendency in the reviews of *A Raisin in the Sun*, literary critic Robin Bernstein explained that the universal and the particular are categories that intersect and are mutually permeable—they are part of a dialectic.[42] Yet "the appearance of a paradox depends on the assumption that universality and particularity are static."[43] Thus, the cultural need to frame them as a paradox derives from a refusal to blur those static boundaries and further, as Bernstein argued, "to stabilize both whiteness and the segregation of Negroes and whites, and thus to produce and enhance white power."[44] Bernstein further argued that this paradox maintains in *A Raisin in the Sun*'s status as a classic American play because the paradox enables it to be viewed as an exception. She writes, "The creation and maintenance of the illusion of the paradox enables some 'exceptional' works by minorities to be declared masterpieces, and simultaneously facilitates the relegation to the back of the bus of artistic works labeled 'non-masterpieces.'"[45]

The paradox between the universal and the particular has parallel implications in *Dutchman*'s reviews, that is, the reviews policed the imagined boundaries between the (white) universal and the (black) particular. Yet they do so by questioning the validity of the black particular's authenticity as presented in the play and linking the question of authenticity to Jones's authenticity as a playwright. In contrast to Hansberry's play, *Dutchman*'s representations unsettle rather than reassure the critics' notion of the black particular through the play's "rage," as multiple reviewers call it. By their assessments, the rage contributes not only to the representations' inauthenticity, but also undermines Jones's merit as an "important" playwright, thereby invoking the boundary between the universal and the particular. Refusing Clay's representation, and especially his monologue, as authentic expressions of black identity, the reviews thematically maintained the imaginary divide between the universal and the particular through their discussion of the characters' authenticity, the shocking nature of the play's language and plot, and the artistic merit of the play and the talent of Jones himself.

In outlining the ways in which the play's representations thematically transgress the universal and particular paradox, the reviews demonstrate the ways in which "those with the power to maintain the illusion of the paradox (e.g., white critics) invent themselves as gatekeepers."[46] Bernstein's insights about the works themselves might be extended to their authors as well, because in policing what constitutes the universal and particular and designating which works are timeless or masterpieces, the minority or nonwhite author of such a work is deemed exceptional. This is the case with theater critics' discussion of both LeRoi Jones as an author as well as the play itself. The reviews demonstrate how critics conflate *Dutchman*'s comment on black subjectivity with the "Negro Question" and frame it as protest or propaganda, which undermines its artistic value. In effect, they maintain a divide between the particular and the universal by refusing to see how the play situates "the relevance of racial particularity and class location without requiring that art serve the prescriptions of social realism or social class."[47]

Similarly, critics reviewing *Dutchman* framed the play's rage as another factor undermining its artistic value. While the reviews repeatedly used the words rage or anger to stand in for Clay's monologue, they do not engage or explicate the monologue itself. But it is important to acknowledge the productive value of the rage informing his monologue. As critic bell hooks argued, rage must be tempered, but it can be a constructive response to oppression and injustice in that it can precipitate actions to resist them; for Clay it enabled his escape from double consciousness and strengthened his resolve to be a poet. Yet she cautioned that denying its transformative potential "creates a cultural climate where the psychological impact of racism can be ignored. . . . Racism can then be represented as an issue for blacks only, a mere figment of our perverse paranoid imaginations."[48] Likewise, the reviews denied the transformative value of Clay's rage in a slightly different register by discounting its artistic value. This enabled them to simultaneously dismiss the monologue and maintain the boundary between the universal and the particular. Though the confrontation and the monologue are essential in detailing his iteration of black identity, critics argued that it hinders its reception as an important play and Jones as an important playwright. In *The New Yorker*'s mixed review in April 1964, Edith Oliver asserted that while Jones is an "original and talented young dramatist," the rage depicted in the play "diminishes its significance and casts doubt on its artistic merit."[49] Similarly, addressing the then–recently published play, Philip Roth claimed in his unfavorable comments in the *New York Times Book Review* that the rage is not of "literary value" and hinted that it may have been inspired by Edward Albee's *The Zoo Story* rather than Jones's own efforts toward depicting the difficulties of asserting black subjectivity.[50] While most of the reviews allowed that Jones had the potential to make a contribution to American theater, they also suggested that *Dutchman*'s perceived effort to retell a previously told story and to allow what Roth called the "luxury" of "the exploited telling off his exploiters" weakened the play.[51] Shifting the play's focus from Clay's iteration of black identity and black autonomy back to the white gaze, Oliver's and Roth's reviews demonstrate precisely the white liberal impulse to control black identity that Clay's monologue exposes.

Significantly, these and other critics conflated the play's representations with the ubiquitous Negro Problem or Negro Question, both euphemisms referencing the political and social unrest around race relations in the United States in the historical moment of the play's production in 1964. It is worth noting that the play opened in the midst of a so-called white backlash against the Civil Rights Act of 1964, which was reflected in American culture in a number of ways. The Alabama governor and avowed segregationist George Wallace, who opposed the law, made a strong showing in the 1964 presidential primaries, gaining nearly 30 percent of the vote in Wisconsin, Indiana, and Maryland. The voters supporting Wallace were primarily second-generation white ethnic immigrants who, historian Dan Carter has argued, "felt psychologically and culturally isolated from the dominant currents of American life in the 1960s" and showed their frustration by voting for Wallace. Yet as *Negro Digest* managing editor Hoyt W. Fuller observed, these frustrations about the "Negro Question" were not limited to working-class white ethnics. Referencing the work of black writers, including LeRoi Jones, who he claimed had figured the white liberal as "a millstone around the Negro's neck," Fuller wrote that "liberals tend to balk and to reject their convictions at the point where Negroes insist on simply being men and women, like any others, with precisely the same rights, privileges, and obligations as any other men and women."[52] In effect, Fuller argued that the sentiments of frustration and alienation reflected in Wallace's strong showing in the North are shared by "friends of the Negro"—white liberals. *Dutchman*'s reviews in the mainstream press not only illustrate Fuller's assertions and articulate a clear sense of fatigue with the Negro Question, but show how critics mitigated the play against preceding representations of black subjectivity. Edith Oliver asserted,

> There is no doubt that this anger is justified, but there is also no doubt, I think, that in this case it is inartistic weakening of the character and the play. Much of what he says, however deeply felt it may be, has been said before. There are echoes of James Baldwin's essays, and even of Adrienne Kennedy's Funnyhouse of a Negro . . . somewhere in the middle of the harangue the rage sounded hollow to me—cooked up rather than real—and I stopped trusting the playwright.[53]

Though Oliver never named what either Baldwin or Kennedy had already said, and perhaps more significantly, how Jones replicated what they had said, she revealed very little about the play itself, but instead reflected on how the play reflected on Jones's merit as a playwright, asserting that he was a "gifted and one-of-a-kind writer" who was "forcing himself into a familiar mold," which undermined both the play and the playwright.[54] Oliver argues that *Dutchman*'s depiction of the difficulties in asserting black subjectivity within and against both white and black cultural norms duplicated the work of other African American writers. At best, Oliver's account proposed that the play's "rage" obstructs a discussion of its merit; at worst, the content of the play itself did not warrant discussion. That "familiar mold" coupled with inauthentic, "cooked up" anger turned to rage, undercut Jones's standing as a playwright. This question around authenticity of both the representations in the play and the playwright himself recurred throughout *Dutchman*'s reviews.

Writer Philip Roth's perspectives, which link the play's "rage" to Jones's failures as a playwright while revealing very little about what occurs in the play itself, resonated with Oliver's. In a *New York Times Book Review* essay evaluating both *Dutchman* and James Baldwin's *Blues for Mr. Charlie*, Roth was troubled by Jones being "hailed in the papers and on television for his anger; for it [was] not an anger of literary value."[55] Echoing Oliver's concerns about the play's originality, he questioned Clay's authenticity as a representation of African American identity, positing that "Clay is not really Negro enough for us to be told that it is for his being a Negro he is murdered."[56] He continued, "Oh, Clay can spout about the predicament of the Negro in this country, but so can I, and so can Richard Nixon, and probably however each of us says it, we will agree that it is awful."[57] Roth's evaluation asserted that there is no difference in the representation of Clay and his comments on African American identity to distinguish his reflections from Roth's or Richard Nixon's—that, in effect, the representation of Clay offers no new insights or revelations on this issue. Despite Clay's ongoing effort to trace the complexities of black identity in his exchange with Lula, Roth reduces Clay's representation to one that can only confirm how "awful" the "predicament of the Negro" is. In other words, he replicated Oliver's contention that *Dutchman* only revisits widely held white perspectives on African American identity and how it signifies in the current historical moment. Roth's implication was that if a collection of people with such politically and socially disparate views as Richard Nixon, Jones's character Clay, and Roth himself could arrive at the same conclusion that the "Negro problem" is "awful," then *Dutchman* has failed to offer a new perspective on what Roth insinuated is an enduring, and possibly tedious, question. Further, and perhaps more importantly, he denied Clay's agency in his self-representation. Yet the means by which *Dutchman* seeks to explore black subjectivity's complexities and to offer a new perspective through the experience of its black middle-class protagonist was summarily dismissed by Roth as an impossibility. What is of note here is less that Roth took the play to task for what he viewed as its artistic failures, but rather that Roth limned an "authentic" and monolithic black identity that Clay fails to represent in arguing that he was not black enough to be murdered. Roth reduced the complexities of black identity to the readily available, known quantity—the "predicament of the Negro"—and likened the play to an out-of-date news story. His closing observation that *Dutchman* is "finally a staged newspaper headline" reiterated that notion.[58]

While Roth discredited the play for its topicality, other reviewers critiqued its profanity and sexual innuendo. From today's vantage, *Dutchman*'s adult language and sexual content might appear only mildly controversial, but the cultural mores in 1964 made it incendiary, and the reviews reflected how unsettling they were to critics evaluating the play. Yet their assessments also underscore the language and sexual content as obstacles that prevent its entry into the universal category and raise questions about how it represents black particularity. Calling it "an explosion of hatred rather than a play," Howard Taubman asserted in the *New York Times* that "everything about *Dutchman* is designed to shock—its basic idea, its language, and its murderous rage."[59] As he further noted that it stages a "mélange of sardonic images and undisciplined filth," he pointed to the artistic implications of such images, arguing that "the impact of Jones' ferocity would be stronger if he did not work so hard and persistently to be shocking."[60] Though he echoed both Oliver's and Roth's contentions that the language undermines the play's potential influence, Taubman differed in his reading of Clay's monologue. Approaching it as a response to Lula's prodding, he said Clay's answer is to "drop the mask of conformity and to spew out all the anger that has built up in him and his fellow Negroes."[61] Taubman continued, "If this is the way the Negroes really feel about the white world around them, there's more rancor buried in the breasts of colored conformists than anyone can imagine."[62] Though the monologue makes clear Clay's rejection of the spokesperson role in his assertion that "they don't need him to claim them," Taubman insisted on a collective black identity for which Clay speaks; he refused the argument for black particularity the monologue makes. Even as he ultimately cosigned the play and Jones as a playwright, observing that of the three works staged at the Cherry Lane Theater, "*Dutchman* is the one that bespeaks a promising, unsettling talent," Taubman's review illustrates critics' impulse to deliberately disregard the representations and even the dialogue offered in the play in favor of imposing their own racial imaginings on the representations on stage.

Even in the play's wholly positive reviews, critics overlooked Clay's iteration of black subjectivity. Reviewing both *Dutchman* and Baldwin's *Blues for Mr. Charlie* in *Vogue*, Henry Popkin's discussion focused on Lula and applauded Jones for succeeding where Baldwin's "dramatic journalism" failed.[63] "Unlike Baldwin," he contended, "Jones has found the experimental technique his rage requires, so he does not pretend to be writing a realistic drama. *Dutchman* is the encounter of not two conventional characters, but of two archetypes—the Negro Square . . . and the white Bohemian."[64] Yet the discussion of Clay is limited to his summary of the monologue, which he called "a furious account of Negro Art as substitute for murder, which would be a more reasonable product of the Negro's tragic condition."[65] Explaining why Lula is preferable to Baldwin's white representations, Popkin asserted, "If the white woman is vicious, she is more interestingly vicious than the white characters of *Blues for Mr. Charlie*: Jones has not confined himself to giving her only plausible vices, but has made her the complete catalogue and storehouse of scornful pseudo-bohemianism."[66] His observations that Jones was "a real dramatist who will be uncomfortable to live with" and had provided "a brilliant part" for actress Jennifer West conclude the review.[67] Though it was favorable, Popkin's review traded in many of the same themes as the others in that it refused to engage Clay's articulation of black subjectivity. Another favorable review appearing in *Newsweek* on April 13, 1964, gave the play and Clay's monologue universal implications: "The interracial hatred and misunderstanding are only the most immediate and dramatic expressions of what is perennial among men: the exploitation of one another for the satisfaction of dreams and hungers. 'Let me be what I want to be' is a cry heard everywhere."[68] Yet even in identifying this universal element of the play, the anonymous review does not take up the "interracial hatred and misunderstanding" that Clay details, or more importantly, how they lend themselves to his iteration of black subjectivity. All of the reviews edged around it, but never addressed it, as they ruminated on the play's rage, how it duplicated the representations offered by other black writers, and linked those to concerns to what they believed constitutes authentic black identity. In so doing, they not only limited the representational possibilities of the black particular, but also reinforced the imagined boundary between the particular and the universal, obscuring Clay's sophisticated enactment of black subjectivity.

Still, *Dutchman* is frequently anthologized and revived on stages across the country. Prior to the Performa13 staging, it enjoyed a revival in 2007 at the theater of its debut, the Cherry Lane. Similar to the March on Washington, the play has become a literary stand-in for the Freedom Struggle era and the same debates about black subjectivity reflected in the play's reviews during the 1960s continue. However, for many critics, both the play and the playwright are relics of a bygone era. Responding to the Cherry Lane revival, cultural critic Stanley Crouch asserted that he "doesn't think [Baraka's] literary standing is very high" and that for most of his career, he has been "more interested in writing propaganda than in writing literature."[69] Yet literary critic Glenda Carpio has suggested that both Baraka's and *Dutchman*'s impact continues to unfold: "People are trying to figure out what his legacy is. A playwright like Suzan-Lori Parks comes out of him, as a negative response to what he's done. He's dated in many, many ways . . . but there's also dialogue that is just outside of time."[70] Writer and theater critic Hilton Als concurred, writing of the 2007 revival that "by bringing so much of America—its myths, its lore, its hatred—onstage in 'Dutchman,' Baraka changed the theater forever. Many of us are still trying to figure out how he did it."[71] Perhaps we can locate Baraka's legacy in not only writing "dialogue that is just outside of time," but in crafting a representation of black identity in a text out of time. Cultural memory both summons and situates *Dutchman* as a furious explosion of black rage indicative of the era's racial turmoil and questions the artistic value of the play and the playwright because of it. But the play shows rage's productive power in Clay's explication of black subjectivity and his prescient interrogation of a monolithic black identity. The representative possibilities Clay makes legible in his monologue endure beyond his death in the possibilities that the conductor and the young man pose at the curtain. His monologue demands that we see them anew. Put alongside Clay, they mark a fissure in the monolithic blackness's landscape in the Freedom Struggle era. As Baraka (then Jones) observed after the play's debut, "I don't think any Negro can represent any mass of Negroes because that's what we've been fighting, the right to be singular, the right to be individual, not to be abstracted, you see, but also the right to choose."[72] Clay compellingly argues for the conductor's, the young man's, and his own right to be singular.

And perhaps it is such a fissure that Rashid Johnson's restaging at the Russian & Turkish Baths expands and makes relevant in the current historical moment. Out of sync with prevailing concepts of black subjectivity in 1964, *Dutchman* speaks, just outside of time, to black subjectivity's complexities in the current historical moment.[73]

CHAPTER THREE

"Ghost(s) in the House!":

Black Subjectivity and Howard Sackler's

The Great White Hope

As discussed in Chapter Two, conceptual artist Rashid Johnson's work wrestles with the intersection of cultural memory—or the media, institutions, and practices that construct a collective past for the nation— and black subjectivity, and I turn to his 2006 photograph, *Self Portrait Laying on Jack Johnson's Grave*, to trace their interplay in Howard Sackler's 1967 play, *The Great White Hope*. In that photograph, Johnson lies across the tombstone of Jack Johnson, the world's first African American heavyweight champion, prone, eyes closed and arms dangling over the sides of the marker in Chicago's Graceland Cemetery. Contrasting his body with the grave marker, Johnson's photograph evokes cultural memory of the heavyweight champion, whose defiance of Progressive Era racial hierarchies transformed the way the nation envisioned black masculine identity. In summoning Jack Johnson, the photograph alludes to the artist Johnson's relationship to cultural memory of the boxer.[1] But beyond their shared last name, how might we interpret the relationship between them? Does the artist Johnson, whose oeuvre similarly challenges normative thinking about black subjectivity, figuratively rest on the shoulders of the Galveston Giant, who contested early-twentieth-century notions of black subjectivity and specifically, masculinity? The image, then, might acknowledge that affinity. Yet Johnson noted that he also took photographs of himself break dancing on the boxer's grave. Those images were not successful, and he instead captured the final image after what he describes as "a fairly long day trying to figure out how to interact with this stone and it happened to be the one that made the most sense."[2] This disclosure offers a potential reading that shifts from honoring his relationship to black masculine identity's cultural genealogies embodied by Jack Johnson to celebrating a break from such ties with his literal dance on his grave. Perhaps the image engages both perspectives and reflects the writer and cultural critic Touré's contention that postblack cultural producers like Johnson grapple with African American cultural figures' spectral presences and their relationship to the current historical moment by asserting that "these people are our history, so honor them, but also, these people are history, so let's move on."[3] Read in that light, Johnson's self-portrait contemplates his own legacy within and against how the boxer signifies within cultural memory and yet claims narrative autonomy as he engages with cultural memory of the boxer.

While Rashid Johnson simultaneously acknowledged and pushed beyond Jack Johnson's spectral proximity to his work and consequently resisted normative notions of black subjectivity in the current historical moment, Howard Sackler's play, *The Great White Hope*, gestured toward parallel cultural work in the midst of the African American Freedom Struggle. After it won the Pulitzer Prize for Drama in 1969, Sackler told the *New York Times* that the play was not "about blacks and whites" and was instead "a metaphor of struggle between man and the outside world."[4] Eliding racial identity's significance, he argued that what made the play compelling was "not [its] topicality, but the combination of circumstances, the destiny of a man pitted against society."[5] Though Sackler drew the play's protagonist Jack Jefferson from events in Jack Johnson's life, he consistently downplayed racial identity's significance in arguing for the universality of the play's characters and themes. In that sense, his argument resonates with *A Raisin in the Sun*'s critics who in their reviews insisted on a boundary between the presumably white universal and the black particular. Yet despite his claim, Jefferson's racial identity and the nation's racial discourse framed theater critics' discussion of the play in both the mainstream and African American press at its 1967 debut at the Arena Stage in Washington, DC, and its subsequent 1968 Broadway opening at the Alvin Theatre. In their turn to the 1960s Freedom Struggle with its social and political unrest, as well as the spectral presences of both Johnson and Muhammad Ali in their evaluations of the play, theater critics resisted Sackler's positioning of universality and topicality as mutually exclusive and rejected racial identity as simply a dramatic device.

This critical impasse between Sackler's assertion of narrative authority and theater critics, who did not deny the play's universality, but instead emphasized its topical comment on 1960s racial politics, offers an opportunity to explore *The Great White Hope* from three vantages. This chapter first considers the tensions and resonances between the play's representation of Jefferson and postblack discourse that refute Sackler's claim of race neutral universality. Second, it considers the play's critique of Progressive

Rashid Johnson, *Self Portrait Laying on Jack Johnson's Grave*, 2006 Durst lambda print 103 x 125 cm / 40½ x 49¼ in, Courtesy the artist and Hauser & Wirth.

Era racial hierarchies and racial uplift ideology—collectively the "racial common sense" of the Progressive Era and its implications for African American subjectivity. Finally, it examines how the play is situated in cultural memory by examining theater critics' reviews of it. Reading *The Great White Hope* through these overlapping trajectories frames it as a play that counters totalizing representations of blackness often linked to the cultural production of the 1960s and that stands as more than a literary anachronism of a bygone era. Instead, Sackler's Jack Jefferson explores black subjectivity by questioning racial uplift's representational strategies. Offering a mode of black subjectivity that emphasizes interiority rather than the dissemination of appropriate racial representations intended to counter the stereotypical images of African Americans circulating in the mainstream public sphere, Jefferson critiques and subverts such Progressive Era representational tactics. Finally, in its reconsideration of uplift ideology's representational strategies as well as their efficacy in assimilating African Americans into the US body politic, *The Great White Hope*'s reading of Progressive Era racial common sense resonates in the post-soul aesthetic.

As discussed in Chapter One, beginning in the late 1980s Greg Tate, Trey Ellis, and other critics examined postblack, or to use their terminology, post-soul texts and their artists as part of a black aesthetic that emphasized a shift from representational modes prevalent in the civil rights era.[6] Expanding this work, critic Bertram Ashe's theorizing of the post-soul aesthetic established a critical framework for the study of post-soul artists and texts and outlined the "post-soul matrix" as a hallmark of both. The matrix includes three features: the "cultural mulatto archetype"—artists or characters who cross traditional racial lines in the development of identity; the use of "blaxporation," which "troubles blackness"; and the "allusion-disruption strategy," which summons and signifies on previous eras of African American history as well as the ideologies and representations linked to those historical moments.

While the post-soul matrix complicates African American identity, Ashe has also pointed to the historical context in which post-soul artists and texts are embedded as a significant factor in the post-soul aesthetic's distinction from other African American literary periods. Allowing that "there are always exceptions to the prevailing literary conventions of the day," he located the difference between post-soul texts and their predecessors in the post-soul artist's "relationship to the idea of freedom."[7] Ultimately, while parallel interrogations of African American identity exist in texts of both the post-soul era and previous eras, the absence of an organized struggle for collective freedom in the post-soul era shifts freedom's emphasis in earlier periods from a fixed, collective black identity to the post-soul period's explorations of such constructions.

I do not invoke postblack discourse to argue for Sackler as a postblack artist or *The Great White Hope* as a postblack text, but rather to emphasize the continuities between the play's exploration of black subjectivity and freedom and, broadly speaking, postblack discourse's figuring of the same. More specifically, the narrative strategies the play employs, including its critique of Progressive Era racial common sense and the race man archetype, are suggestive of the conventions that Ashe has attributed to post-soul texts. Consequently, I read *The Great White Hope* as a text out of time and literary tradition that, through its representation of Jack Jefferson, probes black identity and its relationship to black freedom, and as such, anticipates the post-soul move by complicating reductive iterations of black subjectivity in precisely the historical moment when the aesthetic criteria for and the representations of African American identity in art are described as being restrictive.[8]

Such a reading is further informed by Kevin Everod Quashie's troubling of contemporary critical approaches that are either "aracial" and discount the significance of race or those that are overdetermined by racial identity and in some instances "police the quality of blackness."⁹ Instead, he has offered an alternative criticism that is "interested in race and the discourse of racial difference so long as such is not hindered or simplified by the identity of the writer or characters" as well as one that attends to the characters' interiority and the intersectionality of identity.¹⁰ While identifying Sackler as a white playwright who claimed to have written an aracial play drawn from the life of the nation's first "African American pop culture icon" potentially allows for its dismissal as a cultural relic that positions racial identity as incidental, its treatment of Progressive Era racial common sense undermines Sackler's intent because it demonstrates the centrality of racial discourse to the rhetoric of universality.¹¹ In short, Sackler's attempt to position Jefferson as a racially unmarked figure struggling with the outside world necessitates engagement with questions of black subjectivity, and so the play scrutinizes rather than elides racial identity. Conversely, dismissing *The Great White Hope* as a "cliché of white liberalism" due largely to Sackler's racial identity does a parallel disservice to the play's representations. Instead, my analysis emphasizes a reading of the play between those critical poles and offers an iteration of critical generosity that seeks "to attend to the context and ambition" of the play.¹²

Theatre and performance critic David Román's notion of "critical generosity" signaled an intervention in AIDS theater and performance's discourse that might "rethink the traditional criteria by which evaluations are made but also [to] acknowledge the ideological systems that promote canonical prejudice."¹³ Such an intervention can serve the discussion of black theater and drama by considering representations offered by non–African American playwrights. While mindful of the long history of African American representations proffered by white writers that African American cultural producers have assiduously subverted and with which they continue to reckon, I want to suggest that Sackler's play offers a representation of black subjectivity that moves beyond the dehumanizing representations that have populated American stages and should not be dismissed as such because of the playwright's racial identity or because of his refusal to acknowledge the significance of race and its representation in the play. Similarly, the editors of *The Methuen Drama Book of Post-Black Plays*, Harry J. Elam Jr. and Douglas A. Jones Jr., argue for the inclusion of non–African American playwrights in that volume. Framing non–African American playwrights' post-black representations as a departure from blackface minstrelsy and the early-twentieth-century drama of Eugene O'Neill, Dubose Heyward, and others, they write that their staging "attempts to trouble black-white binaries and, as a result, complicate what it means to be African American."¹⁴ Though it precedes the earliest of the eight plays that Elam and Jones contend "form part and parcel of a concerted movement to 'complicate the discourse around black art'" by forty years, Sackler's *The Great White Hope* offers a representation of black subjectivity that interrogates blackness's meanings.

Jack Jefferson's critique of racial uplift ideology, particularly its attention to class differentiation among African Americans, shifts from an emphasis on developing and sustaining a cohesive black identity in the public sphere as the means of race advancement to foregrounding an interior racial subjectivity that undercuts such an effort. Though often championed as a means of uniting African Americans across class lines in pursuit of social advancement, as noted in Chapter One, uplift ideology hinged on a pernicious contradiction that often colluded with the very race and class hierarchies it attempted to overturn and, as Kevin Gaines has written, "many black elites sought status, moral authority, and recognition of their humanity by distinguishing themselves as bourgeois agents of civilization from the presumably undeveloped black majority."[15] Jefferson, who gains representational currency only after winning the world heavyweight championship, exposes uplift ideology's inherent contradiction that race advancement necessitates proof of humanity through the demonstration of moral purity, ultimately resulting in access to full citizenship for African Americans. As Jefferson rejects both uplift ideology and its tacit outcome of collective black freedom, he privileges black subjectivity as an interior space of meaning rather than a public one and internalizes "the significances of racial differences to the extent that its public expression no longer necessary."[16] This discursive shift privatizes the significance of race.

Further, while the play engages uplift ideology and its reliance upon civility and respectability within the historical context of the Progressive Era, they have implications in the historical moment of the play's staging. Marissa Chappell, Jenny Hutchinson, and Brian Ward argue that respectability and civility refuted white supremacist claims that "segregation was absolutely essential to defend American civilization from contamination by uncivilized blacks with their congenital ignorance, sloth, promiscuity and irresponsibility" during the early 1960s Freedom Struggle.[17] Moreover, notions of "decent behavior," particularly "correct" gender roles and family life, were central to uniting African Americans and to facilitating demands for equality from whites.[18] In effect, though *The Great White Hope* situates Jefferson's critique of respectability and civility within a Progressive Era context, its staging also engages the continued relevance of civility and respectability to African American identity in the midst of the African American Freedom Struggle.

The ongoing significance of "decent behavior" in the 1960s Freedom

Struggle and US culture broadly might also help explain Sackler's use of Jack Johnson's biography. The Jefferson character follows every aspect of Johnson's life, including his conviction and eventual imprisonment through the Mann Act, which sought to curb interstate prostitution. The lone difference between Johnson and Jefferson is Jefferson's relationship with his white girlfriend, Eleanor Bachman. The play's Jefferson continually rejects the unsolicited advances of his former companion and remains in a monogamous relationship with Bachman. Jefferson's normative sexuality—his "decent behavior"—is an antidote to Johnson's indecent behavior, which included gambling, frequenting brothels, and maintaining numerous relationships with other women throughout his three marriages. Though Sackler argued for the play as "theater and not documentary," the cultural currency of decent behavior and how it might shape audiences' perceptions of Jefferson informs his biographical editing and has implications for his claims for the universality of the play's themes and characters.[19] Such an omission in the name of theater aids in ennobling Jefferson as a "Shakespearean tragic hero" with whom audiences might more easily identify, in comparison to Johnson, whose "indecent" sex life demonstrated, as one observer remarked after his arrest for violating the Mann Act, "the disregard of clean morals," and ultimately resulted in a one-year prison sentence for that transgression.[20]

If, as critic Bertram Ashe has suggested, predecessors to the post-soul text are inextricably linked to a collective quest for freedom, one link between *The Great White Hope* and such quests lies in the play's reviews, which repeatedly turned to the 1960s Freedom Struggle to make sense of it. Serving as a contested site of cultural memory, theater critics' reviews also brought the spectral figures of both Jack Johnson and Muhammad Ali to bear on their readings of the play. As they worked to make sense of Jefferson, they consistently turned to the past, where it served as "a point of comparison, an opportunity for analogy, an invitation to nostalgia, a redress to earlier events."[21] Similarly, theater critics drew upon Ali, Johnson, and the 1960s Freedom Struggle as they interpret *The Great White Hope* for their readership by outlining analogies between Ali and Jefferson, taking note of the differences between the historical figure Johnson and the fictional character Jefferson and redressing the injustices done to both Ali and Johnson. Most importantly, by invoking the spectral figures of Johnson and Ali and offering the play as an opportunity to reflect upon the 1960s Freedom Struggle as a moment of national crisis, the reviews subverted Jefferson's exploration of black subjectivity to assuaging that perceived crisis.

The cultural influence of theater critics in the popular press during this era should not be underestimated, because they played a vital role in introducing the American public to theater's merits and their readily available work helped establish them as effective readers of theater.[22] Theatre critics' ruminations on the play served a significant role in how audiences reacted to it and how it has been positioned in cultural memory since its 1967 debut. Consequently, the work *The Great White Hope* does in sifting through the relationship between uplift ideology and black subjectivity has been overshadowed by theater critics' emphasis on the culture and politics of the 1960s, specifically the crisis posed by the African American Freedom Struggle.

Moreover, critics reviewing *The Great White Hope* suggest that the figures of Johnson and Ali haunt the representation of Jefferson precisely because Jefferson was drawn from events in Johnson's life, including the loss of his heavyweight title in what he claimed was a deal with US prosecutors to throw the fight to the final "great white hope," Jess Willard, in 1915 in exchange for a commuted sentence on the Mann Act conviction.[23] Similarly, Ali—who had been stripped of the heavyweight title in April of 1967, eight months before the play's debut, for refusing to be inducted in the US Armed Forces in protest of the Vietnam War—rejected American values through his conversion to Islam and by aligning himself with global struggles for freedom by people of color. While he opposed Johnson's interracial relationships, Ali envisioned himself as the heir to Johnson's dismissal of American cultural politics, illustrated in his comments upon seeing the play in 1968, when he noted to its star, James Earl Jones, that "this play is about me . . . take out the interracial love stuff and Jack Johnson is the original me . . . it's history all over again."[24] His notion of history all over again and his relationship to cultural memory is not lost on theater critics.[25]

The reviews of *The Great White Hope* published in the mainstream and African American press inscribed the figures of both Johnson and Ali within a narrative of race and national identity that shape cultural memory and mediate racial meanings in the past and the present. But the reviews also foregrounded the myriad ways in which they discounted Jefferson's rejection of racial common sense in the service of meditating upon the racial crisis that the 1960s Freedom Struggle presented.

Using bolded lines in the script spoken directly to the audience, *The Great White Hope*'s three acts encompass nineteen locales; include thirty-six characters; and its Progressive Era historical context, particularly that period's concern with respectability and civility as access to social mobility, which informs every aspect of the play. For public figures, both black and white, respectability and civility held significance, but especially so for African Americans, for whom the emphasis on black civic and moral virtue as well as close attention to and incorporation of middle-class American values and ideals were central to creating a case for the inclusion of African Americans in the American plurality. In this regard, Jack Johnson posed a tangle of representational problems for black elites advocating uplift ideology. Though some blacks considered him a hero, his life as a "sport," including his multiple romantic relationships, his ownership of a Chicago cabaret, and his flamboyant personal style—in his title defense with former champion Jim Jeffries, the US flag served as a belt for his boxing shorts—undermined uplift ideology's primary tenets of morality and thrift.[26] Not surprisingly, Booker T. Washington, whose iteration of uplift emphasized industrial education as a means of gaining economic independence for African Americans, viewed Johnson as a threat to uplift's success and his own considerable influence. Framing Johnson's arrest on abduction charges as an assault on race progress in his address to the Detroit Y.M.C.A., Washington asserted, "It is unfortunate that a man with money should use it in a way to injure his own people in the eyes of those who are seeking to uplift the race and improve its conditions."[27] Yet Johnson was unfazed by such critiques from both blacks and whites and pointedly opposed Washington's approach to race relations because he was not "frank in the statement of the problems or courageous in his solution to them."[28]

Likewise, the play's Jefferson positions himself as a figure that not only resists the implicit endorsement of racial hierarchies bound up in uplift ideology, but also challenges African Americans who invested in and sought improved social and political relations through the deployment of it. In short, Jefferson contests his emblematic status in both the African American and white racial imagination and intervenes in efforts to situate him as a racial symbol to advance their own racial imaginings. After his successful title fight in Australia, the search for the great white hope begins and a deceptively innocuous exchange with reporters during sparring practice about his upcoming title defense illustrates his astute critique of uplift ideology.

The press corps' continual presence as Jefferson moves across the country underscores his skillful manipulation of the press to critique uplift ideology and advance his rendering of black subjectivity. Acknowledging uplift's representational freight and limits alongside its implications for his fight strategy as he prepares for his title defense in Reno, Jefferson contends that he has to decide whether to knock out the former champion Frank Brady in the first round or to artificially extend the fight by "juss sorta blockin'" his punches to keep him at a distance.[29] These tactics, he asserts, will be read in one of two ways: if he blocks the punches, spectators will say "ain't that one shif'less nigger, why dey always so lazy" or if he knocks him out in an early round they'll say "no, taint fair, dat po' man up dere fighting a gorilla! **But Ah gonna work it out.**"³⁰

While blackface minstrelsy emerged in the 1830s, its demeaning representations of black identity appeared throughout Progressive Era print culture, usually in an effort to "undermine transgressive images of black power and equality."³¹ Taking up these minstrel stereotypes, Jefferson anticipates and confronts the discourses of black inferiority that underwrite these two widely proliferated images of African Americans as—often simultaneously—indolent and animalistic in American popular culture during the Progressive Era, as well as makes legible the work such images do in maintaining white cultural authority by propagating narrow, racialized caricatures that serve to both literally and figuratively regulate African American subjectivity. Yet while he outlines the racialized representational conundrum he faces for the white press corps, rather than countering those distortions with a positive self-representation and thereby attending to uplift's politics of respectability, he circumvents them through both his embodied ring performance and through "motivated signifyin[g]" which "redress[es] an imbalance of power" and "clear[s] a space rhetorically."³² Positing that he will "work it out" in a direct address—a move that occludes his specific strategies and refuses to validate both the ideology of racial uplift and the white supremacist notions of citizenship informing it—he instead offers signifying as a means of forestalling the imbricated and racialized meanings imposed on his performance in the ring and his rhetorical sparring with the press corps. Consequently, while he signifies full knowledge of the stereotypes and the cultural work they do, he obscures his plans to prevail over such meanings and to secure the heavyweight title, retaining his interiority as a space of racial meaning to enact agency and subjectivity. Jefferson's signifying rhetorically endows him with a means of escape from the representational binary imposed upon him and refutes the authority and power of race and racism in his efforts to maintain the title. As he navigates the public sphere by engaging the racial discourse that the press disseminates, he points to, but does not fully reveal, his interior self, or "the conflicted ways a person imagines themselves in relationship to and distinction with how they are viewed by a social exterior."³³

In the same scene and in an allusion to the racial violence that occurred when he won the title, he acknowledges the potential violent fallout of his win for the broader African American community, saying that "maybe some a them reckon they gonna pay a little high for that belt if Ah take it," still he refuses to pursue those blacks who do not support his bid, telling reporters, "Ah ain't running for Congress! Ah ain't fightin' for no race, ain't redeeming nobody! My momma tole me Mr. Lincoln done that—**Ain't that why you shot him?**"[34] Declining the reporters' figuring of him as a race man who sacrifices autonomy for collective race advancement, Jefferson's signifying reveals uplift's representational limits and the assumptions of the white press corps underwriting them, in several significant ways.

First, it disrupts the notion that holding the heavyweight title translates to full citizenship for African Americans. Though aware of the heightened symbolic significance of the title given the racial violence that took place when he won it, Jefferson maintains that his defense of the title cannot stand in for collective political empowerment nor can it dismantle the systems of racialized oppression in place. He rejects the conflation of the symbolic power of the heavyweight championship and the political influence of race men. Further, in refusing the race man designation, he rejects uplift's implicit claim that an exceptional leader can employ thrift, social purity, chastity, and civility to gain white acceptance of African American humanity and that such an exceptional leader can speak on behalf of or represent a presumed monolithic black population. In effect, he negates racial uplift's premise that black identity must be recuperated by constructing and projecting acceptable representations to demonstrate both African Americans' readiness to be assimilated into the US plurality and their humanity, thereby questioning the efficacy of uplift ideology as well as repudiating the racial hierarchy that informs it.

Additionally, Jefferson's signifying relation to Abraham Lincoln situating him as "the great emancipator" who presumably fought for and redeemed the race by signing the Emancipation Proclamation further demonstrates the personal costs of assuming such a position.[35] In framing the assassination of Lincoln as a retaliatory outcome of creating the historical circumstances enabling African American citizenship, he holds a rhetorical mirror up to the white press corps that indicts their complicity in punishing those who, willingly or not, transgress racial hierarchies as well as refracts their assumptions about monolithic black identity into a parody and critique of such assumptions. The pointed rejoinder to his own figuring of Lincoln as a race man—and in another direct address—underscores the press corps' hypocrisy in soliciting such a representational figure though they are aware of the consequences of that position and their role in exacerbating them. These early exchanges between Jefferson and the press corps demonstrate him as an effective reader of the press's dissemination and fortification of the Progressive Era racial hierarchy and enable his critique of uplift ideology as well as uplift's inadvertent endorsement of it.

But as Jefferson signifies on both the notion of race men and monolithic blackness in his sparring with the white press corps, he engages in a parallel move with African American onlookers who would conflate his success in the ring with race advancement and a collective notion of African American freedom. Just before the start of the successful title defense with Brady, a group of African American men gather at the gates of the fight venue. Though they cannot get tickets to watch the match, a church deacon among them tells Jefferson that "we juss come to pray you gonna win for us, son" and suggests that his defeat of Brady will give them self-respect and make them proud to be black men.[36] Rejecting their foisting of a "race man" banner and arguing that his win cannot significantly alter the social or political oppression of African Americans nor can it provide one purported outcome of uplift—race pride—he responds, "If you ain't there already, all the boxin and nigguhs prayin' in the world ain't gonna get you there."[37] Undeterred, the deacon replies that Jefferson looks "cullud but [you] ain't thinkin cullud" and reiterates his plans to pray for him during the fight. Jefferson replies,

> Tell me you prayin' here! An speck I gonna say
> Oh, thankya, Reveren! You ain't prayin for me!
> ("Star Spangled Banner" in the distance)
> It ain't, Lawd, don' let that peck break his nose,
> Or, Lawd, let him git outa town and not git shot at—
> Ah aint nothing in it but a ugly black fiss here!
> **They don' even push on in to see it workin!**[38]

Against the aural backdrop of the national anthem, which might elsewhere underscore a stable collective national identity, Jefferson launches a critique of uplift ideology that exposes the fissures in the presumed collective group bound by racial identity as well as its costs to both the collective and the reluctant race man. In his suggestion that the prayers are not made to maintain his well-being, but rather to help situate him as an exception to the logic of Progressive Era white supremacy which maintains that African Americans cannot be assimilated into the US body politic, Jefferson reveals uplift's failure to contain the contradictions between a collective pursuit of racial advancement for African Americans and the autonomous pursuit of self-respect as well as exposes one of its ironies. As he chides them for their failure to agitate for admittance to watch the fight that would provide them with racial pride, he situates their investment in the outcome of the fight as a means of positioning his "ugly black fiss" as synecdoche for race advancement. In short, Jefferson argues that the logic of uplift ideology renders him invisible as it displaces his subjectivity for the representational power of his win and the title. But it also renders the men there invisible through its reliance on the uncertain symbolic import of the title for self-respect instead of resisting their exclusion from the audience. Interrupting and redirecting that logic, Jefferson asserts that the only certain return they can gain from his fight is a financial one, telling the small crowd as the scene ends, "Lay your bets, you still got time."[39] While he points out uplift ideology's inherent contradiction, which necessitates that autonomous African American identities be subsumed within a monolithic public identity for black subjects' inclusion in the US plurality, he also signifies on the means and ends of uplift ideology. In other words, if uplift ideology and its emphasis on moral uprightness gamble on white acceptance of African American humanity, for Jefferson, a bet on his win against Brady is the wager most likely to pay out. Ultimately, as he interrogates the logic of uplift, he argues that adherence to its representational strategies holds no guarantee of full citizenship and proposes black subjectivity independent of those strategies as a viable alternative.

Although these tableaux illustrate the ways in which Jefferson clears conceptual space to circumvent uplift's representational confines through both his signifying and his rebuff of the race man designation, his successful title defense against Brady redoubles the efforts of both black and white middle-class elites to regulate the representational power of the title and the national visibility it affords him.[40] By developing race man counternarratives that situate Jefferson as a potential leader of black southern migrants to the North, black and white elites construct the rationale for his containment through the justice system. As law enforcement officials and civic leaders scramble to wrest the title and its representational influence away from Jefferson, they focus on his relationship with Eleanor Bachman, a white divorcée whom he met shortly after winning the title in Australia. Within the Progressive Era context, miscegenation posed "a threat to uplift ideals of family, respectability and class survival" to black elites, while for whites such relationships "remained inadmissible and unspeakable within the reigning terms of black criminality and pure, passionless white womanhood."[41] Yet while Jefferson's liaison with Bachman affronts the bedrock of uplift ideology as well as broader Progressive Era social mores, in *The Great White Hope* it serves as a racial red herring that obscures the perceived threat he poses to a key agent in maintaining the racial hierarchy, the US judicial system.

Led by agent Jim Dixon, federal prosecutors pursue Jefferson for violating the Mann Act, which was passed in 1910 to curb interstate prostitution, despite the fact that they are fully aware that Bachman is over the age of consent and has willingly traveled with him. However, the Mann Act criminalized consensual relationships and therefore, aided in their pursuit of Jefferson. After Dixon arrests him, Jefferson skips bail and leaves Chicago for Europe to avoid prosecution and a three-year jail term. Though the interracial relationship clearly challenges Progressive Era notions of morality, it only provides the occasion for his evasion of the judicial system, which is the more worrisome transgression and warrants immediate suppression. Giving voice to these anxieties, Dixon emphasizes the impact he fears Jefferson has on the underdeveloped black majority and explains why he must use the Mann Act to prosecute Jefferson. He tells fight promoters Cap'n Dan and Pop, who have been charged with offering another title battle to Jefferson in exchange for a lesser jail sentence when he returns to the US, that it is his evasion of the law and its symbolic import for this group that is most threatening rather than his interracial relationship with Bachman:

> When a man beats us out like this, we—the law, that is—
> Suffer in prestige, and that's pretty serious.
> How people regard the law is part of its effectiveness,
> It can't afford to look foolish, and this applies
> Especially now to our Negro population.
> I don't mean the ones who always flout the law,
> And seeing their hero doing it in style
> Act up more than usual—those are police concerns, not
> Ours.
> But though you may not be aware of it yet,
> A very large, very black migration is in progress.
> They're coming up from the fields down there and filling
> Up the slums,
> Trouble's starting in Europe, and our mills and factories
> Have work for them now. And I'm talking of hundreds
> Of thousands, maybe millions soon—
> **Millions of ignorant Negroes, rapidly massing together,**
> **Their leanings, their mood, their outlook, suddenly**
> **No longer regulated by the little places they come from—**
> **Situations have arisen already.**
> We cannot allow the image of this man
> To go on impressing and exciting these people.[42]

Inverting the standard race man narrative that singles out an exceptional leader of black elites striving for race advancement, Dixon's counternarrative establishes Jefferson as an unwitting, and given his earlier responses to the white press corps and African American onlookers, an unwilling race man whose influence over southern black migrants to the North poses an immediate threat to the racial hierarchy that underwrites his legal pursuit of Jefferson. The migration of southern blacks to the North was a source of anxiety for many blacks and whites during the Progressive Era. Often black southerners' relocation to crowded urban neighborhoods in cities like Chicago confirmed black and white perceptions of "laziness, criminality and immorality" among the migrants, but for Dixon, migration also serves to embolden those African Americans who are no longer restrained by southern Jim Crow segregation and its concomitant physical and economic violence.[43] In effect, Jefferson, a migrant who came to Chicago from Galveston, Texas, embodies such perceptions and more importantly, models for black migrants defiance of both the legal system and the racial hierarchy underwriting it.

While Jefferson's evasion of federal prosecution reveals white unease with his potential influence over black migrants, it also uncovers the anxieties of black middle-class elites over his threat to uplift ideology. Though some black elites cited limited jobs and housing in urban areas in their opposition to black southern migration, for many committed to the rhetoric of uplift ideology, it put their own status at risk and was understood as the "antithesis of black progress and respectability."[44] Similarly, in the response to Dixon's race man counternarrative, the participation of an unnamed African American doctor in the efforts to prosecute him illustrates the black elite's investment in uplift and the class differentiation among African Americans that drives it. After one of the men among the civic leaders pursuing Jefferson attributes his defiance of the Mann Act prosecution to his racial identity rather than his resistance to the uneven application of the law, saying "**you know how niggers are**," the doctor responds by both underscoring class differentiation within uplift ideology and tracing the myriad representational complications Jefferson poses to the black elite:

> We can't pretend that race is not the main issue here.
> And, as you imply, sir, the deportment of this man
> Does harm to his race. It confirms certain views of it
> You may already hold: that does us harm.
> But it also confirms in many Negroes the belief
> That his life is the desirable life, and that
> Does us even greater harm. **For a negro today,**
> **The opportunity to earn a dollar in a factory**
> **Should appear to be worth infinitely more**
> **Than the opportunity of spending that dollar**
> **In emulation of Mr. Jack Jefferson.**

But this I assert: the majority of Negroes
Do not approve of this man or of his doings.
He personifies all that should be suppressed by law,
And I trust that such suppression is forthcoming.[45]

Alluding to a collective racial "us" as he sanctions punishing Jefferson's errant behavior, the doctor allows that Jefferson's evasion of the law "substantiates" widely held views of African Americans that are drawn from the minstrel stereotypes Jefferson circumvents in the earlier scene. However, such "confirmation" is eclipsed by Jefferson's failure to model appropriate racial behavior for black migrants that is aligned with uplift ideology's standards, including thrift and propriety. Put differently, while the doctor seemingly concurs with Dixon, he does so with an important revision. Jefferson's most egregious transgression is his affront to uplift ideology through migrants who might mimic his penchant for the sporting life, not that he flouts the law. In the doctor's race man counternarrative, black southern migrants emulating Jefferson risk troubling the distinction elites seek to make between themselves and such migrants in two ways. First, uplift ideology hinged on the perception of black elites by both blacks and whites as middle class, though their material conditions belied such status more often than not.[46] In effect, while the black elite might aspire to bourgeois respectability through possession of a home and other material goods that would outwardly mark elite status, black southern migrants' acquisition of the same in mimicking Jefferson makes them indistinguishable from the elite. As a successful entrepreneur who owns Café de Champion in Chicago and as a property owner at the Beau Rivage resort in Wisconsin, Jefferson has already troubled this distinction and attempted to pass as elite. Second, and perhaps more threatening to uplift ideology, are the migrants who, in emulating Jefferson, follow his rejection of middle-class values such as thrift and propriety. If Dixon's "millions of Negroes" embrace "the sporting life" and its affront to bourgeois values, uplift's project of race advancement is in jeopardy. Echoing Booker T. Washington's warnings about Johnson, the doctor's reminder that most blacks do not support Jefferson then serves to reify him as an aberration from the monolithic public black identity that must be secured in order for uplift ideology to propel elites and cooperative migrants into the US plurality. In short, while Jefferson might hold the markers of elite status, the doctor makes clear that he and his potential imitators are unwanted interlopers in the black public sphere.

These scenes illustrate Jefferson's noncompliance with the racial common sense that informs the Progressive Era public sphere, but they also show Jefferson's estrangement from the communities that support and advance those ideologies. Reminiscent of the post-soul aesthetics' "cultural mulattos," who by Trey Ellis's definition refuse to "deny or suppress any part of [their] complicated and sometimes contradictory cultural baggage to please either white people or black," Jefferson's negation of the cultural politics of representation within the public sphere leaves him without an easily recognizable cultural home.[47] His displacement signals a crisis of racial anxiety in which he turns to Progressive Era racial common sense to interpret his experience and to settle the unstable racial ground on which he attempts to stand.

The stateside consolidation of both uplift's proponents and the US justice system in containing the threat Jefferson poses to each of their projects strains the relationship between Jefferson and Bachman. After their arrest on charges of violating the Mann Act, he jumps bail and travels across Europe with Bachman. While there, Jefferson refuses a fixed fight in Havana with "The Kid" in exchange for a lesser jail sentence, and nearly out of money, they retreat to Juarez, Mexico. Though Bachman encourages him to accept a deal because his ongoing pursuit by Dixon drives his actions and he is "not [his] own man any more," Jefferson again refuses and directs her back to Chicago.[48] It is in this moment of crisis that he accepts the racial hierarchy sustaining racial common sense and uses it to both explain and end his relationship with her. Advising Bachman to "stay wid your own lady," he holds her accountable for their situation rather than the racial hierarchy that spawns his legal pursuit by the US justice system.[49] However, replicating the logic of Progressive Era racial common sense is untenable for Bachman, and shortly after this exchange she commits suicide.

Her death mobilizes Jefferson and redirects his efforts toward undermining that logic, and so he agrees to a fixed fight brokered by Dixon that allows him to serve only six months in prison for violating the Mann Act and provides him $100,000 of the purse providing he goes down in the eighth round. But in defiance of the agreement, he continues to fight through the eighth and goes down for the count in the eleventh round. Not only does his rejection of the agreement enact agency and resistance that emphasizes interiority and autonomy as he refuses to accept the racist premises that inform the offer of a fixed fight, the play reiterates his struggle for autonomy within the public sphere debates about black subjectivity through the absence of his voice during the fight. The only speakers during the course of the match are the spectators, promoters, and trainers who narrate the fight's action within the rhetoric of restoring racial order by returning Jefferson to his appropriate place within the racial hierarchy. His silence signals both an illumination and defense of his interior self. In effect, Jefferson both asserts and defends his interiority in order to enact black subjectivity outside of the Progressive Era public sphere. Losing the heavyweight title in the racial spectacle staged with The Kid marks the development of black subjectivity forged outside of the public sphere where both uplift ideology and the white supremacist racial hierarchy collide and in some instances collude. When Jefferson finally speaks in the last lines of the play after the fight ends, he tells a reporter who knew of the agreement and asks why he lost, "He beat me dassall."[50] Pressing him further for a reason for his loss, the reporter asks, "But why, Jack? Really." Jefferson responds, "Ah ain't got dem reallies from de Year One. . . . **An if any a you got em, step right down an say em. No . . . you new here like Ah is—**."[51] His signifying response once again seeks to redress the balance of power by challenging the reporter to reveal his own complicity with the fixed fight and its white supremacist underpinnings. More importantly, it inaugurates an alternative discursive and conceptual space where the logic of both uplift ideology and the Progressive Era racial hierarchy have no traction. Jefferson's refusal to take a dive in the eighth round and his subsequent loss of the fight on his own terms, rather than those of Progressive Era racial common sense, marks the failure of such logic and enacts black subjectivity that defies it. In asserting that he and the reporter are "new here," he establishes "here" as an alternative space to the public sphere's "real" that depends upon the deployment of uplift ideology and racial hierarchies for its authority and validity.

Yet if Jefferson articulates an alternate discursive and conceptual space for the enactment of black subjectivity in the play's final lines, its final images acknowledge both the persistence of the Progressive Era racial hierarchy and its waning authority in the public sphere. Following Jefferson's response to the reporter, The Kid is carried out of the fight venue on the shoulders of his supporters "immobile in his white robe, with one gloved hand extended, the golden belt draped around his neck and a towel over his head—his smashed and reddened face is barely visible—he resembles the lifelike wooden saints in Catholic processions."[52] While such pageantry illustrates that Jefferson's struggle for subjectivity is contested by the unrelenting racial hierarchy The Kid embodies, his bloodied face undercuts its representational power.

Further, The Kid himself is in some ways as constrained by representation as Jefferson was before turning to interiority as a space for racial meaning. He never speaks during the match and does not have a single line in the play. Consequently, as his supporters joyfully "parade him before the audience and with a final cheer fling their straw hats into the air" just before the curtain that would seemingly restore the authority of the Progressive Era racial hierarchy, his likening to a religious icon is an oxymoron that speaks to its instability and ephemerality.[53] Figured as a wooden effigy offered up for public consumption, The Kid can instantiate but never materialize the white supremacy he represents within the public sphere. Put alongside Jefferson's interior enactment of black subjectivity and The Kid's battered body, these signposts collectively map the racial hierarchy's vulnerabilities and its dependence upon representations of white supremacy, no matter how threadbare, to sustain itself. In the Progressive Era public sphere, in which both uplift ideology and racial hierarchies are embedded, Jefferson's public defeat on his own terms marks the interiorization of black subjectivity and the rejection of the public sphere as a viable space to enact it. By repudiating the public

The Great White Hope. 1969 Alvin Theater Playbill. Collection of the author.

sphere discourse of racial common sense and its attempts to regulate black identity, Jefferson offers interior black subjectivity as the only feasible alternative.

The Great White Hope's debut in December 1967 came at the height of the Black Arts/Aesthetic Movements and during an era of African American theater history that depicted "a variety of African Americans never seen before."[54] Aided by the development of black theater companies in the 1960s, this new range of representations was exemplified in the staging of Peter Weiss's *Songs of the Lusitanian Bogey*, Wole Soyinka's *Kongi's Harvest* and six other plays by the Negro Ensemble Company, while its rival, the New Lafayette Theatre, produced Ron Milner's *Who's Got His Own*, Ed Bullins's *In the Wine Time*, and Athol Fugard's *Blood Knot* during the 1967–1968 season.[55] But African American actors were also prominent on stages beyond black theater venues, including at the world premiere of *Hair* in October 1967 at Joseph Papp's Public Theater and in Charles Gordone's *No Place to Be Somebody: A Black Black Comedy* at the Sheridan Square Playhouse in the following month.[56]

Yet aside from the employment opportunities they provided for black performers, critic Hoyt Fuller asserted that it was difficult to "drum up a great deal of enthusiasm" for those productions.[57] Like Fuller, critic Peter Bailey was skeptical of such productions because they were not relevant to, as he and other Black Aestheticians argued, black theater that is "written, produced, and financed by blacks, located in black areas, and geared to black audiences" and instead sought "to attract that theater-going, we shall overcome, black and white together crowd."[58] Fuller and Bailey aptly summarized the perspectives of many Black Aestheticians who approached such productions warily and rejected claims by mainstream critics that they constituted evidence of an "upsurge in black theater."[59] These concerns about *The Great White Hope*'s relevance to black theater notwithstanding, it did draw black audiences, and according to Jane Alexander, who portrayed Eleanor Bachman at the Arena Stage and the Alvin Theatre, it elicited different responses from black and white spectators. She recalls that at the outset of its Broadway run, audiences were primarily white and "patting themselves on the back for their racial understanding," but "by the end of the year, they were predominantly black" and cheering at Bachman's suicide.[60]

While some of the reviews attended to these questions of audience reception and racial identity, most theater critics worked to interpret the play and Jack Jefferson within the context of the African American Freedom Struggle's social discord, largely ignoring its exploration of black subjectivity. However, there were two notable exceptions. One was the *Chicago Daily Defender*'s Harry Golden, who took up Jefferson's explication of racial uplift ideology and the burden of racial representation he rejects, contending that Sackler's play presents a point of view too often ignored in "the tumultuous events surrounding the civil rights struggle."[61] He continued that "not everyone can be a citizen twenty-four hours a day, nor should they [and] not every individual can bear the standard for his race."[62]

Similarly, writer Toni Cade Bambara emphasized its contributions to discussions of black subjectivity. In a review originally published in *Obsidian*, she wrote that while the play presents white liberals with "a chance to flagellate themselves and perpetuate their guilt ridden nightmares," its "sense of history and immediate relevance" provides the standard by which "our attempts to compile a canon of nationalist literature need to be judged."[63] Calling *The Great White Hope* "a fine play . . . a fine production . . . a fine lesson," she identified it as a departure from the impulse in some plays that seek to "move the conscience of white America" with "pitiful-po-me intimations just beneath [their] stormy invectives."[64] Bambara concluded that the Jefferson character, buoyed by James Earl Jones's performance, enables a "sense of the mythic, the epic, of timeless history" and showcases a complexity that is "brooding, defiant, cunning, gentle, primordial. . . . There is an ambience as well as a person that strikes us; it is familiar to the gut, but we've seldom seen it with our eyes. Jones' man becomes a great deal more than fiction."[65]

These exceptions aside, most critics alluded to the civil disturbances across the country, and in some instances directly referenced Muhammad Ali's arrest and conviction for his refusal to be inducted.[66] Noting the play's topicality by linking Jefferson to Ali, Clive Barnes observed in the *New York Times* that "in these liberal times, we can accept a black heavyweight champion, but can we accept a *Black Muslim* heavyweight? It is a question that seems to lurk like a silent ghost in the very corridors of Mr. Sackler's play."[67] Echoing Barnes, Alan Bunce pointed out in the *Christian Science Monitor* that the case of "current 'ex' champion Muhammad Ali inevitably comes to mind."[68] Likewise, *The Nation*'s Julius Novick wrote of initially fighting the play's implications and that he "had it in his mind to accuse Sackler of catering to a dangerous kind of Negro paranoia," but that he relented after thinking, first, of US House member Adam Clayton Powell, and second, "Cassius Clay."[69] Novick concluded that the play "demands of us, in urgently dramatic terms, that we examine the whole [race] question and our stake in it" and that further it should be shown in schools, the House of Representatives, and "other places where immature minds seek to cope with the problems of our day."[70] Each of these critics spoke to the interplay of race and representation in the past and the present and alluded to its then-current implications but do not speculate on what those implications might be.

While they frame *The Great White Hope* as an important, but perhaps indecipherable, historical lesson about representations of blackness and their meanings in cultural memory, other critics offer the play's discussion of race and racism as a marker of American theater. *The Nation*'s Harold Clurman described its racial spectacle as "vulgarly and excitingly American" and the *Los Angeles Times*'s Cecil Smith wrote that the play comes from "the very loins of America. . . . [It] flows out of the lifeblood of this country, out of the pompous bigotry that led to black revolution."[71]

However, if its treatment of race makes it a quintessentially American play, several writers took it to task for enabling the amnesia of presumably white audiences about the impact of white supremacy on American cultural memory. Arguing for the play as a "drama of contrition" that "asks playgoers to share guilt for the oppression of the Negro," the anonymous critic in *Time* suggested that it provides a "false catharsis" that "eases the conscience without facing the tragedy."[72] Similarly, in the *New Republic*, Richard Gilman asserted that it refuses to reconcile "Jefferson who is being shamefully whittled down [with] what we are now" and ultimately called out the play as "a splendid liberal occasion, an opportunity for self congratulation on the part of whites . . . in which we look back and see how we done them wrong."[73] Clurman advised that its setting in the distant past provides the audience "a chance to view the depicted events as an episode in the history of our shame for which it need not feel personally guilty."[74] Finally, as she speculated on the play's positive reception among white audiences, the *New York Amsterdam News*'s Cathy Aldridge remarked that they "may not have known why they were standing and applauding with tears in their eyes. They may not have known they were watching themselves. We can only hope."[75] Aldridge read and critiqued the significance of sentiment in the play's reception among white audiences in ways that echo *A Raisin in the Sun*'s reception discussed in Chapter One.

In the collective economy of these reviews, theater critics revealed apprehension about white audiences' ability to identify what constitutes the play's meaning within the context of the African American Freedom Struggle and the expense of failing to do so. More importantly, they demonstrated anxiety about audiences' capacity to see their complicity with institutions that put what the *Time* reviewer named "the tragedy" in motion. The irony here is that the critics themselves didn't elucidate the play's tragedy or its consequences in that historical moment and they were silent on what is at stake in the interplay between *The Great White Hope*'s Jack Jefferson and the spectral identities of both Johnson and Ali that the critics themselves summoned.

One way to account for this is that in 1968, the Freedom Struggle itself was ongoing, with no temporal designations and without a master narrative detailing successes and failures to frame it as a historical moment worthy of critical reflection. But the mainstream press reviews themselves narrated a drama of contrition. In demonstrating regret for historical wrongs against Johnson and linking them to Ali in the then-current moment, *The Great White Hope*'s reviews served as a racial repentance that ultimately elide the complexities of African American subjectivity as they are staged in the play. Theatre critics' preoccupation with Johnson and Ali directed attention away from the representation of Jack Jefferson and the ways in which it held up blackness for examination by rejecting the pursuit of black freedom through uplift ideology.[76]

Drew "Bundini" Brown, who served as Muhammad Ali's cornerman for much of his career, was known to chant "Ghost in the house! Ghost in the house! Jack Johnson is here, ghost in the house" during Ali's fights.[77] Similarly, despite Sackler's claims for its "aracial" universality, *The Great White Hope* summons Jack Johnson and the ubiquity of Progressive Era racial common sense, but does so to prompt the exploration of black subjectivity in a historical moment that is figured as limiting it. Most importantly, what a reconsideration of the play's representation of Jefferson and the reviews of *The Great White Hope* as an archive of cultural memory illustrate are the ways in which cultural memory often obscures the very cultural operations it seeks to illuminate.

CHAPTER FOUR

Gathering Black Subjectivities and Cultural Memory in Alice Childress's *Wine in the Wilderness*

In his foundational essay, "The New Black Aesthetic," critic and writer Trey Ellis counted photographer and conceptual artist Lorna Simpson among the era's most important postblack innovators. Perhaps best known for her photograph, *Waterbearer* (1986), Simpson has long been identified with postblack aesthetic practices. Her 2011 exhibition at the Brooklyn Museum, *Lorna Simpson: Gathered*, comprised two photograph installations titled "57/09" and "Please remind me of who I am" and one video called "Easy to Remember." A meditation on memory and history, the collection of images combined original photographs and drawings as well as found photo booth images of unidentified African Americans, primarily women, collected from e-Bay and flea markets. In line with much of her work over her nearly thirty-year career, *Gathered* marked both history's collision and its continuities between and across the images depicted in the work, yet it also undermined the static and singular meanings often conferred upon archival materials.

She suggested in these works that the photographs are not objective documents of history, but instead allude to cultural memory and identity's collision across history. In one installation of 308 gelatin silver prints entitled "57/09," Simpson juxtaposed found black and white photographs of an amateur African American pinup in 1957 Los Angeles in a range of poses including at a piano and talking on a telephone with images of Simpson herself restaging many of the pinup's poses in 2009. At first glance, it is difficult to identify the differences in the images and only upon further examination do the subtle distinctions become clear, suggesting both continuities and disconnections across history. Similarly, in "Please remind me of who I am," Simpson juxtaposed the eighty-two heavy, bronze-framed found photographs of a spectrum of anonymous African American women from the 1920s through the 1970s, with sixty-eight small abstract ink drawings. Arranged in a constellation-like formation with a dense cluster of photographs at the center, the installation recontextualizes the historical moments from which the photographs are drawn and, put alongside the abstract ink images, they suggest new, sometimes contradictory meanings in the current historical moment.

Though bringing the disparate images together speaks to the commonalities of their composition—they are all African American women who took photo booth photographs to archive themselves in that particular moment— yet the collection and display of images resist legibility within the African American collective it depicts, as the photo booth images alternately fade and darken, remaining anonymous to audiences, and the abstract ink drawings also defy static signification. At the same time, they serve the larger constellation of images in creating a narrative whole that viewers construct with history and memory. Finally, the video segment "Easy to Remember" offers a black and white recording of fifteen mouths humming the 1935 Rodgers and Hart song of the same name, offering yet another iteration of memory and history as multivalent. Throughout *Lorna Simpson: Gathered*, Simpson summoned history and memory to simultaneously reaffirm and interrogate a notion of African American history and community that is always contingent and contested in cultural memory and that mirrors what she suggested about individuals and their relationship to communities. As she observed,

> People have opportunities in the way they construct themselves and if you're not reliant on the society around you to provide you with that construction then you can make yourself or construct yourself any way you'd like. So it's the idea that individuals can build communities but in such a way that they are not reliant on a status quo to confirm for them who they are.[1]

Likewise, Alice Childress, author, actor, director, and playwright, who is perhaps best-known for her 1973 award-winning young adult novel, *A Hero Ain't Nothin' But A Sandwich*, summoned history and memory in her oeuvre. Over her forty-year career, she wrote plays devoted to questions of race and racial identity that she did not see addressed elsewhere on theater stages which challenged expectations about black identity's representation in much the same way as Simpson. Her first play, *Florence*, was staged in 1949 at the American Negro Theatre (ANT), which she helped to form with Abram Hill and Frederick O'Neal in 1939 and where she became a student in its studio training program because of an absence of roles for African American actors.

Explaining that she and other black actors, including ANT graduates Sidney Poitier and Harry Belafonte, rejected the parts they were offered as "all that stereotypical stuff," Childress intervened in the dearth of black representations on stage by writing her own plays.[2] Her essay "For A Strong Negro People's Theater," published in both the Communist Party USA's *Daily Worker* and in the American Marxist monthly *Masses and Mainstream* in February 1951, issued a call that anticipated demands made by Black Aestheticians for African American self-representation in theater production roughly fifteen years later. Pointing out the lack of "interest in the cultural or historical background of the Negro people," her essay argued for representations in an African American theater drawn from the lives of "our neighbors, the community, the domestic workers, porters, laborers, white-collar workers, churches, lodges and institutions" that would "create a complete desire for the liberation of all oppressed people."[3] Shortly after her essay's publication, she was placed on the Federal Bureau of Investigation's subversives list and remained under surveillance until 1973.[4]

Mindful of her call to put African American cultural history in the service of African American theater, this chapter frames Childress's 1969 teleplay, *Wine in the Wilderness*, as a counternarrative to cultural memory's master narrative of the Freedom Struggle era. Refuting a narrative of declension that poses the Black Power/Black Arts Movement as a cynical response to the so-called heroic era of the Civil Rights Movement, *Wine in the Wilderness* strategically deploys African American cultural history to rewrite cultural memory. In its iteration of allusion-disruption strategy that summons iconography, images, events, and figures of an earlier moment to trouble blackness as well as to oppose reductive iterations of blackness, the text disrupts the standard ideas associated with it and, consequently, creates a new meaning. It does this in three significant ways. First, in its intraracial exchange among the Harlem community members, it offers a model for cooperation across gender and class lines that draws on African American fraternal organizations. Second, it engages and critiques both the Moynihan Report's contentions about black female identity as well as the Kerner Report's assertions about African Americans' role in the civil disturbances of the mid-to-late 1960s. Finally, it unpacks the intraracial ideological hierarchy that underwrites some Black Arts/Aesthetic expression. In creatively addressing and rewriting cultural memory of the 1960s in the midst of that era, *Wine in the Wilderness* approximates postblack cultural production.

Amiri Baraka's *Dutchman*, discussed in Chapter Two, alludes to the African American class divide as it surfaces in Clay's defense of himself to Lula as "authentically" black. His insistence that he is no less black because he

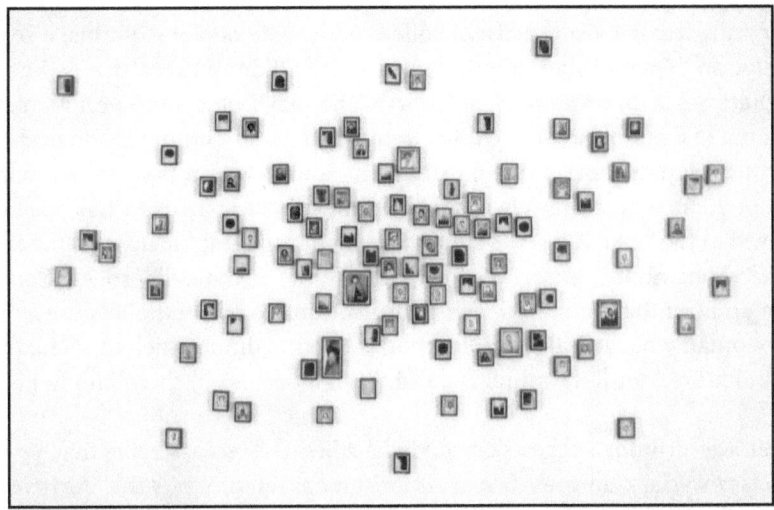

Lorna Simpson, *Please remind me of who I am*, 2009, 100 total bronze elements: 50 ink drawings, 50 photo booth images, dimensions variable upon installation. Courtesy of the artist and Salon 94, New York.

aspires to the black middle class is a direct response to the premise that the African American middle class is somehow less authentically black than the African American working poor. Yet *Dutchman* stages an interracial debate about class rather than an intraracial discussion and interrogates the existence of a black middle class that Lula challenges. Some forty-five years later, this argument about class status and its relationship to so-called authentic black identity finds resonances in the current historical moment's postblack discourse. Engaging a range of African American cultural producers, the writer Touré observed that in order "to codify Blackness, many Black minds create a hierarchy of authenticity" and he vigorously challenged this impulse, particularly the tendency to gauge black authenticity in terms of its "proximity to the ghetto experience."[5] While Touré laid bare a historically intraracial discussion about the relationship between class status and black identity in the twenty-first century, *Wine in the Wilderness*'s representations spoke to similar concerns in 1969, as the play shares both postblack discourse's rejection of "Black life experiences as rankable" as well as an insistence upon situating the multiplicity of black subjectivities "on a continuum where all experiences are equally valuable, equally Black."[6]

Following the call in "For a Strong Negro People's Theater" for representations that embody a range of black identities, *Wine in the Wilderness* depicts a cross-section of middle- and working-class Harlemites—Tomorrow Marie, or Tommy, a thirty-year-old blue-collar dress factory worker; Bill Jameson, a formally trained visual artist; a college educated couple—Cynthia, a social worker and Sonny-Man, a writer; and, finally, Edmond Matthews, known as Oldtimer, a sixty-something laborer. The play's plot hinges on a chance meeting in a bar between Cynthia, Sonny-Man, and Tommy in the midst of the 1964 Harlem riot. While Cynthia and Sonny-Man retreat to the neighborhood bar, where they encounter Tommy, whose apartment has been destroyed in the riots, Bill is developing his own iconographic interpretation of "black womanhood"—a triptych he calls "Wine in the Wilderness." Sonny-Man and Cynthia phone Bill and invite Tommy to his studio to pose as the lost woman who, as Bill tells Oldtimer, is "a poor, dumb chick that's had her behind kicked until it's numb . . . and the sad part is . . . there's no hope for her."[7]

Bill's description suggests critic Michael Eric Dyson's assertion that "seething class warfare" in the African American community pits the "Afristocracy" against the "Ghettocracy." The Afristocracy—or the black elite and upper middle classes comprised of intellectuals, artists, bankers, civil rights leaders, entertainers, and athletes—rails about the "pernicious habits of the black poor" and has support of the black middle classes.[8] However, he pointed out that the black middle class itself is multifaceted, arguing that "there are many black middle classes: the one barely a paycheck or two from poverty; the one a notch above, with jobs in the service economy; the one more solidly in the middle, with low-level professional jobs; and the one in the upper stratum, with high-level professional employment and the esteem such labor entails."[9]

Conversely, the "Ghettocracy"—or the black poor—is populated by "the desperately unemployed and underemployed, those trapped in underground economies, and those working poor folk who slave in menial jobs at the edge of the economy . . . [and] extends into the ranks of athletes and entertainers . . . whose values and habits are alleged to be negatively influenced by their poor origins."[10] Dyson argued that "class in black America has never been viewed in strictly literal economic terms; the black definition of class embraces style and behavior as well."[11] Similarly, *Wine in the Wilderness* situates Tommy and Oldtimer within the "ghettocracy" and Sonny-Man, Cynthia, and Bill within the black middle class Dyson details. Tommy, a dress factory worker who has had no education beyond the eighth grade, reveals to Cynthia that she "come from poor people" and that her mother raised her and her siblings on very little money. Explaining her lack of education to Cynthia, she asserts that she was tired of her subsistence on "on grits, or bread and coffee" and sought "a job. Later for school."[12] Likewise, Oldtimer, an itinerant worker whom Bill chastises for collecting clothing and food left in the wake of the riot, laments his lack of education to Bill, telling him "my day we didn't have all this grants and scholarships like now."[13]

Stage direction, dialogue, and personal style affiliate Bill, Cynthia, and Sonny-Man with the black middle class. The stage direction describes Cynthia as being dressed in clothing that is "tweedy and in good, quiet taste" and Sonny-Man as wearing a dashiki and slacks.[14] Similarly, Bill's tastes speak to middle-class status as his Harlem studio reflects "a beautiful, rather artistic state of disorder," with arts supplies, trinkets from around the world, and portraits of and books about historical figures.[15] Further, as he laments to Tommy, he grew up in a solidly middle-class household as the son of postal workers in the Long Island suburbs, where all the homes in his neighborhood had ducks on their aluminum screen doors; hedges and crabgrass populate his bad dreams. Though such details about their personal styles signify what might be called middle-class tastes, what links them most closely to the black middle class are their jobs and educational backgrounds. All three hold college degrees, and the successful pursuit of higher education places them squarely within the black middle class. Most often, their class status is signified through the dialogue between these characters and Tommy. In particular, their emphasis on academic phrases and other markers of what might be called cultural literacy that she doesn't understand illustrates this point. Tommy, whose eighth-grade education heightens the class differences between her and Cynthia, Sonny-Man, and Bill makes her awareness of these differences clear in several scenes.

After Sonny-Man and Bill leave to get food for her to eat while she poses for the triptych, she is left alone with Cynthia and they begin to discuss Bill. Tommy takes note of class markers in his studio, observing the "books, books, books everywhere" as well as Cynthia's place within the class structure when she tells her, "You a social worker, I know that mean college."[16] Tommy then reveals that she was raised in a single-parent household headed by her mother, and Cynthia frames it as evidence of "the matriarchal society." She responds:

TOMMY: What's that?
CYNTHIA: A matriarchal society is one in which the women rule . . . the women have the power . . . the women head the house.
TOMMY: We didn't have nothin' to rule over, not a pot nor a window. And my papa picked hisself up and run off with some finger-poppin' woman and we never hear another word 'til ten twelve years later when a undertaker call up and ask if Mama wanta come claim his body.[17]

Here Cynthia provides an academic definition, buttressed by *The Negro Family: The Case for National Action*, published by the US Department of Labor's Office of Policy Planning and Research in 1965, in her framing of the matriarchal society. Widely known as the Moynihan Report after its author, Daniel P. Moynihan, who was then the assistant secretary of labor, it asserted that black women's success in education and employment, black families with men in the household "dominated by the wife" in addition to black households headed by single black mothers put undue pressure on black men and ultimately impeded the social progress of black families.[18] Yet Tommy mediates her relationship to the phrase in her counternarrative. She argues that if the logic of the matriarchal society presupposes subjects who can be "ruled," then by definition her family does not follow that logic. In effect, she rejects both the phrase and its definition and instead provides the social context that gave rise to their iteration of the so-called matriarchal society by providing a narrative that denies the validity of the logic used to circumscribe black female identity. Tommy's resistance to such framing intervenes in the discourse of African American class struggle.

Another aspect of the discourse of intraracial class struggle that she addresses moves beyond her resistance to academic phrases circumscribing black female identity and markers of cultural literacy that Cynthia, Sonny-Man, and Bill employ in educating her. Tommy offers a rebuttal to Cynthia's framing of style and behavior within the class struggle's discourse. As she begins to realize that the reason she has been asked to Jameson's studio has nothing to do with a potential romance between the two, she asserts that Cynthia doesn't think he would "go for" her. Initially, Cynthia attempts to remain diplomatic about Tommy as a partner for him, gently suggesting that Bill may not be Tommy's type. Continuing to straighten up Bill's studio, Tommy finally asks Cynthia, "What's wrong with me?" Relenting, Cynthia replies with a laundry list of behaviors and style concerns that might better serve the romantic ends Tommy seeks, including allowing "the black man [to] have his manhood again," yet her instruction also takes up Tommy's appearance:

> CYNTHIA: Leave the room alone. What we need is a little more sex appeal and a little less washing, cooking, and ironing. (*TOMMY puts down the room straightening*) One more thing, . . . do you have to wear that wig?
> TOMMY: (*a little sensitive*) I like how your hair looks. But some of the naturals I don't like. Can see all the lint caught up in the hair like it hasn't been combed since know not when. You a Muslim?
> CYNTHIA: No.
> TOMMY: I'm just sick-a hair, hair, hair. Do it this way, don't do it, leave it

natural, straighten it, process, no process. I get sick-a hair and talkin' 'bout it and foolin' with it. That's why I wear the wig.
CYNTHIA: I'm sure your own must be just as nice as or nicer than that.
TOMMY: It ought to be. I only paid nineteen ninety five for this.
CYNTHIA: You ought to go back to usin' your own.
TOMMY: (*tensely*) I'll be giving that some thought.

I want to momentarily put aside Cynthia's sex appeal comment to focus on the discussion about Tommy's hair and how it informs both notions of black masculinity and Black Power rhetoric. As the discussion of Beneatha and the significance of her Afro in Chapter One suggests, it offers a range of cultural significations. Both Sonny-Man and Cynthia wear Afros, which were often considered to reflect radical political affiliations for African Americans. Historian Robin Kelley has asserted that market forces had much to do with the proliferation of the Afro in the 1960s and 1970s, and the availability of products to "make one's natural more natural" influenced its popularity, but its roots can be found in "the bourgeois high fashion circles in the late 1950s."[19] What Kelley describes is a transformation within its cultural genealogy or, as he puts it, "Once associated with feminine chic, the Afro suddenly became the symbol of black manhood" that rendered women invisible.[20] Steering Tommy away from the wig, Cynthia frames the Afro as a means of allying herself with Bill and restoring his masculinity. Within this context, Cynthia's comments about sex appeal come into focus since some iterations of Black Power and Black Arts rhetoric hinged on the idea that women could best serve the movement in support roles to male leadership and that the masculine power denied to black men by means of institutional racism could be partially restored through the support of black women.[21] In his best-selling memoir, *Soul on Ice* (1968), the Black Panther Party's minister of information, Eldridge Cleaver, exemplified this impulse, contending that only through "the liberating power of [the black woman's] re-love" could black manhood be redeemed.[22] Cynthia's suggestion that black women need more sex appeal in order to both attract black men and restore their manhood alludes to this notion and links Tommy's acceptance of the Afro to a shift in its cultural genealogy that effaces women.

Once again offering a counternarrative to Cynthia's framing of the Afro and its political and cultural import, Tommy rejects Cynthia's usage and suggests that in being "sick-a talkin' about it and foolin' with it," she prefers to circumvent these potential meanings altogether by wearing a wig. Yet by the play's end, the stage direction points out that she decides to stop wearing it, dictating that after the wig is removed, her natural hair "must not be an accurate, well-cut Afro . . . but should be rather attractive natural hair."[23] While acknowledging the symbolic import and genealogy of the Afro, the play insists on Tommy's revision of it to serve her iteration of black female identity by rejecting the meanings that Cynthia suggests inhere within that cultural marker but lays claim to its transformative possibilities. In other words, Tommy puts the cultural marker in the service of her own representation of black female identity that deemphasizes the affiliations to which Cynthia alludes in their discussion.

Like *Dutchman*, *Wine in the Wilderness*'s climactic scene hinges on a confrontation between the characters. When Oldtimer inadvertently reveals to Tommy that she is the model for the "messed up chick" in Bill's triptych, she delivers a scathing critique of the entire group. Realizing that Tommy defies the narrow categories that he, Cynthia, and Sonny-Man have assigned to her, Bill apologizes. However, in responding to Bill's admission, she asserts her complicity with their class-based perceptions, likening her behavior to the Uncle Tom figure: "Trouble is I was Tommin' to you, to all of you. . . . Oh, maybe they gon' like me. . . . I was your fool, thinkin' writers and painters know moren' me, that maybe a little bit of you would rub off on me."[24] Still, she insists on her knowledge as a source of agency by emphasizing the ways that their perceptions fail them. As she puts it, she is only a fool for believing that writers' and painters' cultural work and the knowledge they produce is by definition more valuable and valid than her own. However, when she is confronted with the reality that they believe she embodies Moynihan-escue black pathology, she exposes how such framing provides Sonny-Man, Cynthia, and Bill narrative authority of the black collective and effaces the black poor:

> TOMMY: If a black somebody is in a history book, or printed on a pitcher, or drawed on a paintin' . . . or if they're a statue, . . . dead, and outta the way, and can't talk back, then you dig 'em and full-a so much-a damn admiration and talk 'bout "our" history. But when you run into us livin' and breathin' ones, with the life's blood still pumpin' through us, . . . then you comin' on 'bout how we ain' never together. You hate us, that's what! *You hate black me!*[25]

Identifying echoes of racial uplift ideology, which hinges in part on "reforming the character and managing the behavior of the black masses," Tommy reveals the ways that Sonny-Man, Cynthia, and Bill put an African American historiography in the service of maintaining a class divide between the black middle class and the black poor and reads their framing of her as the lost woman as a reflection of their refusal to broaden their class-conscious notions of black community.[26] Throughout the play, Bill in particular, but also Sonny-Man and Cynthia, demonstrate resistance to reading either Oldtimer or Tommy as "living and breathing" agents within an African American collective community. Instead, both must be rehabilitated under their tutelage as evidenced throughout the play, including Cynthia's instruction to Tommy on hair and sex appeal as well as Bill's and Sonny-Man's hectoring of Oldtimer for his misappropriation of the people's revolution. Yet before Tommy introduced herself to him, they didn't know Oldtimer's real name—Edmond Lorenzo Matthews.

Further, when Tommy frames her voter activism and her knowledge of Adam Clayton Powell, Martin Luther King, and Malcolm X as a contribution to the revolutionary history he reveres and displays in his apartment—books about Monroe Trotter and portraits of Frederick Douglass and John Brown—he corrects and rejects her assertions, saying that she can best serve black people as the representation of the lost woman that he has envisioned. In short, Tommy's scolding reveals the trio's duplicity in framing a revolutionary history and action and points to the ways that Bill, Sonny-Man, and Cynthia circumscribe Oldtimer and Tommy's participation in both. Her climactic calling out of Bill, Sonny-Man, and Cynthia issues a call to action that effects change; as the stage direction notes, Bill is "stung to the heart, confused and saddened by the half truth which applies to himself."[27] Her willingness to engage their trio results in the group's reconsideration of the ways they frame revolutionary history and action; Bill scraps his earlier representation and begins a new canvas that represents "the real beautiful people"—Edmund, Sonny-Man, Cynthia, and Tommy—which reflects a broader African American historiography and places them on "a continuum where all experiences are equally valuable, equally Black."[28]

Bill's triptych serves a central role in advancing the play's multiple counternarratives, as it both enables a shift in consciousness among the group and offers a representation of the reconfigured group. Not only do Sonny-Man, Cynthia, Oldtimer, and Tommy contribute to class and race discourse around the painting's representations and, through those discussions, aid Bill in clearing out the "junk room" of representations utilized in his first version of the triptych; they also embody the black collective community for which Tommy advocates and that Bill represents on the painting's panel at the play's end. In short, the triptych traces and enables the development of a radically transformed community collective, and as such, it catalyzes the group. Yet the triptych's earlier representations also enable a counternarrative to the framing of Africa within Black Arts expression. When Bill initially shows the painting's two completed canvases to Oldtimer—one depicts "a charming little girl in Sunday dress and hair ribbon" that he calls "black girlhood," the other features a beautiful black woman in regal headdress and draped in African cloth—Bill remarks that this second panel represents "Mother Africa, regal black womanhood in her noblest form . . . perfect Black womanhood."[29] The blank third panel will portray what he describes as "the lost woman . . . what the society has made out of our women . . . as far from my African queen as a woman can get . . . as close to the bottom as you can get without cracking up . . . ignorant, unfeminine, coarse, rude . . . vulgar . . . a back-country chick right outta the wilds of Mississippi. . . . Born in Harlem, but back country."[30] Upon its completion, he hopes to display it in a public place so that its "Black queen will look down from the wall so the messed-up chicks in the neighborhood can see what a woman ought to be."[31]

Bill's "Mother Africa" image illustrates the sometimes conflicting cultural politics informing Black Arts expression that *Wine in the Wilderness* critiques. Historian James Smethurst has argued that within Black Arts cultural production, the trope of Mother Africa, often serving as a "touchstone of essential blackness who renew[s] the identity of black men," bore considerable influence on Black Arts ideologies.[32] Thus, in the triptych's panel, Bill constructs the black queen as an analogue to Mother Africa, who not only models authentic black female identity for "lost women" in order to fortify black masculinity, but who also cannot not deviate from or complicate this image. Serving as both an antidote to and an aspiration for the lost woman, the black queen's identity is fixed and restrained within a narrow framework of "authentic" black femininity. Through its representation of Tommy, however, the play critiques such an imposition on black women in Black Arts cultural production and thereby contributes one thread in its counternarrative to cultural memory.

Not only does his work employ a narrow aesthetic of cultural purity in an attempt to depict and fix authentic black womanhood, but in addition, that effort is buttressed by echoes of the Moynihan Report, which asserted that the black family's matriarchal structure "seriously retards the progress of the group as a whole, and imposes a crushing burden on the Negro male and, in consequence, on a great many Negro women as well."[33] In offering the literal and figurative rehabilitation of the lost woman through the representation of the black queen, Bill alludes to the broadly circulated claims about black women made in the Moynihan Report's "tangle of pathology."[34] Similarly, a vision of reconstructing and revolutionizing the heteronormative black family that emphasized male supremacy alongside the trope of Mother Africa significantly influenced some iterations of Black Arts expression.

Consequently, Bill's work engages the report's premise that black women unwittingly undermine black social progress, and this, coupled with his reliance upon cultural purity aesthetics in developing the triptych, exposes an ideological fissure that Childress's Tommy exploits in critiquing Black Arts representational strategies and in constructing a counternarrative to cultural memory of civil unrest in the 1960s.

As discussed above, though, the confrontation between Tommy and the others initiates a shift in consciousness. The backdrop for this shift—the Harlem riot—is as significant as the shift itself. The civil disturbances that occurred during the mid-to-late 1960s across the United States are a key aspect of cultural memory's declension narrative that *Wine in the Wilderness* critiques. That narrative is both troubled and confirmed by the National Advisory Committee on Civil Disorders—better known as the Kerner Commission. President Lyndon B. Johnson formed the eleven-member committee in July 1967 to explain the riots that had occurred each summer in cities across the United States since 1964 and to make recommendations on how to prevent their reoccurrence. The committee's report, issued in February 1968, made three fundamental critiques of media coverage of civil disturbances. First, the commission found "a significant imbalance between what actually happened in [our] cities and what the newspaper, radio and television coverage of the riots told us happened"; second, it found that the "news media [have] failed to analyze and report adequately on racial problems in the United States"; and, finally, the report said that contrary to mainstream media coverage depicting the disturbances as large-scale, black-white conflicts, "nearly all the deaths, injuries and property damage occurred in all-Negro neighborhoods, and thus . . . were not 'race riots' as that term is generally understood."[35] Yet while the commission critiqued the mainstream national media, it also took calls for black consciousness and solidarity—key tenets of the Black Power Movement—to task as well. In a survey of rioters that the commission conducted to assess their racial attitudes, the committee found that "rioters have strong feelings of racial pride, if not superiority" and interpreted those sentiments as evidence of the "frustrations of powerlessness" and a longing for inclusion in the American plurality.[36]

In short, the Kerner Commission Report traces the contours of civil unrest's mediated master narrative that frames rioting in urban areas across the country as more destructive as well as more widespread than they actually were and as a purely interracial phenomena. However, it significantly misconstrues calls for racial solidarity and demonstrations of racial pride as a plea for inclusion in mainstream American society, which overlooks how such sentiments point to the desire for self-representation of African American identity in the public sphere that underwrites much of the African American Freedom Struggle's cultural production. Challenging the report's contentions, *Wine in the Wilderness* situates the Harlem riot during which the play takes place as a site enabling productive reflection on and reconsideration of what constitutes black identity through its counternarratives. In contrast to the master narrative's figuring of riots as a site of interracial conflict, the play foregrounds black identity discourse and an intraracial discussion of black identity's signifiers and markers. Despite the Kerner Report's findings, it does so through a call for community that does not envision inclusion in mainstream American society as its ultimate goal, nor does it impose a monolithic black identity to develop community. Instead, the play's counternarratives enable community through the confrontation between Tommy and the others in the group.

Further, it emphasizes continuities across the play's representations of the community members' lived experiences rather than valorizing personalities or specific events. As it underscores the revolutionary potential of the lumpen proletariat or the working class in locating those continuities, it also signals revolutionary possibilities by drawing on an unlikely and often overlooked institution of the heroic era as a model for those efforts—black fraternal organizations. In its discussion of the Improved Benevolent and Protective Order of Elks of the World, or the Elks, the play intervenes in African American Freedom Struggle historiography by situating the Elks' activism as a radical form of community solidarity that built bridges across classes and occupations during the period when Black Power ideologies purportedly undermined heroic era advances.

Before Tommy discovers she is the model for the lost woman, she argues with Bill about her reticence to pose for him. Echoing the Moynihan Report, he tells her that "the matriarchy gotta go," advises her to stop "fighting" him, and attributes her caginess about posing to a host of flaws in black women including being "too damn opinionated" and wanting to "latch on" to men; he then seeks to put her at ease, asking her to tell him "something ... anything about herself."[37] Tommy earlier revealed to Cynthia that her formal education ended in eighth grade and that she grew up poor in a single-parent household with her mother and siblings, a stark contrast to the college-educated and solidly middle-class Cynthia, Sonny-Man, and Bill. Yet she counters those credentials with her instruction from her immediate and extended family's involvement in African American fraternal organizations, including the Prince Hall Masons, The Order of the Eastern Star, and The Improved Benevolent Protective Order of Elks. Her knowledge of the Elks not only allows Tommy to engage Bill intellectually, but also to do so in a sub-

Abbey Lincoln as Tommy and Israel Hicks as Bill in Alice Childress's *Wine in the Wilderness* produced for WGBH. Courtesy of the WGBH Media Library & Archives.

ject where he purportedly has expertise signaled in both the history books in his apartment and the history lessons he offers to Tommy. In short, her knowledge of the Elks provides her with the cultural currency to instruct Bill. African American fraternal organizations have been sorely understudied, but according to sociologists Theda Skocpol and Jennifer Lynn Oser, they built black communal interaction as they "bridged classes and locations and offered many opportunities not only for group self-help but also for public assertion and leadership on social and civil rights concerns."[38] In tracing a fraternal order history for Bill, Tommy offers these organizations' advocacy as a model for the black collective community cooperation she envisions.

After she explains that the white Elks organization sued its black counterpart to prevent it from using the same name, "over fifteen hundred Black folk went to jail for wearin' the Elk emblem on their coat lapel . . . that's what you call history," she continues, describing how the black Elks bought the farm where abolitionist John Brown had trained participants in the Harpers Ferry insurrection, building an outdoor theater and erecting an eternal light in Brown's memory.[39] Bill is unaware of this history, and upon asking Tommy how she knows of it, she reveals that she learned it from her uncle, who was an Elks member, and her cousin, to whom the organization provided a college scholarship after she wrote an essay about its history.

In emphasizing the black Elks' history, Tommy points to the productive ways that the organization models both interracial and intraracial activism across class divides. Further, she situates black fraternal organizations as a key, but often overlooked, player in African American historiography that Bill, Sonny-Man, and Cynthia seek to educate her about. Fraternal organizations played a significant role in building community across class and gender divides, and as sociologist Joe Trotter has noted about the unacknowledged influence of these organizations, they were "deeply rooted in patterns of cooperation and conflict that accompanied the growth of multiclass black institutions, culture, and social networks during the nineteenth and twentieth centuries."[40] Ultimately, Tommy's historiography shifts the class- and education-based economy of power within the group, which not only provides her with the educational capital to more effectively confront Cynthia, Sonny-Man, and Bill about their complicity with the narrow modes of representation discussed, but also enables all of them, and Bill specifically, to see her, as the stage direction suggests, "with new eyes."[41]

While she identifies a black collective community as she hails the "we-ness" of the "nitty-gritty" crowd in her final monologue, Tommy predicts Lorna Simpson's contention that "individuals can build communities but in such a way that they are not reliant on a status quo to confirm for them who they are" by deconstructing the iconography of Bill's painting:

> Bill, I don't have to wait for anybody's by-your-leave to be a "Wine in the Wilderness" woman. I can be it if I wanta, . . . and I am. I am. I am. I'm not the one you made up and painted, the very pretty lady who can't talk back, . . . but I'm "Wine in the Wilderness" . . . alive and kickin' me. . . . And Cynthia, if my hair is straight, or if it's natural, or if I wear a wig, or take it off, that's all right because . . . they're just what you call . . . accessories . . . somethin' you add or take off. The real thing is takin' place on the inside . . . that's where the action is.[42]

Although throughout the play she has advocated for a black collective community, Tommy refuses to sacrifice her sense of self or her ways of knowing in order to become part of the black collective community that the trio offers. In short, she rejects their confirmation of who she is and asserts the primacy of her ways of being. However, by aligning herself with Bill's iconography of "perfect Black womanhood" and arguing that it is one among many subject positions that she occupies in her efforts toward self-representation, Tommy allows for black identity's multiplicity. As she refutes the trio's framing of black female identity as singular, which marks their attempts to serve as black identity's gatekeepers, she imagines and enacts a black collective community—a "we-ness"—that refuses to rank black experiences according to class hierarchies informed by education or style.

If the alternate history Tommy provides in this scene enables Bill, Sonny-Man, and Cynthia to see Tommy in a different light, a second scene, shortly after she discovers her role in the triptych, broadens that effect as it takes up a critique of Sonny-Man's mode of address that points to one peculiarity of the language of Black Arts cultural production and Black Aesthetic criticism. After Tommy's outcry about her designation as the lost woman, Sonny-Man remarks that "the sister is upset." Their ensuing exchange foregrounds yet another ideological disconnect within Black Arts aesthetics and practice:

> TOMMY: And you stop calling me "the" sister, . . . if you feelin' so brotherly why don't you say "my" sister? Ain't no we-ness in your talk. "The" Afro American, "the" black man, There's no we-ness in you. Who you think you are?
> SONNY-MAN: I was talking in general er . . . my sister, 'bout the masses.
> TOMMY: There he go again. "The masses." Tryin' to make out like we pitiful and you got it made. You the masses your damn self and don't even know it. *(Another angry look at Bill.)* Nigger.[43]

Here Tommy identifies and refutes the intraracial division embedded in Black Arts poetics. Critic Philip Brian Harper has contended that such practices issue Black Nationalist calls to unity that frequently deploy the second person pronoun "you" who is addressed by a speaker who "can be distinguished as a politically aware, racially conscious, Black Nationalist subject" in contrast to the addressed "you"—to whom the appeal is made to take part in a Black Nationalist collective and who has not yet achieved Black Nationalist identity.[44] In taking note of the use of the definite article "the" in Sonny-Man's speech that sets him as the speaker apart from the black subjects he references, whether they are "the masses" or "the sister," Tommy both makes the divide legible and troubles Sonny-Man's concepts of nationalist unity underwriting his speech as an obstacle impeding her notion of community and also critiques how he situates himself as a conscious subject who speaks for her and frames her as an unconscious object. Her reading of Sonny-Man's speech also implicates Cynthia and Bill, as it calls attention to their efforts to construct themselves as enlightened black subjects who can educate Tommy, whom they frame as a presumably uneducated and unconscious black object. By pointing out how Sonny-Man appropriates an iteration of black nationalism's rhetoric to demarcate class boundaries within the group, Tommy illuminates how Sonny-Man's recitations undermine the intraracial unity it purports to seek as well as illustrates how she acts on her own behalf within the collective's social structure. Ultimately, Tommy's reading resists black middle-class social control over working-class blacks who ostensibly undermine black upward striving intimated in Sonny-Man's rhetoric of unity.

Redoubling her critique, Tommy calls Bill "nigger." A source of ideological struggle between Tommy and Bill throughout the play, their conflict over its meanings reaches its apex when she directs it at him. He insists on its static meaning as he summons his fifth grade teacher's definition of the term and turns to a dictionary to educate Tommy:

> BILL: I'm telling you it's a low degraded person. Listen. *(reads from book)* Nigger, N-i-g-g-e-r, . . . A Negro . . . A member of any dark-skinned people. . . . Damn. *(amazed by dictionary description)*
> SONNY-MAN: Brother Malcolm said that's what they meant . . . nigger is a Negro, Negro is a nigger.
> BILL: *(slowly finishing his reading)* A vulgar offensive term of hostility and contempt. Well, so much for the fifth grade teacher.
> SONNY-MAN: No, they do not call low, degraded white folks niggers. Come to think of it, did you ever hear whitey call Hitler a nigger? Now if some whitey digs us . . . the others might call him a nigger-lover, but they don't call him no nigger.
> OLDTIMER: No, they don't.
> TOMMY: *(near tears)* When they say "nigger," just dry-long-so, they mean educated you and uneducated me. They hate you and call you "nigger," I called you "nigger" but I love you. *(there is dead silence in the room for a split second)*[45]

Tommy argues that nigger's deployment in white mainstream culture ignores the African American class divide in order to subordinate blacks on either side of it, while her usage in this instance looks toward transcending that divide. Her usage here and throughout the play anticipates sociolinguist Geneva Smitherman's findings that African Americans use nigger in four different ways: to identify other blacks; to disapprove of their behavior; to signify shared values and experiences; and, finally, as a term of endearment.[46] Drawing on Smitherman, legal scholar Randall Kennedy concluded that its meaning is "contingent, changeable, [and] context-specific."[47] Tommy uses the term nine times in each of the four contexts that Smitherman detailed. Consequently, her usage throughout the play demonstrates its contingency, but most significantly, it demonstrates her refusal to submit to the subordination typically ascribed to it by white mainstream culture or to Bill's attempt to eradicate it from her lexicon to serve his pedagogical purposes.

Tommy makes parallel use of the term that signifies in three registers. First, as an expression of her frustration with the ideological paradoxes around class in her struggle with Cynthia, Sonny-Man, and Bill over the representation of black female identity, it speaks to the gap between the rhetoric all three use in reference to her and their literal efforts to figure her as the representation of the messed up chick. In effect, it levels the ideological playing field for the group. Second, in juxtaposing her use and the "dry-long-so" or everyday, ordinary use of the term in mainstream white culture deployed to dehumanize and demean African Americans, she points out how she uses it to show her personal affection toward Bill rather than as a means of limiting identity as signified in the 'dry-long-so" usage of it often found in broader culture. In this rhetorical turn, she rejects Bill's figuring of it as an entirely negative term that requires the more politically correct alternative he offers earlier in the play—Afro Americans.

Finally, her explication of the term's use in broader culture demonstrates the futility of putting class status in the service of assessing black identity. She argues that in spite of their figuring of her as the triptych's messed up chick, their education does not prevent them from being situated as "niggers" in white mainstream culture. In addition, she equates their efforts to limit her identity through the triptych to the efforts of the broader culture to limit their identities through the use of "nigger" despite their education and class status. Further, Tommy's use points to her desire for community that does not rely on class status as a marker of authentic black identity. She deploys the "tragicomic sensibilities" attached to the word that acknowledges the complicated history of African Americans in the United States and the often-contested intraracial relations between African Americans. In so doing, she exposes the many fissures in terms of representation within the African American community. This exposure undercuts notions of monolithic African American identity in its staging of the class divide and ultimately offers an alternative means of bridging it.

Tommy's earlier alternative historiography and her skillful reading of Sonny-Man's speech does, as theater and performance critic Soyica Diggs Colbert has contended, "shift the consciousnesses of the middle-class characters and refocus the relationship among the people in the apartment and their neighbors rioting outside at the beginning of the play," as *Wine in the Wilderness*'s final scene stages Bill's reworking of the triptych, throwing out the completed panels—remnants from what he calls "the junk room" of his mind—and beginning anew to include Tommy, Cynthia, Sonny-Man, and

Edmund Matthews—Oldtimer—in a the painting that reflects that shift in consciousness.[48] Continuing by acknowledging that his earlier version of the triptych was painted "in the dark, all head and no heart," Bill convinces Tommy to pose for the center panel, so that when people see it they'll say, "Hey, don't she look like somebody we know?"[49]

Through confronting Bill, Cynthia, and Sonny-Man about the ways in which they employ cultural markers to identify authentic black identity, Tommy prompts them to reconsider how they read the markers as well as encourages them to recognize the impact of their assessments on the people who are being read. By persuading Bill to revise his "statement"—or his representation of the African American community, she recreates the artistic process as a collective one. Cynthia, Sonny-Man, Edmond Matthews, and Bill all contributed to and are represented in the revised painting. Although Tommy suggests that she could walk away from her encounter with Cynthia, Sonny-Man, Bill, and Oldtimer with "much more than [she] brought in," the collective embodied in Bill's revised triptych also walks away with much more than they brought in—a more nuanced and complicated understanding of African American identity. As these scenes demonstrate, Tommy ably navigates and evaluates the sometimes contradictory representational politics within Black Arts cultural production and contributes to the devel-

The cast of Alice Childress's *Wine in the Wilderness* produced for WGBH. Courtesy of the WGBH Media Library & Archives.

opment of black female identity in the interstices of the African American Freedom Struggle's master narrative.

Wine in the Wilderness was produced by Boston PBS station WGBH-TV as the first installment of a groundbreaking, fifteen-hour National Educational Television (NET) series written, produced, and acted by African Americans and called *On Being Black*. Collecting a range of black cultural expression in addition to Childress's play, which starred singer and actor Abbey Lincoln as Tommy, the series also featured other well-known actors and playwrights. It included the plays *Johnny Ghost*, by Philip Hayes Dean; Luther James's *Alton Flipped*; Clayton Riley's *The Record is 21 Minutes*; and *Basis of Need*, with Mary Alice and Al Freeman Jr; J. E. Franklin's *Black Girl*; Rose Jourdain Hayes's *The Candidate*, featuring Billy Dee Williams; *Face in the Mirror*, by Conrad Bromberg; Charlie Russell's *Men Are Not Made of Steel*, with Moses Gunn and Lou Gossett Jr.; Bill Ford's *Say It Out Loud*; and *Danger Zone*, by Lonne Elder III. It also featured a comedy special, *Laughing to Keep From Crying*, with Moms Mabley and Dick Gregory, as well as performances of Alvin Ailey's *Revelations* and Talley Beatty's *Black Belt*, by the Alvin Ailey American Dance Theatre.[50] Originally broadcast in Boston between January and September 1969, *On Being Black* later aired in cities across the country. However, its broadcast was banned on Alabama Public Television station WBIQ due to the presence of "lewd, vulgar, obscene, profane or repulsive material."[51] Though complaints lodged against the Alabama Educational Television Commission (AETC) argued that the station systematically censored black-oriented programming offered by the NET, the AETC insisted that a total of 217 hours of programming during a relevant period "either were integrated or involved a Negro complement entirely." However, 155 of those hours were devoted to morning and afternoon showings of *Sesame Street*.[52]

It may be no surprise that the representations of black identity put forward in the play elicited a blackout in Alabama, the so-called cradle of the Confederacy. Yet the AETC's action spoke to the Kerner Report's claim that national and local media's refusal to show an "understanding or appreciation of—and thus have not communicated—a sense of Negro culture, thought or history. . . contributed to the black-white schism in this country."[53] Further, the commission found that "news organizations have failed to communicate to both their black and white audiences a sense of the problems America faces and the sources of potential solutions."[54] Arguing that perspectives on the African American experience are seldom conveyed, the commission asserted that such omissions illustrated that the mainstream media "repeatedly, if unconsciously, reflects the biases, the paternalism, the indifference of white America."⁵⁵ As it called on both national and local media outlets to offer "plays and programs whose subjects are rooted in the ghetto and its problems," the commission concluded its findings about the mainstream media and race relations with a demand for "fair and courageous journalism: commitment and coverage that are worthy of one of the crucial domestic stories in America's history."⁵⁶

In light of these urgent calls, it might seem that *Wine in the Wilderness*'s premiere more than eighteen months after the Kerner Commission Report's release on February 29, 1968, and as a segment in a NET-developed program, would gain the mainstream media's attention as the report itself garnered media attention and made the *New York Times* best-seller list. Yet despite the play's distribution to180 public television stations across the country, just three mainstream publications reviewed it—two at its initial broadcast in 1969 and the other at a rebroadcast in 1971. While *Christian Science Monitor*'s Nora E. Taylor described *On Being Black* as "a series of one-hour dramas written, performed and produced by blacks which explore[s] many of the situations faced by black Americans," she was silent on the play itself, remarking only that singer and actor Abbey Lincoln portrayed Tommy in the production.⁵⁷

Taylor's column did, however, include the details of two new National Educational Television programs for pre-school children—one called *Mr. Roger's Neighborhood* and the other called *Sesame Street*. She observed that the new *Sesame Street* program would include "live-actions films and guest stars against a continuing background of a street that might be anyone's our street in our town."⁵⁸ Outlining the purpose of the program, she asserted that the new show is designed "to equip little ones with knowledge that will be helpful to them when they start school."⁵⁹ Through the new show, Taylor explained, the NET hoped to "deliver to children the kind of program they have shown they like and understand and one from which they are able to learn."⁶⁰

Taylor also glosses the premieres of two other NET programs: *The Advocates*, which would use a courtroom format to raise such questions as, "Should the principal of a high school report known marijuana-using students to the police?," and *Theatre America*, which would provide a "tour of six geographically separate and stylistically different concepts of what theater in America is doing today."⁶¹ She closed with a discussion of Paul Foster's installment in the series called *Heimskringla or the Stoned Angels*, an experimental piece which "incorporates 'videospace' or almost all the surreal effects television knows how to produce today."⁶²

It is hard to escape the irony that in Taylor's reading of *Sesame Street* as a children's show that emphasizes its location "in anyone's our street in our town," in the very same column she neglected a series that attempted to accomplish the same goal in relation to the African American experience. In electing to discuss at length a host of other premiering NET programs and effectively disregarding *Wine in the Wilderness*—or any of the *On Being Black* programs, Taylor participated in precisely the kind of media indifference the Kerner Commission's report outlined.

Though it more fully engages the play, Jack Gould's *New York Times* review was nearly as blind as Taylor's to the play's significance. Gould summarized the play as the story of "a self-satisfied artist and a bitter undereducated girl in search of identities by which to live" and asserted that Childress has "superimposed distinctions in black society on a fitful romantic theme."[63] In closing, he turned to the play's structure, which he described as "rather abrupt in raising its issue and conventional in reaching a resolution" but allows that it nonetheless offers "some insight into black tensions."[64] By the end of the review, the identities by which Bill and Tommy seek to live, as well as the issue that the play has raised and its insight into black tensions that Gould claims it provides, remain unexplored. He fails to address or engage any of the seemingly significant assertions he makes about the play and its themes. In short, while Gould's cursory review took the play's broadcast more seriously than Taylor's, it still failed to fully engage with the play's representations and themes. What is perhaps even more significant (and more disappointing) about Gould's assessment is that while he took the time to identify at least three potentially fruitful entries into a discussion of the play and its representations, he gave it a superficial reading, devoting most of his column inches to the first installment of *NET Journal* on the increasing use of drugs among youth called "Speak Out On Drugs."[65] He asserted the program underscored the need for "turning on the younger generation with fresh ideas, fundamental changes in perspectives and especially things to do that are productive and worthwhile."[66]

The only review that comprehensively engaged with the play's representations and themes was Alan Kriegsman's *Washington Post* assessment of a rebroadcast of *On Being Black* in 1971.[67] Kriegsman immediately took note of the complexity of the representations in the play, asserting in the first lines of the review that "the 'black experience' is not just a simple matter of black and white, a truism viewed from a number of interesting perspectives in the teleplay 'Wine in the Wilderness.'"[68] He continued in this vein, emphasizing the gradations within the performances of "blackness" and African American identity that the play sought to showcase as he identified key questions that the play takes on: "What is blackness really all about—chic slogans, a kind of attire, revolutionary lingo? What are the deeper sources: Where does niggerhood end and Negritude begin? Such are the sticky questions to which 'Wine in the Wilderness' addresses itself, with no little candor and insight."[69] Kriegsman located the significance of the play's representations in the questions they raise about the nature and sources of African American identity as he pointed out that *Wine in the Wilderness*'s representations move beyond trading in Black Power/Black Arts symbols and signifiers by tracing their cultural genealogies to dislodge them from essentialized notions of African American identity. Further, by situating "niggerhood" and "Negritude" on the same cultural continuum, rather than as opposing categories, Kriegsman frames *Wine in the Wilderness* as an exploration of black identity that echoes Tommy's assertions about it in the play. Emphasizing the relationship between Tommy and Bill and her transformation in the play, Kriegsman asserted that Bill "looks upon [Tommy] as an interesting specimen and uses her admiration to draw out her attitudes, dreams and obsessions," while Tommy views Bill as more than a man, but also as "an embodiment of upper-crust sophistication which she both fears and covets."[70] Identifying the transformative possibilities enabled by their confrontation, Kriegsman wrote that "she lashes out with all of her former bitterness, furious at her own gullibility, angrier still at Bill's hypocrisy. But with her rage comes the spark of self-discovery, the realization that her own identity is no less precious—and no less black—than Bill's despite the differences in vocabulary, status, and lifestyle that divide them."[71] While he suggested, as Gould did in his review, that the play's resolution "seems too easy and glib," he argued that this shortcoming "really doesn't matter much, for the guts of the piece lie elsewhere,"[72] locating them in its themes. Accordingly, he asserted that "most new plays, especially the thematic ones, have an excess of style and a paucity of substance. . . . The fact that the reverse is true for *Wine in the Wilderness* doesn't detract much from its impact."[73] Although he described the play's use of setting, characterization, and dialogue as "strictly kitchen sink realism" and continues that in terms of dramatic technique it "breaks no ground," he presumes that these minor shortcomings are "more than redeemed by an authenticity of feeling" that the cast captures with "unswerving intensity."[74] Kriegsman concluded by applauding the performances of all of the actors, but he was especially impressed by that of Abbey Lincoln as Tommy, describing her performance as one that "seems not to miss a single nuance of the character's turbulent transformation."[75]

Yet *On Being Black* producer Luther James, a former CBS television executive producer who left his post there to work on the series, challenged Kriegsman's contentions regarding the play's conclusion and its "kitchen sink realism" and champions drama's heightened capacity for transformation in contrast to other modes of representation, asserting that it "can illuminate human experiences in ways that cannot be realized by documentaries, by coverage of demonstrations or by the airing of grievances."[76] James's observation pointed to the prospects that plays like *Wine in the Wilderness* enable in effecting change in lives of their audiences. His notion echoed Lorraine Hansberry's notion of "genuine realism," which considered "not only what *is*, but what is *possible* . . . because that is part of reality too."[77] Childress herself affirmed those transformative possibilities, asserting in an 1969 appearance on WGBH's *Say Brother* broadcast that "we live in a day when everyone says tell it like it is—I want to tell it like it's going to be, because I'm hoping for something a little better than what we've been through."[78] *Wine in the Wilderness* offers a model for the possibilities that Childress and Hansberry discussed, whether or not mainstream critics heralded them.

While the mainstream press effectively ignored the broadcast, the African American press in Chicago, Los Angeles, and New York embraced the play's television premiere; in both Chicago and New York, they advocated for the play's stage debut shortly after it appeared in the series. The *New York Amsterdam News*'s Vivian Robinson urged readers to see the double bill *Wine in the Wilderness* shared with Childress's *Mojo*, staged by the newly formed New Heritage Repertory Theatre in Harlem, observing that while Tommy is introduced as an "object of ridicule," she "drastically changes the lives of those she meets."[79] Similarly, the *Los Angeles Sentinel* noted that Bill and Tommy's relationship "reveal[s] much about the difficulties inherent in the black experience."[80] Finally, the *Chicago Daily Defender* observed that the inaugural production of the newly established Black Theatre Workshop at Northern Illinois University offered an opportunity for reflection as it "does not just attack whites and white society but rather stresses the involvement of the truth among blacks" and contends that Tommy sparks a transformation among the group and "ends up teaching them a lot about black womanhood."[81]

These reviews not only illustrated the Kerner Commission's contention that "large news organizations would do well to establish better lines of communication to their counterparts in the Negro press," but also that the African American press took *Wine in the Wilderness*'s transformative possibilities seriously and made them accessible to its readership through its reviews.[82] Further, in announcing community theater productions of the play that occurred shortly after its television debut, they participated in and supported black theater that responds to Childress's 1951 call in "For A Strong Negro People's Theater" to work toward "the understanding and projection of Negro culture."[83] Most importantly, in writing about the opportunity to witness and reflect upon representations that speak to both an African American collective and individual African American identities, the black press contributes to enhancing the ways that African Americans understand themselves. The black press's work indicts the mainstream press and shows that the commission justly censured the national press for abdicating its duties to both white and black citizens to provide "a sense of the problems America faces and the sources of potential solutions."[84]

Ultimately, the black press's and Kriegsman's reviews recognized *Wine in the Wilderness*'s critique of normative gender and class representations as they have been framed within the African American Freedom Struggle. In so doing, they facilitated both Tommy's and Childress's anticipatory enactment of an African American community, a collective, which would embrace its complexities and contradictions. They set into a motion a representational pivot clearing the way for the collective Lorna Simpson gathered some thirty years later.

CHAPTER FIVE

Prefiguring Postblackness in Charles Gordone's *No Place to Be Somebody: A Black Black Comedy in Three Acts*

After his move from Santa Monica's multicultural, but primarily white, social context to the predominantly African American and Latino West Los Angeles community of Hillside, Gunnar Kauffman describes how his status in Santa Monica as "the whitest Negro in captivity" fails to translate to the visual and corporeal rhetoric of black identity in Hillside's social spaces.[1] Paul Beatty's 1996 novel, *The White Boy Shuffle*, traces Gunnar's coming of age and awkward mastery of Hillside's black identity rhetoric. While his initial status there is bleak, or as he asserts, "In a world where body and spoken language were currency, I was broke as hell," Gunnar's simultaneously painful and humorous experiences in Hillside ultimately enable his own iteration of black identity.[2] Yet his self-fashioning only comes after he pries blackness apart from the currency—the body and spoken language—that elude him when he arrives in Hillside and adapts that currency to suit his needs. The novel inscribes Gunnar's unwieldy, but still successful, navigation of Hillside in his default "barely acceptable" dance step, the white boy shuffle.[3] Though it does not enable a full translation into Hillside's social space, the move allows him to remain in, but not fully of, that social space, or as he describes it, "I wasn't funky, but I was no longer disrupting the groove."[4] As a cultural mulatto who troubles blackness and "hold[s] it up for examination," Gunnar locates himself within Hillside's social space yet navigates its contingencies by both engaging and critiquing its groove—or its framing of black identity.

Gabe Gabriel similarly engages and critiques Johnny's Bar and the intraracial social space of Greenwich Village in Charles Gordone's 1969 Pulitzer Prize–winning play, *No Place to Be Somebody: A Black Black Comedy in Three Acts*. Interrogating blackness and suggesting that black identity does not exclusively reside in the bodily currency Gunnar discusses, Gabe contends,

> Yes! They's mo' to bein' black than meets
> The eye!
> It's all the stuff that nobody wants but
> Cain't live without!
> It's the body that keeps us standin'! The
> Soul that keeps us goin'! An' the spirit
> That'll take us thooo!
> Yes! They's mo' to bein' black than meets
> The eye!

Both Gunnar and Gabe argue that there is more to being black than the visual rhetoric read in and on black bodies. Offering themselves as iterations of the cultural mulatto figure that "worr[ies] blackness, . . . stir[s] it up, . . . touch[es] it, feel[s] it out and hold[s] it up for examination," they challenge critic Madhu Dubey's framing of the cultural mulatto as "the tragic 'victims' of the Civil Rights movement, caught between two worlds and burdened by anxieties about their racially ambivalent status."[5] Instead, they escape the conundrum Dubey describes through their explorations of blackness in their respective texts that enable them to comfortably occupy their own concepts of black identity. Still, their examinations of blackness are met with varying degrees of suspicion and hostility from within and outside of the various social contexts in which they are embedded in both texts, as both protagonists encounter ridicule, censure, and in some instances both, for their refusal to embody blackness according to what each social space and context demands. As a result, both Gabe's and Gunnar's "blaxplorations" invite questions about their iterations of blackness, and in particular, whether or not their self-fashioned blackness is "authentic."[6] In other words, they put their blackness in jeopardy and risk having their "black card" revoked by enacting their notions of black identity outside of those social spheres' standards.

Charles Gordone's own blaxplorations met similar ends. After the critical and financial success of *No Place*, which ran on Broadway for more than a year and went on a national tour for three years, he staged a one-man show, *Gordone Is a Muthah*, in 1971. At the end of *No Place*'s national tour, he continued writing and directing in community theater across the country, staging his play *Anabiosis* by the City Players of St. Louis in 1979. By this time, Gordone was struggling with alcoholism, which he would later blame in part on his early successes and difficulties in completing work in a form that he felt was polished enough for production.

After gaining sobriety in 1985, Gordone found an academic home teaching in Texas A&M University's Theatre Arts Department in 1987. At nearly the same time, he was awarded a D. H. Lawrence Fellowship from the University of New Mexico, where he would live at the Lawrence Ranch in the Sangre de Cristo Mountains. The residency there initiated an exploration of the late 1980s Western revival, specifically cowboy songs and poetry that he would pursue until his death in 1995. Immersing himself in cowboy gatherings held in Texas, Colorado, New Mexico, and Wyoming, Gordone sought to "remythologize" the West by seeking out African Americans' presence in the story of "how the West was won."[7] He looked toward providing a legacy to others in search of African American history in the West, writing that he wanted "the coming generations to know there were such men" as York, a member of the Lewis and Clark expedition; Moses "Black" Harris, a fur trader and trapper; Edward Rose, the son of a white trader and an African American and Cherokee woman who helped build a fort at Big Horn and lived with the Crow Indians; Jim Pierce, an expedition cook and guide; and James P. Beckwourth, a fur trader and explorer who discovered Beckwourth Pass through the Sierra Nevada Mountains and who was, by Gordone's estimation, "a figure suited to the making of Western legend,"[8] and his final works engaged this legacy. Set on a ranch in the Kansas prairie, his final completed play, *Roan Browne & Cherry*, staged in 1988, traces the romantic relationship between the African American ranch hand Roan and Cherry, the Native American and white daughter of his widowed and bankrupt white employer. At the time of his death, Gordone was working on a new play called *The Fugitive*, which was inspired by figures such as Beckwourth. Speaking to his concerns about the African American presence in the West, he envisioned the play's protagonist, Ben Factor, "as an African American who will take his logical place with those whose names have been immortalized in American history."[9]

Yet Gordone's explorations served his insistence on a multicultural and integrated theater relying upon the stories of all the country's racial and ethnic groups to create what he called a truly "American" theater. He was a proponent of color-blind casting, or in his preferred phrase, "seeing casting," in productions of *Night of the Iguana*, *A Streetcar Named Desire*, *The Iceman Cometh*, and other classic plays with his life-partner Susan Kouyomijian at Berkeley's American Stage from 1977 through 1982. Framing his investigations into the African American presence in the American West as one facet in his efforts to "resurrect [its] multicultural power" and to "establish a richer connection with the present for all Americans," he argued for the black experience as part of an untold national story, or as he suggested in an interview, he understood the "American experience as an American theater."[10] In relating that experience, however, Gordone rejected a stand-alone African American theater tradition, instead relocating it to the multiethnic American theater tradition he sought to advance. Continuing that challenge to racial boundaries, he often self-identified as a "man of color" whose multiethnic ancestry, "part Indian, part French, part Irish and part nigger," made him quintessentially American.[11] Those and similar assertions about his racial identity, black theater, and the relationship between blacks and whites in the United States drew the ire of critics and cultural producers taking part in the Black Arts/Aesthetic Movements still in progress at the time of *No Place to be Somebody*'s production. Though he situated both himself and what many critics have called his alter ego, Gabe Gabriel, as interrogating racial identity's boundaries, contending that "the black experience isn't all black and the white world isn't all white," such assertions put Gordone's racial integrity at risk with Black Arts practitioners, including poet and playwright Amiri Baraka and critic Clayton Riley. Insisting at the play's debut that he was unfazed by African American cultural producers who accused him of race treason, toward the end of his life Gordone admitted that he had been "dazed, hurt, confused and filled with self-pity" by their response to him and his play and felt he was "ironically . . . left with no place to be!"[12] Consequently, Gordone echoed here the conundrum Beatty's cultural mulatto, Gunnar Kauffman, discusses about his zero cultural balance in Hillside. Likewise, Gabe Gabriel's parallel assertion in *No Place to Be Somebody* that there is more to being black than meets the eye causes his cultural displacement by the play's end. Yet Gabe's exploration of black subjectivity beyond its imagined boundaries also illuminates its postblack resources. While Gunnar's white boy shuffle marks a kind of provisional revision of Hillside's black identity rhetoric and his awkward trading in its spoken and bodily currency, Gabe's solo performances trouble the black identity rhetoric of the Freedom Struggle era and consequently mobilize his iteration of black subjectivity. Locating himself within the black social and discursive spaces of the 1963 March on Washington and Black Arts cultural nationalism, Gabe's performances navigate blackness's contingencies by engaging and critiquing black identity's framing within those spaces.

Cultural critic Michael Eric Dyson has argued that the long-standing African American strategy against racial oppression in the United States to "prove in word and deed that we were not the savages [whites] said we were" sacrificed "the depth of variety for the breadth of unity" within African American identity's discourse.[13] In effect, disproving white supremacist ideologies about African American identity diminishes the complexities and contradictions inherent within African American identity and its representation. While racial uplift ideology's prominence in the late nineteenth and early twentieth centuries, as well as its continued relevance through the present moment, demonstrates one strategy of contending with those white supremacist ideologies, cultural producers of the postblack era still resist its remainders. Conversely, cultural nationalism within the Black Arts/Aesthetic Movements of the 1960s presented another set of ideologies that, while it sought to develop authentic African American cultural expression wrested free from a Western aesthetic model, was potentially just as restrictive in its impact on black representation as disproving white supremacist ideologies through a strategy like racial uplift ideology.

Larry Neal's foundational essay, "The Black Arts Movement" (1968), provides one example among several aesthetic statements indicative of the era's sometimes narrow framing of African American identity. Turning to Jimmy Garrett's *We Own the Night* (1968), Ben Caldwell's *Militant Preacher* (1967) which was later staged as *Prayer Meeting, or the First Militant Minister* in 1969, and Ron Milner's *Who's Got His Own* (1966) as exemplars of a black aesthetic, Neal argued that these plays begin with "the premise of a well-defined Afro-American audience ... that must see itself and the world in terms of its own interests."[14] He continued by outlining what the movement will *not* do—repeat the failures of the Harlem Renaissance of the early twentieth century—and asserted that the artists and writers of that era neglected addressing themselves to "the mythologies and the life-styles of the Black community ... the struggles of that community" and thus failed to become "its voice and spirit."[15] In identifying a unifying premise of the plays, Neal posed the Black Arts Movement's artistic production as a response to a monolithic black community's needs and that further, Black Arts cultural producers should speak to and for that monolithic black community and its needs. However, it is precisely that notion of black identity as monolithic and that requires representative speakers and texts for its correct or authentic representation which both produced the cultural conditions that bring postblackness into being and that postblack critics and writers reject. In short, while postblack cultural producers respect the advances wrought during the Black Arts Movement by statements like Neal's, they also seek to explore blackness from new vantages that reveal, as critic Wahneema Lubiano has asserted, "what it looks like when you're no longer caught by your own trauma about racism and the history of black people in the United States ... [and] everything is up for grabs as a possibility."[16]

This chapter argues that Charles Gordone envisioned such possibilities in *No Place to Be Somebody: A Black Black Comedy in Three Acts* and in so doing crafted a play that provides an ideological pivot to postblack subjectivity discourse. By framing the play's protagonist, Gabe Gabriel, as a cultural mulatto who disrupts Black Arts' notions of a monolithic black community and by employing an iteration of allusion-disruption ideology that reimagines the 1963 March on Washington for Jobs and Freedom, *No Place to Be Somebody* interrogates racial boundaries and worries blackness in ways that anticipate postblack identity discourse.

No Place to Be Somebody traces an interracial group of patrons and em-

No Place to be Somebody: A Black Black Comedy. 1970 Arena Stage Playbill. Collection of the author.

ployees of Johnny's Bar in Greenwich Village and follows the increasingly contentious and ultimately deadly relationship between Gabe Gabriel, an often unemployed African American writer and actor, and the bar's African American owner, Johnny Williams, over Johnny's planned attempt to take over gambling, prostitution, and drug trafficking activity in the Village from the white crime bosses there. Johnny's intended partner in the takeover, his mentor Sweets Crane, discovers—upon his release from jail after serving ten years on a racketeering conviction—that he is terminally ill and reveals to Johnny that he no longer wants to participate in the takeover. However, Johnny is insistent that they continue with the plan despite Sweets's and Gabe's pleas, which leads to a violent confrontation between Johnny and Gabe and, ultimately, to Johnny's death at Gabe's hands.

Though theater and performance critic Harry J. Elam Jr.'s discussion of the play did not explicitly name the play as a precursor to postblack identity discourse, it gestured toward such a move. Arguing that the play's protagonist, Gabe Gabriel, engages the tendency in 1960s Black Arts/Aesthetic discourse toward a narrow concept of black identity, Elam read three of his five solo performances within the play as interventions that simultaneously "critique and celebrate those romanticized and essentialized ideals."[17] Contending that these performances "simultaneously blur and extend the space between theatrical illusion and reality," Elam asserted that Gabe's moves outside of the immediate context and action of the play enable a "productive ambivalence" allowing him to "reflect and comment on the action and on race in ways that a position of merely being inside the representation could not afford him."[18] Expanding Elam's contentions, I argue that each of Gabe's performances serves as allusion-disruption moments in which he offers alternate readings of both the Black Arts/Aesthetic Movements' as well as the Civil Rights Movement's implications for black subjectivity. Each solo performance comments upon the play's action preceding the solo performance or foreshadows its ensuing action in crafting its iteration of black subjectivity. Ultimately, Gabe casts black subjectivity into relief by demonstrating how the African American Freedom Struggle's most familiar tropes fail to contain or signify his complex meanings.

The first act and scene cue those efforts as Gabe argues for the play's truth rooted in his lived experience, which he simultaneously writes and performs: "Might not believe it but I'm gonna make it all up in my head as I go along. Before I prove it to you, wanna warn you not to be thinkin' I'm tellin' you a bunch'a barefaced lies. An' no matter how far out I git, don't want you goin' out'a here with the idea what you see happenin' is all a figment of my grassy imagination. 'Cause it ain't!"[19] While as Elam suggested, Gabe argues here for

March on Washington for Jobs and Freedom. August 28, 1963. AP Photo.

his dual role as both writer of and actor in the play, or as an ambivalent representation that reveals the playwright Gordone's art and artifice to the audience, Gordone's alter ego, Gabe, also advocates for the narrative's veracity and his own reliability as both an actor and narrator.[20] By framing the play as one that departs from conventions in ways that might cause the audience to perceive it as a fabrication or a drug-induced hallucination, Gordone and Gabe insinuate that *No Place* will challenge the dramatic, narrative, and racial conventions with which the audience is familiar and prepare them for the ways in which the play might defy their notions of blackness and black subjectivity. Ultimately, they argue for a willing suspension of disbelief in dramatic, narrative conventions that might impede the interventions the play offers, beginning with a watershed event of the Civil Rights Movement, the 1963 March on Washington for Jobs and Freedom.[21]

As Gabe's performance troubles a master narrative of the civil rights era that has come to "dominate American social memory," it similarly deconstructs the monolithic, unified black community alluded to in Larry Neal's "The Black Arts Movement," as well as the monolithic black community underwriting the success of the March itself.[22] Beginning with the *Brown v. Board of Education* Supreme Court decision in 1954, the heroic period continues with public protests such as the March on Washington, marks the passage of the Voting Rights Act of 1965 as the era's apex and, finally, and locates the Civil Rights Movement's decline in the Black Power/Black Arts era heralded by Student Nonviolent Coordinating Committee (SNCC) activist Stokely Carmichael's calls for black power in 1966.[23] Historian Jacqueline Dowd Hall goes further to discuss the master narrative's reliance upon "bowdlerized heroes" such as Martin Luther King, who she contends is, in the current historical moment, "frozen in 1963, proclaiming 'I have a dream' during the march on the Mall."[24] Recounting, but reimagining the March in a solo performance poem, Gabe offers a counternarrative to the broader Freedom Struggle master narrative that pits such heroes against Black Arts/Aesthetic villains as well as deconstructs the master narrative's representation of a monolithic black community on the Mall on August 28, 1963. He instead emphasizes the tensions and ambiguities underlying the mediated representations of the March by first reconsidering its participant/observers at the Lincoln Memorial; second, by recasting King's "I Have a Dream" speech; and, finally, by speculating on the representational strategies the March employs in its pursuit of racial equality.

Just after Gabe counsels the audience on the willing suspension of disbelief's necessity in engaging the play's representations, he takes up the degree to which the March on Washington's representations sacrificed "the depth of variety for the breadth of unity."[25] After he appears at the bar and shares the news that he has failed to be cast in another production, Cora, one of the regulars, asks him to perform "one o' them crazy po'ms," and Johnny instructs him to "make it sump'm you know."[26] Gabe's poem initially reconstructs the March as a racially inclusive and unifying event, very much in the same vein as most of the five organizations sponsoring the event attempted to frame it. The Southern Christian Leadership Conference (SCLC), National Association for the Advancement of Colored People (NAACP), Congress of Racial Equality (CORE), the Urban League, and the Student Nonviolent Coordinating Committee (SNCC) emphasized unity among the organizations, but there was ongoing behind-the-scenes discord about the means to that end. As an example, at a meeting to organize the March, both Roy Wilkins of the NAACP and Whitney Young of the Urban League threatened to withdraw their support if the openly gay Bayard Rustin was appointed to head it. As a result, A. Philip Randolph, president of the Brotherhood of Sleeping Car Porters and originator of the idea for the March, became its official head, but Rustin remained responsible for all of the organizing.

Further, for both the NAACP and the Urban League, the March's purpose was to support President Kennedy's civil rights bill, while for CORE and the SCLC, economic issues including employment were just as important as effective civil rights legislation. Consequently, Wilkins, one of the March speakers, insisted on banning placards that were critical of the Kennedy administration and argued for capitulation to other demands made by the administration as a condition of the NAACP's participation.[27] Additionally, SNCC was hesitant to provide its support for the March largely because the group viewed it as a means of containing rising black militancy. However, the group and its new president, John Lewis, acceded to the wishes of its local organizers, who were enthused by the March's prospects; ultimately, SNCC was unwilling to break the unity of the Freedom Movement.[28] Yet even on the day of the March, Lewis was forced to considerably revise his speech and soften its critique of the Kennedy administration in order to placate Wilkins as well as Washington, DC's archbishop, Patrick O'Boyle, who was slated to give the invocation and who threatened to pull out of the event if Lewis's speech wasn't revised.[29]

Yet the ambivalence reflected in SNCC's stance toward the March finds resonances in Gabe's recounting of it. Situating himself as a participant in and observer of the event, he suggests that he shares SNCC's concerns about it. He initially advances the notion of unity at the outset of his performance, contending

> *They met on the banks of the Potomac, the rich, the great and the small!*
> *It's impossible to tell you, should'a been there an' seen it all!*
> *They came by train, by plane, by bus an' by car!*
> *Bicycle an' tricycle from near an' very far!*
> *On mule an' on horseback!*
> *With greasy bag an' kroker sack!*

He continues, addressing the cross section of onlookers and participants:

> *Carts with motors, an' trams!*
> *Wheelchairs an' wheelbarrels an' women pushing prams!*
> *Little boys on scooters! Little girls on skates!*
> *Beatnicks, hippies, an' hoboes, most of them had come by freights!*
> *We had walked in light-footed an' barefooted, had walked all out'a*
> *Our shoes! Some hopped it on crutches for days!*
> *An' then we got the news, some black power agitators was arrested along the*
> * way!*[30]

In sketching the crowd gathered there, Gabe finally notes that there were *"a lotta Cadillacs an' Buicks, rich people showin' off,"* but says he *"didn't pay that no min,'"* since he took "comfort in the thought that we needed people of every kin'!"³¹ Gabe takes pains to denaturalize representations of the March in cultural memory by emphasizing the broad range of people in attendance as well as the many modes of transportation utilized by grassroots participants and observers who came to Washington, DC, to take part in it. Many of the March's 250,000 participants and observers were bussed in from across the country on some 2,000 buses, 21 special trains, and 10 aircraft. Others, particularly DC residents, used the modes of transportation Gabe outlines, but significantly, he draws attention to those participants and observers who are not rich or showing off, as he puts it.³² Rather than focusing on the mediated images of the speakers and celebrities who participated in the onstage action at the March, as much of the media coverage of the event did, Gabe shifts attention to the everyday, ordinary people on the ground there. In so doing, he highlights the ways in which it encompassed participants from a broad range of social backgrounds and political perspectives. Yet as he continues his reimagining of the March, King's marquee speech fuels his increasing uneasiness about its coalition politics, the monolithic black community that his speech implies, and the March's emphasis on King as the bowdlerized hero who becomes central to cultural memory of the event.

The coalition had been held together in large part by the linchpin of direct nonviolent protests—the representation of a unified black public through protestors' demonstrations of respectability and civility. Participants in sit-ins and other actions were told to dress in their Sunday best and to remain cordial and polite at all costs according to historians Marissa Chappell, Jenny Hutchinson, and Brian Ward. Respectability and civility refuted white supremacist claims that "segregation was absolutely essential to defend American civilization from contamination by uncivilized blacks with their congenital ignorance, sloth, promiscuity and irresponsibility" during the early 1960s Freedom Struggle.³³ Nearly every aspect of the March alludes to this strategy of emphasizing respectability and civility as a means of inclusion in the American body politic, and it is reflected in "An Appeal by the March Leaders" that was widely distributed ahead of the event and read in part that the March "will be unified in purposes and behavior, not splintered into groups and individual competitors."³⁴ Still, it focused on leadership to help encourage unity and that leader was King. Alluding to his introduction to the stage, Gabe contends,

> *Said they had on han' the speaker of our choice!*
> *Said this black man was a black man of black deeds an' black fame!*

(I'll be damned to hell, I disremember his name!)
Then a hush fell on them people that night,
'Cause we was there for one thing, our civil right![85]

Once again, Gabe deemphasizes the necessity of key figures in the movement by suggesting that he cannot remember the name of the March on Washington's key speaker who had, seven years beyond the success of the Montgomery Bus Boycott, gained national and international fame. But he also points to the question of leadership within the Freedom Struggle by framing the hush when King takes the stage as reverence for his ensuing speech as a course of action in obtaining social equality. In effect, the participant/observers he sketched at the outset of the poem await instruction from *"the blackman of black deeds an' black fame."*[36] Those instructions call for African Americans to set aside intraracial differences, to rally around King, and finally to reject militancy as he asserts, *"unite an' not roam to other orguzashuns who jus' wanted to fight white people an' get what they can in a country that would soon give liberty an' 'quality to every man!"*[37] Recounting the payoff for compliance with the instructions, Gabe conveys King's assertion that *"if we worked long an' hard, he admitted it'd be rough! But he said, black unity an' solidarity would be enough!"*[38] Reminding the audience that he will "try to remember what [King] said," Gabe performs skinning a team of mules that stand in for African Americans' wide-ranging social locations and political perspectives that undermine the notion of a monolithic black community:

Hya!
You, Afro-Americans!
Hya!
You, American Afros!
Hya!
You Muslims an' nay-cee-pees!
Hya!
You so-called Negroes!
Tan liberals!
Black radicals!
Hya!
You respect-rabble black boorwahzees!
Hya!
Black Demos an' Publicans,
Git back on the track!
You Nash-na-lissys and Marx-a-sissies

Who all been pin-pointin' black!
Hya!
You half-white pro-fesh-nals!
Hya!
Civil rights pro-sesh-nals!
Hya!
You cursed sons-a-ham!
Don't rock no boat!
Don't cut ne'r tho'oat!
Be a beacon for some black magazeen!
Come doctor!
Come lawyer!
Come teacher!
Black employer!
An' keepers of white latrines![39]

Likening King to the mule driver and participants/observers to the mule team, Gabe proposes that King demonstrates dominance over the African American team in order to advance notions of black respectability and civility underwriting the representation of African American unity to satisfy the white normative gaze. However crass such imagery might be, particularly in the year marking the centennial anniversary of the Emancipation Proclamation, it remains that Gabe's solo performance works here in two ways. First, it serves as a critique of the top-down leadership model for the pursuit of racial equality that SNCC had initially opposed but that became central to the March's behind-the-scenes wrangling. Second, his performance throws into relief the impossibilities of a monolithic black community by showing the incongruence among the team members that undermines a narrative of black unity. His reimagining argues that the team pulling the Civil Rights Movement's wagon runs the social and professional gamut—from janitors to doctors, teachers, and lawyers, as well as the full political scope of possibilities—from the apolitical, NACCP activists, Marxists, cultural nationalists, to Republicans and Democrats. But in his performance as King, Gabe also recasts such diversity as requiring rehabilitation—it has led African Americans off course, which necessitates a call for them, in Gabe's performance of King, "to git back on track."[40] Significantly, Gabe points out that each team member, no matter the political or social vantage, seeks to "pinpoint" black or to singularly identify and fix black subjectivity, and his performance within the performance as King suggests that King himself attempts to rehabilitate and rein in black identities by forging a monolithic black identity that is then pressed into respectability and civility's service. In effect, Gabe outlines the conundrum of black representation in his counternarrative to the 1963 March: cultivating and performing a monolithic black community as a condition of full citizenship exposes the hypocrisy of white leaders and institutions bestowing those rights because it diminishes black subjectivity's complexities in its expulsion of dissenting perspectives and representations to secure them.

Gabe's poem proposes that the "living petition" of the March sacrifices "the depth of variety for the breadth of unity" in its representation of African American subjectivity and in so doing offers a postblack intervention to the politics of civility and respectability underwriting the Civil Rights Movement. Critic Bertram Ashe points to characters that traverse racial boundaries in the development of black subjectivity and that summon and signify on previous eras of African American history as well as the ideologies and representations linked to those historical moments in his theorization of postblack—or what he calls post-soul—texts.[41] However, the primary distinction between postblack texts and their predecessors resides in the post-soul artist's "relationship to the idea of freedom."[42] In short, the absence of an organized struggle for freedom in the post-soul era shifts freedom's emphasis in earlier periods from a fixed, monolithic black identity to the post-soul period's explorations of such constructions. Yet Gabe's reimagining of the March on Washington for Jobs and Freedom exposes and explores precisely such a shift.

A turn to the poem's final three stanzas helps to illustrate the ways in which he explores constructions of African American identity within the African American Freedom Struggle's historical context and proposes a shift in black subjectivity's relationship to the idea of freedom. Continuing his earlier critique of bowdlerized heroes and African American leadership, Gabe's recounting of King's speech traces both the monolith's unraveling and the possibilities it provides:

> *What's needed to save us*
> *Is not Some-a-Davus*
> *Or even Benjammer O.!*
> *Giddy-up! Yippeee-ay! Or Kidney Poteeay!*
> *They already got they dough!*
> *Now, here are the bare facks,*
> *Grab yo'selves by the bootblacks!*
> *Leave Heroin Manderson on the side!*

Speaking as King, Gabe critiques the prominence of African American celebrities including Sammy Davis Jr., Marian Anderson, and Sidney Poitier in the March's proceedings, as well as political figures such as U.S. Air Force General and commander of the Tuskegee Airmen Benjamin O. Davis, who helped draft the executive order integrating the U.S. armed forces that President Harry Truman signed in 1948. Framing their prominence as a distraction from the pursuit of economic empowerment for all African Americans, as "they already got they dough," and in a willing suspension of disbelief that asks the audience to traverse 1963 and 1968, Gabe signifies on King's "Remaining Awake through a Great Revolution" sermon at the National Cathedral in March 1968. In that sermon, King dispelled what he called an "over reliance on the bootstrap philosophy," which argues that African American freedom from discrimination and segregation demands that blacks lift themselves out of oppression by their own bootstraps.[43] Yet Gabe's signifying on King's sermon acknowledges both the myth and its rebuttal as an interminable dispute that the March and any ensuing legislation cannot resolve. In other words, the March's performance of a monolithic black community does not engage the means of economic empowerment for most African Americans—"the small"—as he refers to them at the outset of the poem; it instead circumscribes representation of the black community for the sake of the March and its premise that it must be "unified in purposes and behavior" in order to serve its "living petition" for civil rights.[44] What, then, do "the small" gain in return for their compliance with the March's living petition? Gabe speculates:

> *We'll have invented a machine that delivers*
> *A cream to make crackers pay the debt!*
> *Now junkies don't dilly*
> *You husslers don't dally!*
> *Don't waste yo' time smokin' pot*
> *In some park or some alley,*
> *'Cause Cholly is watchin' you!*[45]

As he acknowledges the white normative gaze with "Cholly is watchin' you!"—Uncle Charlie or, effectively, the white public—Gabe makes protest's futility legible. Signifying on George Schuyler's 1931 novel, *Black No More*, which satirizes the invention of a serum that turns black skin white and its impact on the nation, Gabe facetiously asserts that March leaders and organizers can produce a cream compelling the nation to repay its debts—

both economic and moral—to African Americans. In short, by satirizing the means of compelling the debts' repayment within a performance of the March, Gabe illustrates that a bid for equality that demands the politics of respectability and civility for its success is just as fanciful as the discovery of a cream that would force the debts' repayment. Moreover, he insists that the uncertain transactions offered—a monolithic black community bound up by respectability and civility in the March's performance in order to secure full African American citizenship—cannot address the underlying social challenges faced by "the small," drug addicts and petty criminals who potentially undermine that performance. In sum, Gabe points to the ideological shortcomings of the March specifically, and of protest broadly construed. Emphasizing its contingency as it relies upon white consent "to grant and guarantee complete equality in citizenship," Gabe recognizes that the March's emphasis on civility and respectability to gain that consent may not elicit the results it seeks.[46] Likewise, that recognition resonates with Black Arts/Aesthetic practitioners' framing of protest's failures. Critic Etheridge Knight defined the act of protest as "the belief that a change will be forthcoming once the masters are aware of the protestor's 'grievance.'"[47] At the poem's close, he returns to his position as an observer of the March and details his and the other observers' response to King's speech, calling further attention to the monolith's unraveling:

> *When he sat down wasn't a clap ner a soun',*
> *Couldn't tell if he'd got to the end!*
> *A cracker preacher there, then said a prayer!*
> *Said civil rights you could not fo'ce!*
> *By this time I was so confused my head was in a spin!*
> *Somebody else got up with a grinnin' face!*
> *Said to leave that place like we found it!*
> *Tha's when I reached in my pocket an' pulled out my packet an' before everybody took a sip'a my wine!*
> *Then we lef' that place without ne'r trace!*
> *An' we didn't leave ne'r chit'lin' behin'*
> *Everyone laughs and claps his hands.*[48]

Shifting back to his role as an observer reveals further ambiguities in the programmatic direct action protest the March proposes and in the unified black community underwriting it. By the speech's end, Gabe and the other observers are unsure of what African Americans' course of action might be as it is not revealed or detailed by King; they cannot determine whether he has finished his speech, which leaves the appropriate course of action as an unanswered and, finally, unresolvable question. Further, though the March's living petition aims to assuage warnings from a range of constituencies that civil rights cannot be forced, the preacher's continued support of moderate progress echoes Knight's contentions about protest's failures. In effect, the preacher's refusal demonstrates that despite its meticulous planning and execution, the March's performance fails to compel a change in perspectives even among the purported supporters taking part in the events on stage. Alluding to the white participants who refused to congratulate SNCC's John Lewis even after he revised his speech, Gabe reads the impossibility of a singular course of action for African Americans in the March's wake. His attempt to navigate the convergences and the discontinuities among the range of ideological perspectives on civil rights represented on the March stage leaves him bewildered, with his head *"in a spin."*[49]

His cynicism finds resonances in the debate over and passage of Civil Rights Act of 1964. In a June 1963 speech just over two months before the March, President Kennedy called for civil rights legislation banning discrimination in public accommodations but did not include other provisions that civil rights activists had demanded, including protection from police brutality and discrimination in private employment as well as empowering the Justice Department to pursue desegregation and job discrimination lawsuits. However, the Judiciary Committee of the House of Representatives strengthened the bill to include those provisions, and it was then referred to the Rules Committee in November 1963, where its segregationist chair, Virginia's Howard W. Smith, vowed to let it languish. In spite of this, President Kennedy's assassination later that month changed the national mood toward the bill and in light of that shift, Smith relented, enabling its approval by the committee. Still, the bill met resistance on the Senate floor, where it was stalled by a fifty-four-day Senate filibuster conducted by the Southern Bloc, consisting of eighteen southern senators who vehemently opposed the bill's passage. This resulted in Minnesota senator Hubert Humphrey's introduction of a weaker compromise bill that attracted enough Republican swing votes to end the filibuster, and the compromise measure was signed into law by President Lyndon Johnson on July 2, 1964. Gabe's skepticism speaks to a fundamental duplicity on full citizenship for African Americans illustrated not only in the bill's debate and passage, but in the preacher's deferment in his March address as well. Though the Civil Rights Act of 1964 ultimately became law, it was opposed at nearly every turn, and its passage was viewed by many as a memorial to President Kennedy's assassination, not a national mandate on civil rights. Despite his cynicism about the March's aims and the confusion it provokes as he and the other observers emerge from the Mall, Gabe traces how the discontinuities across perspectives represented on the March stage can be read as productive for black subjectivity beyond a collective expression of respectability and civility. Problematizing the March on Washington's master narrative in cultural memory as a univocal and ideologically unified event, Gabe's performance of the March deconstructs notions of intraracial and interracial unity undergirding those narratives, clearing discursive space for the iteration of black subjectivity offered at the play's end.

But while legislation fell short of the civil rights organizations' demands and the March's performance attempted to constrain African American subjectivity, in the final lines of the poem, Gabe and the other observers reject the binary opposition between respectability and full citizenship offered in the March's representational strategies. Gabe's sip of wine at the March's close alludes to the state of emergency declared in Washington, DC, on August 28 that closed all bars and liquor stores in the city. Mindful of claims by the *Washington Daily News* that "the vandals are coming to sack Rome" and NBC News's *Meet the Press* moderator Lawrence Spivak's assertion that "it would be impossible to bring more than 100,000 militant Negroes into Washington without incidents and possibly rioting," Gabe's sip marks a disavowal of the March's representational strategies. It disregards both the white mainstream press's insinuation that full citizenship necessitates a prerequisite demonstration of black respectability at the March and the capitulation of March organizers to such an implication.[50] Building on his credibility as an effective critical reader of the March's pitfalls and promises, Gabe acknowledges the utility of unity in leaving the Mall as they found it, but renounces the fear and hysteria around the gathering of black people there. In a final signifying read of the March, Gabe turns to one African American culinary tradition—chitlins—to underscore that black unity put in the service of pursuing racial equality need not expunge African American folkways, nor must it accept the assumption that African Americans are incapable of demonstrating civic responsibility.[51]

In the end, Gabe Gabriel as solo performer and Charles Gordone as playwright offer a reading of the March on Washington that draws upon multiple social and political contexts as a viable means of developing identity that refuses to be moored to any singular mode of representation or any one political ideology. It calls for African Americans to turn their critical lenses inward and to reconsider the ways in which the heroic period of the Civil Rights Movement shapes African American cultural production to both productive and counterproductive ends. Not unlike other representations of African American identity, the heroic era of the Civil Rights Movement does not speak univocally and upon examination reveals the competing ideologies within the heroic era in ways that uncannily prefigure postblack discourse and identity.

While Gabe's initial solo performance's deconstruction of the March on Washington's representational strategies might gesture toward the cultural nationalism embraced by Amiri Baraka, Larry Neal, and other Black Arts Movement critics and writers, his short monologue in the first act's second scene addressing what he calls "social protest jive" refuses such an association. Gabe's performance of the March on Washington locates its limitations in its capitulation to the politics of respectability, while the play's second scene identifies rage as a flaw in cultural nationalism that likens it to a strain of protest. Though he does not dispute its validity or its value and acknowledges the productive power of rage informing some iterations of Black Arts expression, the monologue opening the second scene frames his tenuous relationship to rage and its expression.

Echoing *Dutchman*'s Clay, Gabe locates the roots of his rage about racial injustice in his social isolation, which initiates reflection on "all manner of treachery an' harm" he imagines awaits him beyond his home.[52] Revealing that he has been alone for two months, he asserts "sometimes I git to feelin'—like I get so vicious, I wanna go out an' commit mass murder."[53] Yet even as he identifies as a black playwright and acknowledges his rage, Gabe intervenes in a frequently invoked and reductive association between black playwrights and racial propaganda best reflected in critic Martin Gottfried's contentions about the cultural nationalism reflected in black theater companies such Robert Hooks and Douglas Turner Ward's Negro Ensemble Company as well as the work of playwrights such as Ed Bullins and Amiri Baraka. Gottfried argues that black playwrights' compulsion to "write about black people and the racial situation," which on one hand offers "the intensity of black anger [that] gives their plays a special drive," also impedes artistic expression or, as Gottfried asserts, "is a restriction on content that deprives these writers of an independent existence as artists."[54] He concludes that such deprivations negatively impact the plays' artistic value and dangerously approaches social protest as it "encourages propaganda and inevitably leads to agit-prop plays."[55]

But as critic bell hooks has argued, rage precipitates actions to resist oppression and offers an opportunity for transformation. Further, she has warned that denying its transformative potential "creates a cultural climate where the psychological impact of racism can be ignored. . . . Racism can then be represented as an issue for blacks only, a mere figment of our perverse paranoid imaginations."[56] In a play that began with Gabe's directive that its content is not a figment of his "grassy imagination," reading his discussion of rage through the prism of the transformative possibilities that hooks describes has multiple implications.[57] First, while he acknowledges his rage at racial injustice, he also posits that it does not impede or consume his artistic vision; he is not "hung up on crap like persecution an' hatred."[58] As a result, Gabe simultaneously hails rage's transformative capacity as well as a representation of black subjectivity beyond the limits of rage's expression. In other words, Gabe provides a glimpse of what black subjectivity might look like, as critic Wahneema Lubiano would have it, "when you're no longer caught by your own trauma about racism and the history of black people in the United States."[59] Second, Gabe's contention that in both the play and his solo performances he elects to "leave that social protest jive to them cats who are better equipped than me" speaks once again to protest's failures, but in contrast to his critique of the March on Washington, which focused on monolithic black identity, this reference frames Black Arts' cultural nationalism as social protest by a different name. His signifying read then, aligns the work of critics including Baraka, Neal, Knight, and others with social protest, a form that they vehemently denounced as anti-black and counterrevolutionary. Still, Gabe's framing of Black Arts' cultural nationalism significantly differs from Gottfried's in its refusal to deny protest's artistic merits. In short, while Gabe critiques and ultimately rejects protest as an appropriate vehicle for his expression, he does not dismiss its viability for other artists. Proclaiming his vantage as a black playwright and tracing black subjectivity beyond the boundaries enforced by both black and white critics, Gabe not only eludes their limitations on black expression; he also clears discursive space for black subjectivity's iterations that interrogate those boundaries by the play's end.

Mapping and establishing the play's aesthetic and ideological terrain by reimagining the March on Washington and reframing black rage in his first two solo performances, Gabe continues to limn black subjectivity in the remaining three solo performances. Further interrogating racial categories, Act Two opens with Gabe's spoken word interpretation of the Protestant church hymn *Whiter Than Snow*, which addresses his family's experience of residential desegregation. His performance of the hymn unsettles the binary racial categories black and white and, as Elam has observed, "negotiate[es] the space between the two, to find a space for his own identity."[60] Moreover, Gabe's negotiation of the space between those categories turns on his reading of race's spatialization within the performance. Juxtaposing the family's move from a "dirty-black-slum" to a "clean-white-neighborhood" to illustrate those categories' imagined boundary, Gabe traces how his family traverses the boundary or how "the tracks" purportedly contains and confines those categories.⁶¹ Yet as the performance exposes the boundary's permeability as well as the categories' instability, it also points to the social costs of transgressing the categories and their boundary. Though they remain in the "clean-white-neighborhood" long enough to gain the acceptance of their white neighbors, they ultimately realize that "the world was not clean and white" and return to the "dirty-black-slum," where Gabe recounts that their neighbors "Denied us! Disowned us! And cast us out!"⁶² In framing his family's experience as one that leaves its members without a cultural home, he clears discursive space for black subjectivity's representation that refuses those categories.

Likewise, Act Three's solo performance specifically probes the construction of African American identity. Alluding to the civil uprisings across the country in cities including New York, Los Angeles, and Detroit during the mid- and late 1960s, the play's stage direction calls for a table with a folded newspaper that reads "Negroes Riot!" as well as a Molotov cocktail, an automatic pistol, a plate, and a fork. A banner resembling the US flag stands next to Gabe as he begins his spoken word performance. These visual signposts not only frame black identity's exploration in the performance; they also mobilize his deconstruction of black subjectivity's boundaries. Turning to African American vernacular culture in his solo performance, Gabe's sermon on "they's mo' to bein' black than meets the eye" echoes "The Blackness of Blackness" sermon in Ralph Ellison's *Invisible Man* (1952). While that novel's sermon conceptualizes and locates black identity within the tension between its visibility and invisibility, Gabe's sermon looks toward disentangling black identity from the visual markers and cultural practices that limit its representation. Deliberately engaging black cultural practices and visual markers laden with always already-inscribed notions of blackness's meanings, Gabe's sermon troubles them by situating black subjectivity within the tension between the practices and markers he references. Closing the sermon, he conceptualizes black subjectivity as simultaneously instinctive yet factual, necessary yet unwanted:

> *Yes! They's mo' to bein' black than meets*
> *The eye!*
> *It's all the stuff that nobody wants but*
> *Cain't live without!*
> *It's the body that keeps us standin'! The*
> *Soul that keeps us goin'! An' the spirit*
> *That'll take us thooo!*
> *Yes! They's mo' to bein' black than meets*
> *The eye!*⁶³

Seated at the table as he ends the sermon, Gabe cuts and takes a bite from the gun, which he follows with a sip from the Molotov cocktail. As Elam has argued, consuming those representations of violence enables Gabe to "demystify and deactivate their power and authority."[64] I further suggest that Gabe's subsequent request, "Bru-thas an' sistahs! Will ya jine me!,"[65] not only upends those visual signposts of black rage, but also offers communion over his conceptualization of black subjectivity detailed in the sermon. In short, Gabe's communion seeks to unite individuals and groups through his conceptualization of black subjectivity. Yet his concept rejects blackness as a programmatic and didactic concept and instead offers it as a matrix that anticipates postblackness's framing of African American subjectivity.

After he kills Johnny, who embodies rage's stagnancy and inhibits its transformative possibilities, Gabe stages his final solo performance in *No Place to Be Somebody*'s Epilogue as the Black Lady in Mourning to underscore black subjectivity's fluidity. Offering his female impersonation, or drag performance, as a spectacle that draws attention to gender's conventions and expectations and intervenes in Black Arts' masculinist tendencies, he asserts, "Your capacity for attention is very short. Therefore, I must try to provoke you. Provoke your attention. Change my part over and over again."[66] Gabe emphasizes here both black subjectivity's ephemerality and spectacle's service in black subjectivity's explorations of racial meanings in each of his performances, but particularly his drag performance. Yet as he exposes how it might function as provocation, or even protest, recalling his earlier arguments about protest's futility, Gabe acknowledges its failures, asserting that, "I will weep, I will wail, and I will mourn. But my cries will not be heard. No one will wipe away my bitter tears. My black anguish will fall upon deaf ears."[67] Despite both provocation's and protest's failures, Gabe's mourning gestures toward a different possibility: "I will mourn a passing! Yes! The passing and the ending of a people dying. Of a people dying into that new life. A people whose identity could only be measured by the struggle, the dehumanization, the degradation they suffered. Or allowed themselves to suffer perhaps. I will mourn the death of a people dying. Of a people dying into that new life."[68] Gabe's Freudian expression of the loss of a love object, "the passing and the ending of a people dying," marks his grief as the Black Lady in Mourning.[69] Yet his mourning not only recognizes the inherent regenerative potential that protest's death offers, but also its implications for black subjectivity free of protest's representational freight. His mourning speaks to a departure from a normative attitude toward black subjectivity that limits its meanings to struggle and resistance. As he mourns the death of black subjectivity likened to "the dehumanization, [and] the degradation [black people] suffered," he poses the death of such associations as a rebirth of black subjectivity that offers new prospects for its representation beyond African American experience's historical trauma. Clearing conceptual space for iterations of black subjectivity in his final solo performance, Gabe enables new possibilities for its representation. Similarly, Charles Gordone's *No Place to Be Somebody* and Gabe Gabriel's solo performances collectively offer a meditation on black subjectivity beyond the African American Freedom Struggle. As Gabe and Gordone expand black subjectivity's limits in the play, they

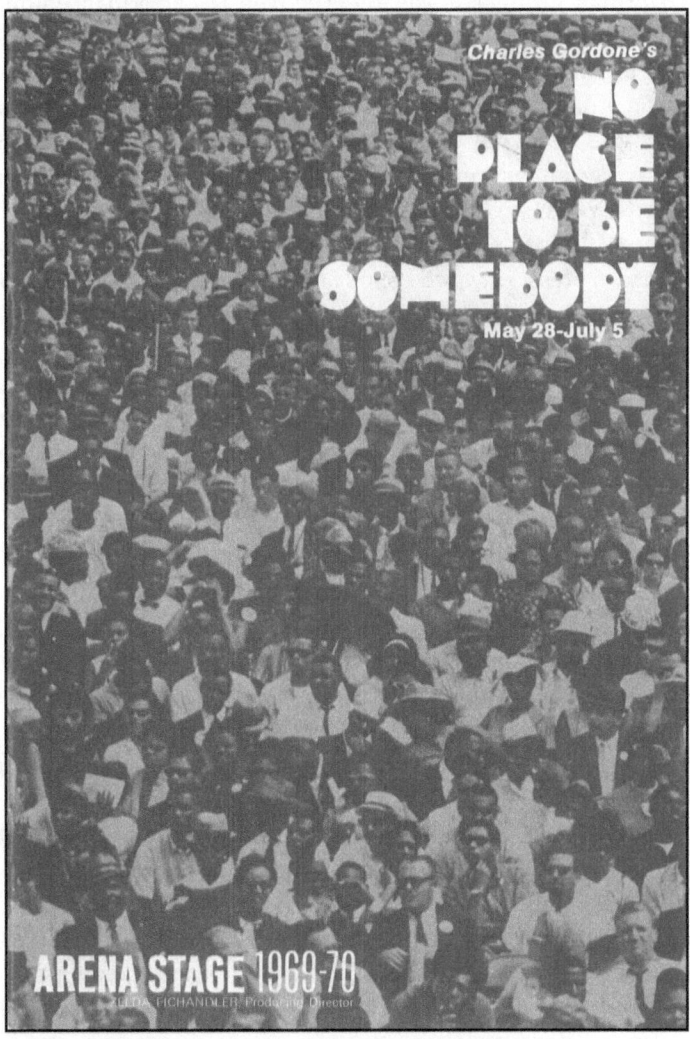

No Place to be Somebody: A Black Black Comedy. 1970 Promenade Theatre Playfare. Collection of the author.

imagine, as Lubiano would have it, "what it looks like when you're no longer caught by your own trauma about racism and the history of black people in the United States . . . [and] everything is up for grabs as a possibility."

Gordone started work on *No Place to Be Somebody* in 1960 and staged an early version of it at the Sheridan Square Playhouse in November 1967. Two years later, it appeared as a three-weekend showcase production at Joseph Papp's Other Stage at the Public Theater in March 1969. *No Place to Be Somebody* moved in May to the New York Shakespeare Festival's Public Theater for a 248-performance run, and was followed by a 15-performance limited engagement at Broadway's American National Theater and Academy (ANTA) that ended in January 1970. Following its success in those venues, Gordone directed three national touring companies of the play from 1970 and 1977. Speaking to the *New York Amsterdam News*, producer Joseph Papp argued that the play warranted immediate staging at an already financially strapped Public Theater because Gordone was a playwright "with something to say to both the races."[70] Most of *No Place*'s reviews in both the mainstream and African American press conveyed Papp's palpable enthusiasm for Gordone and his play. Walter Kerr proclaimed in the *New York Times* that Gordone was "the most astonishing new playwright to come along since Edward Albee," describing *No Place*'s representations as "complex, rich, garish, improbable, overburdened, defiant, and successful."[71] Similarly, the *New York Amsterdam News*'s Simon Anekwe praised Gordone's writing for its "ability to reveal the inner motivations of blacks and whites as they mingled in the relative racially tension-free West Village."[72] Molly Haskell also commended Gordone in the *Village Voice*, describing the play as a "sprawling, searching play, as messy and convulsive as the muddy truths it deals with and as multiple in message styles as there is shades of gray."[73]

Yet others insinuated a premature move from workshop to full-scale production reflected in both its writing and its staging. Theatre critic George Oppenheimer left feeling that he had seen "several plays, none of which was satisfactory," while Clive Barnes criticized the three and a half hour performance as "rather too long and certainly too episodic for its own good."[74] Mel Gussow complained that the second act's flaws apparent at its Public Theater run remained at the ANTA staging, where "the action turns quickly into something resembling a James Cagney movie."[75] Finally, Martin Gottfried asserted that *No Place* was "long, clumsy and confused" due largely to its "overpraise into a major production."[76] Despite its shortcomings, Gottfried concurred with every other critic in both the mainstream and black press that the play signaled Gordone as "an extremely talented playwright."[77]

While black critics similarly recognized Gordone's talent in their reviews, intimations of race treason or racial inauthenticity accompanied those acknowledgments. Asserting that the play's white director, Ted Cornell, and its white producer, Joseph Papp, "do not know what [Gordone] is about" and that Papp has "a limited grasp of the milieu involved in *No Place to Be Somebody*," Clayton Riley further argued in the *New York Times* that "Brother Gordone is an eminently gifted and hard-working artist who has fallen prey to that lamentable inclination of black men in America to trot along someone else's road."[78] Referencing the narrative dissonance between Gabe's solo performances and the play's ongoing action at Johnny's Bar, Riley blames Cornell's staging for the lack of a "workable marriage between the playwright's prose and his poetry."[79] Closing his review, Riley condemns the "rather bad news" he discerns in the play—"suspicion of self-hatred here, a hint of contempt for black people there," and asserts that while Gordone stumbles in his desire to "say too much—indeed, say it all—in this his first play," his most egregious error lies in "allowing the Public Theater to get at his play."[80] In the same vein, *Negro Digest* editor and critic Hoyt Fuller revealed uncertainty about *No Place to Be Somebody*'s racial politics that was resonant with his observations about the play itself, writing that "[it] reflects a good bit of inherent ambiguity on its own. Nevertheless, there is no denying the inherent power of the play."[81] While he commends the performances of Ron O'Neal as Gabe and Nathan George as Johnny, Fuller contends that the play paints a bleak picture of both interracial and intraracial relationships, positing that "the action proceeds in a world where tenderness is suspect and is therefore inadmissible."[82] Finally, critic Peter Bailey, Fuller's colleague at *Negro Digest*, expressed doubt about the play's and Gordone's racial credibility in an opinion that merits quoting at length:

> White critics were ecstatic about it, but many Blacks have expressed misgivings about this work which is filled up with self-loathing, Greenwich Village "Negroes" going through changes with each other and their weirdo white friends. Playwright Gordone, who describes himself as part-Indian, part-French, part-Irish, and part-nigger, and who wrote in the New York Times that "I believe the idea of Black theater is dead," is obviously writing about people he knows well. They can still be seen in Village hangouts. *No Place* is well written and the acting is superb. Nathan George, as Johnny Williams, gave the best acting performance I saw all year. Nevertheless, Black people had best beware while laughing at the dialogue and marveling at the acting. *No Place* is full of cold contempt for us.[83]

Offering Gordone's racial self-identifications and his view of black theater as evidence that puts the playwright's own claim to black identity in jeopardy, Bailey's review insinuated that such assertions undermine the play's racial veracity. In short, neither Gordone nor the play is "authentically" black. Limning an intraracial boundary as he cautions black viewers who laugh at the dialogue and who marvel at the acting of *No Place*'s contempt for "us," Bailey imposed precisely the monolithic black subjectivity that the play seeks to expand. Put differently, Gordone's play interrogates the construction of an African American "us" while Bailey's review attempted to police those explorations by framing the play as both a contemptuous and an inauthentic representation of black subjectivity written by an inauthentically black subject. Similarly, those of "us" engaging the representations by laughing at the dialogue and marveling at the acting put their own blackness in jeopardy, and his review served to warn black audiences about the racial contempt and self-hatred informing the play's representations. Though Bailey conceded Gordone's writing talent, his review delivered a cautionary tale about the pitfalls of interrogating black identity in the play—authentic blackness hangs in the balance.

While these reviews collectively recognized Gordone's possibilities as a compelling playwright, they exposed anxiety about his attempts to explore racial boundaries and situate these efforts as markers of black self-hatred. *No Place* emerged within the historical context of a burgeoning black theater scene that saw the opening of Amiri Baraka's Black Arts Repertory Theatre and School (BARTS) in 1965, Robert Macbeth and Ed Bullins's New Lafayette Theatre (NLT) in 1966, Robert Hooks and Douglas Turner Ward's Negro Ensemble Company (NEC) in 1967, and Barbara Ann Teer's National Black Theatre (NBT) in 1968. They were founded in response to what Ward called a "screaming need" for a theater "concentrating primarily on themes of Negro life, but also resilient enough to incorporate and interpret the best of world drama—whatever the source," and consequently would appear to offer a potential home for *No Place*.[84] Yet Gordone claimed that he first approached the NEC's Robert Hooks about producing the play before working with Joseph Papp and was turned away because he refused to eliminate the white characters; furthermore, no other black theater company showed interest in it.[85] Moreover, if the NEC and other black theater companies sought to portray black life and the black experience, it would seem that despite the presence of white characters, *No Place to Be Somebody*'s most important relationship is the one between the two African American characters—Gabe and Johnny—and would therefore meet the aesthetic criteria to represent the black experience to black audiences. The motives driving the institution of these black theater companies during the mid-to-late 1960s were quite obviously justified and, indeed, necessary given the grave circumstances and difficulties African American theater practitioners faced in attempting to stage work reflecting the black experience in the United States. Gordone was acutely aware of these challenges, as his work with CORE's Committee on the Employment of Negro Performers indicates. Certainly, the NEC and other black companies' decision to pass on *No Place* can be attributed to a host of aesthetic concerns. At the same time, the refusal to stage a production like *No Place* because of its white characters ignored Ward's own call for a theater providing a home for black playwrights who examine "the contours, the contexts, the depths of his experiences from an unfettered, imaginative Negro angle of vision."[86] Though by most assessments, Gordone's play demonstrated his talent, his exploration of blackness's meanings and contexts posed questions that some black theater critics and companies could not, or would not, accommodate, and seemingly his provocations, as Gordone himself put it, left him with no place to be in 1969. Despite the specters of inauthenticity raised in the reviews, Charles Gordone's *No Place to Be Somebody* offers in Gabe Gabriel a compelling iteration of black subjectivity that anticipates Bertram Ashe's cultural mulatto. Gabriel pried apart and explored the relationship between black subjectivity and the African American Freedom Struggle of the 1960s in order to define his relationship to freedom on his own terms. Placed within the expansion of blackness's boundaries that a postblack critical framework enables, Gordone's "text out of time" perhaps, finds a home that embraces an individualized notion of blackness and allows black cultural producers and their products "latitude, freedom and the benefit of the doubt."[87]

CODA

Postblackness's Ancestors and Relatives or "The Past Pushing Us into the Present"

> "But perhaps you will understand when I say [Richard Wright] did not influence me if I point out that while one can do nothing about choosing one's relatives, one can, as an artist, choose one's 'ancestors'"
> —Ralph Ellison, "The World and the Jug" (1963)

> "This post–Civil Rights movement generation has somehow transcended double consciousness. Their articulations of this aesthetic are no less than self-generated, black-on-black emancipation proclamations."
> —Bertram Ashe, "Theorizing the Post-Soul Aesthetic: An Introduction" (2007)

All five plays discussed in *Prefiguring Postblackness* have been staged in a range of venues over the last ten years. With actor Denzel Washington starring as Walter Lee Younger, *A Raisin in the Sun* returned to Broadway in 2014 and earned a Tony award for the year's best revival of a play or musical. The other plays were revived Off-Broadway or in university or regional theaters. *Wine in the Wilderness* was staged at Seattle's ACT Theatre in 2006, and two Cleveland theater companies, Karamu House and Ensemble Theatre, along with Akron's Weathervane Community Playhouse, co-produced *The Great White Hope* in 2010. In 2013, Penn State University's Pavilion Theatre staged *No Place to Be Somebody*, and as discussed in Chapter Two, Performa13 showcased *Dutchman* at the East Village's Russian & Turkish Baths and at Chicago's Red Square Russian and Turkish Baths in 2014.

Critics reviewing the plays approached them as cultural artifacts, unpacking them as they might the contents of a newly opened time capsule. Locating the artifact's import in the current historical moment, they historicized the productions and situated them as markers of a pivotal era in the nation's history and its narrative about race. In effect, the plays become a history lesson about the African American Freedom Struggle. In some instances, critics found that the artifact cannot be meaningfully translated in the current moment and discussed it is an anachronism. Bob Abelman's review of *The Great White Hope* asserted that both the supporting players' acting and "the dated theatricality of the material itself" undermined what is otherwise "an important tale to tell."[1] Similarly, Ted Hoover observed of *No Place to Be Somebody* that "'Hip/cool' plays, which *No Place* must have certainly been at one time, tend to age badly, and this one most certainly has."[2] Yet neither offered insight on what those tales' significance might be.

In other reviews, critics engaged the historical and cultural legacy the plays bequeath to a younger generation and positioned the plays as speaking to enduring truths of the African American experience in the United States. But as they argued for the historical significance of the plays, they—like the critics writing about these works in the Freedom Struggle Era—elided the representation of African American identity's complexities present in the play. Reviews of *A Raisin in the Sun*'s 2004 Broadway revival, which garnered Tony Awards for Phylicia Rashad and Audra McDonald for their portrayals of Lena and Ruth, respectively, aptly illustrated this point. Putting the play's representations aside, critics focused on the audience that hip-hop impresario Sean Combs drew in his appearance as Walter Lee Younger. Though like many other critics, Ed Siegel panned Combs's performance, he noted that Combs made the play "a bona fide event in New York's black communities and thereby introduced both an American classic and the uniqueness of live theater to some people who might never have experienced either."[3] He attributed the predominantly African American audience at the performance to Combs and asserted that it was the first time there had been a majority of African American attendees at "any New York play [he's] attended."[4] While increasing African American audiences at Broadway performances is a worthwhile, even necessary, endeavor, James Baldwin made a parallel observation at the play's 1959 debut, writing that he had "never in [his] life seen so many black people in the theater," which suggests that the play has always attracted black audiences.[5] Playwright Anna Deveare Smith's review of Hansberry's play also recognized the significance of Combs's stage debut, which she said was "infused with hope," but suggested that despite its age, *A Raisin in the Sun* "come[s] to us with a sense of urgency . . . sometimes repetition makes things more real, more vibrant, more apparent."[6] For Smith, the play's revival marked historical progression, or what she called an instance of "the past pushing us into the present."[7]

Ben Brantley's review of the 2014 revival restated Smith's assertions about the relationship between the past and the present moment, observing that despite the audience's likely familiarity with the play, Kenny Leon's direction enabled the audience "to get to know the family without having to squint to see the real people behind the social archetypes. And a drama often presented as something monumental, to be approached with awe and piety, becomes refreshingly accessible."[8] And while Leon's direction and the actors' performances clearly infused what Brantley named an "estimable production" with new energy, much of the play's dynamism was embedded in the representations themselves.[9] Both Brantley's and Smith's reviews acknowledged the representations' power and remained mindful of, but not burdened by, cultural memory's framing of them.

Still, what binds many of the recent reviews is the underlying assumption that audiences are so familiar with these plays and their narratives that there is no need to reflect on either of them because cultural memory's synthesizing and summarizing of them to support the dominant narrative of the Freedom Struggle era expediently completes that work. In effect, audiences already understand how and what those representations signify. While the past pushes us toward the present, it does so through the dialectic between remembering Freedom Struggle era representations that support its dominant, consensus narrative and forgetting, or sometimes deliberately overlooking, the errant representations that might unsettle it. The recent reviews have duplicated that dialectic, alternately remembering, forgetting, and overlooking the plays' wayward representations. *Prefiguring Postblackness* has aimed to show that cultural memory in both the Freedom Struggle era and the current historical moment often cloaks such disruptive representations and to encourage us to reconsider what we think we know about the representations and the plays this work discusses by drawing attention to those disruptions.

This study has also sought to explore postblackness's literary genealogies, or more specifically, to consider how the plays it studies might constitute a potential literary relative to postblack discourse. Appearing in *The New Leader* in December 1963, just four months after the March on Washington, Ralph Ellison's "The World and the Jug" refuted critic Irving Howe's claim that Richard Wright's racial identity alongside his literary prominence established him as an influence on Ellison's work. Choosing Ernest Hemingway, T. S. Eliot, Fyodor Dostoyevsky, and William Faulkner as literary ancestors while claiming Langston Hughes and Wright as literary relatives, he asserted his right to determine which aesthetic values and traditions informed his work. Ultimately for Ellison, shared racial identities did not necessarily constitute shared aesthetic values. Yet his rejection of a strictly race-based literary genealogy and his positioning of Wright and Hughes as literary relatives resonates with critic Bertram Ashe's summation of postblack artists' work as "black-on-black emancipation proclamations" in that both articulate a relationship to black culture and aesthetic practices that draws upon those practices but are not limited to them. Just as Ellison traced his own literary genealogy in 1963 to include white writers "if [we] please or don't please," Trey Ellis proclaimed post-soul freedom in 1989, asserting that postblack artists "no longer need to deny or suppress any part of our complicated or sometimes contradictory cultural baggage to please either white people or black."[10] Ellison and Ellis have argued for artistic autonomy in their rejection of imposed aesthetic genealogies; the only distinction between them is the historical context in which those proclamations were delivered. Ashe contended that those historical contexts make a vital difference, and that while cultural production prior to the post-soul era might resemble its explorations of black identity, in the end, their emergence within the previous era undermines those explorations because their "ideological bottom line—or the ideological interpretative context often thrust on them—was the African American struggle for freedom."[11]

Yet *Prefiguring Postblackness* has worked toward demonstrating both the ideological bottom line and the ideological interpretative context's permeability by emphasizing the plays' critique of how the Freedom Struggle's representative strategies limited black identity's representation. In the same way that Ellison and Ellis resisted the contexts imposed upon them, the representations under consideration have defied the ideological interpretative context imposed by the Freedom Struggle era as well as theater critics' insistence on the import of those contexts.

Rather than foisting a literary genealogy upon postblack texts or refuting the undeniable value of naming and theorizing a postblack aesthetic, *Prefiguring Postblackness* has instead explored the resonances between the explorations of blackness's representation in the Freedom Struggle era and the postblack era. Such an investigation offers an intervention in the Freedom Struggle era's framing within postblack discourse that challenges the sometimes reductively drawn relationship between postblack texts and the African American Freedom Struggle. In other words, the Freedom Struggle era's representations were not monolithic, and they offer more than the primary point of departure for postblackness's narrative tropes, which trouble static notions of African American identity. Not only do the representations that *Prefiguring Postblackness* examines envision and represent African American identity beyond the pursuit of collective freedom informing the African American Freedom Struggle, they break cadence with a lockstep march toward collective freedom and reimagine its interpretative context.

Ultimately, these Freedom Struggle era texts reaffirm Ellison's instructive response to Howe's question of how a black writer "can achieve personal realization apart from the common effort of his people to win their full freedom."[12] Speculating on post–Freedom era representations in his answer, he wrote, "I suggest that he ask himself in what way shall a Negro writer achieve personal realization (as writer) *after* his people shall have won their full freedom? The answer appears to be the same in both instances: he will have to go it alone!"[13] Likewise, while the works discussed in *Prefiguring Postblackness* remained mindful of the Freedom Struggle's necessity and significance and engaged it as a point of departure for their explorations of black identity, their authors simultaneously pushed their representations beyond the Freedom Struggle era's burden of representation and the ideological interpretative contexts it imposed. By challenging both racial uplift's and cultural nationalism's significant influence on African American representations of the Freedom Struggle era, these playwrights had to go at exploring black identity from unexpected vantages alone. Most often, the mainstream reviews sought to situate those so-called inauthentic representations within a more familiar ideological interpretative context. And while the African American press usually applauded their representations, in at least one instance they were censured and the playwright's racial authenticity questioned. Both the mainstream and the African American press sought to recontextualize them within fixed categories of identity, despite the challenges they posed to those categories. As a result, cultural memory of the Freedom Struggle era most often frames these plays as nothing more than a relic of that bygone historical moment. Yet they remain at the ready to speak to questions of black identity in the current moment for those who are willing to suspend their disbelief in their capacity to do so. Rashid Johnson seemingly saw that possibility in Baraka's *Dutchman*; perhaps others might follow his lead in rethinking the continuities across time and through drama, cultural memory, and the African American Freedom Struggle of the 1960s.

While postblack discourse may not claim these representations as literary ancestors, this analysis has argued for their consideration as literary relatives through their parallel interrogation of black identity's boundaries. Whether they continue to go it alone or are acknowledged, the representations offered in *A Raisin in the Sun, Dutchman, Wine in the Wilderness, The Great White Hope,* and *No Place to Be Somebody* uncannily anticipated postblack representations. In their explorations of blackness and how it signifies within an era often figured to consolidate black identity's meanings, they merit our reconsideration. They offer an opportunity to broaden our understanding of the African American Freedom Struggle's representations of black identity and their relationship to its representation in the current historical moment.

NOTES

Introduction

1. Jeanne Theoharis, *The Rebellious Life of Mrs. Rosa Parks* (Boston: Beacon Press, 2013).
2. Barbie Zelizer, "Journalism's Memory Work," in *Cultural Memory Studies: An International and Interdisciplinary Handbook*, ed. Astrid Erll and Ansgar Nünning, 379–87 (Berlin: Walter de Gruyter, 2008).
3. Ibid., 384.
4. Theoharis, xi.
5. Ibid., x.
6. Ashley Southall, "Statue of Rosa Parks Is Unveiled at Capitol," *New York Times*, February 27, 2013, http://mobile.nytimes.com/2013/02/28/us/politics/statue-of-rosa-parks-is-unveiled-at-the-capitol.html (accessed June 30, 2013).
7. Ibid.
8. Elizabeth Spelman, *The Fruits of Sorrow: Framing Our Attention to Suffering* (Boston: Beacon Press, 1998), 205; "Honoring the Legacy of Rosa Parks," Mitch McConnell Speech at Rosa Parks Statue: Dedication on February 27, 2013, http://uneditedpolitics.com/mitch-mcconnell-speech-at-rosa-parks-statue-dedication-22713 (accessed September 3, 2013).
9. "Honoring the Legacy." McConnell also noted that Parks "lives in America's collective memory in a pair of rimless glasses, hair pulled back, neatly dressed in a simple hat and dress" and limited her impact to "a simple act of courage." On an "otherwise ordinary evening in Montgomery, she did the extraordinary by simply staying put."
10. Theoharis, ix.
11. Further, as both the secretary of Montgomery's chapter of the NAACP as well as its Youth Chapter leader, Parks's case was handpicked by that organization to become the initiator of a legal challenge to the segregation laws because of her commitment to ending segregation. Yet she also downplayed her activist roots, submitting to the gendered image of the exhausted seamstress that became central to the fable. While Montgomery teens Claudette Colvin's and Mary Louise Smith's stands against segregation preceded Parks's own, she never sought to downplay their importance to the movement and her stand. Though not mentioned in cultural memory's framing of her, she was aware of and spoke

to how gender and class politics shaped interpretations of the movement and her stand. Considered a "good Christian woman" who "was a tireless churchgoer of working-class station and middle-class demeanor" and who therefore represented the virtues of civility and respectability that were central to the success of the Civil Rights Movement, she had to strategically use those characterizations in the service of the boycott and especially how those politics shaped the experiences of her teenage forerunners. Colvin and Smith had been arrested for their refusals in March and October respectively, but Colvin had been a NAACP Youth Council member and became acquainted with Parks through the latter's leadership of it. She asked Colvin to tell the story of her arrest to her and other youth council members again and again and was incensed by the abuse Colvin endured.

12. Attorney General et al., Supreme Court of the United States, Argued February 27, 2013, Decided June 25, 2013. Arguing that the legislation was intended to address a voter suppression problem in the South that no longer exists, Justice Antonin Scalia observed that it was "a perpetuation of racial entitlement" that had outlived its relevance in 2013, even as African American voters in Alabama found their names unjustly removed from voting rolls and as voters in predominantly black and Latino precincts in Florida waited for more than seven hours to vote in the 2012 presidential election. On June 25, Section 4 of the Voting Rights Act requiring that the federal government approve any changes in election laws in nine mostly southern states was struck down by the Supreme Court. Justice Scalia further emphasized the changed racial climate in the US South, saying that "no one can fairly say that it shows anything approaching the pervasive, flagrant, widespread, and rampant discrimination that clearly distinguished the covered jurisdictions from the rest of the Nation in 1965."

13. Shelby County, *Alabama v. Holder*, Attorney General et al., Supreme Court of the United States, Argued February 27, 2013, Decided June 25, 2013.

14. Rebecca Wanzo, *The Suffering Will Not Be Televised: African American Women and Sentimental Political Storytelling* (Albany, NY: SUNY Press, 2009), 30.

15. Stephen Colbert brilliantly illustrated and critiqued this tendency in his "The Word: Black and White" segment of *The Colbert Report*, which aired shortly after the fortieth anniversary of Martin Luther King's death on April 10, 2008. In it, he bemoaned former Newark mayor Corey Booker's, scholar Cornel West's, and columnist David Brooks's questioning of the way we remember King as a kind of benevolent Santa Claus. In the sketch, Colbert refused to let those "scrooges" tell him how to remember King. Arguing for maintaining the simplistic representation of King and rejecting the FBI's contention that he was the most dangerous man in America, Colbert asserted, "If he was the most dangerous man in America, would he be made into this collectible figurine? Adorable. That is a king everyone can embrace for just $16.99. [plus shipping and revisioning] Now, best of all the Santa Clausification of Martin Luther King means we don't need to ruin his legacy with his humanity." He concluded,

"I don't want to hear about his anger, his frailty, his self-doubt, I want him to be magic. [Presto civil rights-o] Because if he's magic, that will inspire each of us to stand up and say there was a great man, no way I could do what he did, I mean nobody could. You see with the Santa Clausification of Martin Luther King, we can just be good for goodness' sake and wait for someone greater than ourselves to come down the chimney in the middle of the night and bring us peace and brotherhood. [some assembly required] And that's the word." http://www.colbertnation.com/the-colbert-report-videos/165434/april-10-2008/the-word---black-and-white (accessed June 27, 2013).

16. Theoharis, xi.

17. Ibid. For example, cultural memory attributes Parks's resistance to her physical fatigue rather than recognizing it as a deliberate decision that she made in response to the continued racial injustice imposed on her and other black Montgomerians. As both the secretary of Montgomery's chapter of the NAACP and its Youth Chapter leader, Parks's case was handpicked by that organization to become the source of a legal challenge to the segregation laws because of her commitment to ending segregation. Yet she also downplayed her activist roots, submitting to the gendered image of the exhausted seamstress that became central to the fable.

18. Ibid.

19. In addition to Ward and Street, George Lipsitz, Lee Raiford, Renee Romano, Margo Natalie Crawford, Lisa Gail Collins, Peniel Joseph, James Smethurst, and Tanisha Ford, among other scholars, have advocated for the centrality of culture in the Civil Rights Movement and the Black Arts/Aesthetic Movements, which I am referring to collectively as the African American Freedom Struggle of the 1960s.

20. Joe Street, *The Culture Wars in the Civil Rights Movement* (Gainesville: University Press of Florida, 2007), 14.

21. Brian Ward, ed., *Media, Culture, and the African American Freedom Struggle of the 1960s* (Tallahassee: University Press of Florida, 2001), 10.

22. David Román, *Performance in America: Contemporary U.S. Culture and the Performing Arts* (Durham, NC: Duke University Press, 2005). Román argued for the centrality of the performing arts in US culture and pointed to theater critics' key role in interpreting works produced on stage, as they "played a vital role in introducing the American public to theater's merits and their readily available work helped establish them as effective readers of theater." Ibid., 297.

23. Zelizer, 379–87.

24. Marianne DeKoven, *Utopia Limited: The Sixties and the Emergence of the Postmodern* (Durham, NC: Duke University Press, 2004), 229.

25. bell hooks, "Postmodern Blackness," in her *Yearning: Race, Gender, and Cultural Politics* (Boston: South End Press, 1990), 29. Mark Anthony Neal, *Soul Babies: Black Popular Culture and the Post-Soul Aesthetic* (New York: Routledge, 2002), 3.

26. Bertram Ashe, "Theorizing the Post-Soul Aesthetic: An Introduction," in *Post-Soul Aesthetic*, ed. Bertram Ashe, special issue of *African American Review* 41, no. 4 (2007): 609–23.

27. Marisa Chappell, Jenny Hutchinson, and Brian Ward, "'Dress modestly, neatly ... as if you were going to church': Respectability, Class, and Gender in the Montgomery Bus Boycott and the Early Civil Rights Movement," in *Gender and the Civil Rights Movement*, ed. Peter J. Ling and Sharon Monteith, 69–100 (New Brunswick, NJ: Rutgers University Press, 2004).

28. M. A. Neal, 3; Ashe, 614; and Michael Eric Dyson, Foreword, "Tour(é)ing Blackness," in Touré, *Who's Afraid of Postblackness: What It Means to be Black Now*. (New York: Free Press, 2011) xi.

29. M. A. Neal, 2–3.

30. Ibid.

31. Román, *Performance in America*, 11.

32. Ibid.

33. Ibid.

34. Ibid.

35. Ibid.

36. Lorraine Hansberry, *A Raisin in the Sun*, intro. Howard Nemiroff (New York: Vintage, 1994), 104.

37. Nita N. Kumar, "The Logic of Retribution: Amiri Baraka's *Dutchman*," *African American Review* 37, nos. 2–3 (2003): 271–79.

38. Larry Neal, "The Black Arts Movement," *Drama Review*, 12, no. 4, (Summer 1968): 29–39.

39. Trey Ellis, "The New Black Aesthetic," *Callaloo* 12, no. 1 (1989): 233–43.

40. United States Kerner Commission, "Reporting of Racial Problems in the United States," *Report of the National Advisory Commission on Civil Disorders* (New York: Bantam, 1968), 383–86.

41. Ibid.

42. Harry J. Elam Jr., "The Performance of Blackness and the Black Performer," in *African American Performance and Theater History*, ed. Harry J. Elam Jr. and David Krasner, 296–97 (New York: Cambridge University Press, 2003).

43. Charles Gordone, *No Place to Be Somebody: A Black Black Comedy in Three Acts*. (Indianapolis, IN: Bobbs-Merrill, 1969): 115.

44. Patricia Bosworth, "From Nowhere to 'No Place,'" *New York Times*, June 8, 1969, D1.

45. Ellis, "New Black Aesthetic," 233–43.

Chapter 1

1. Lorraine Hansberry, "A Raisin in the Sun," Original Play Script with Annotations, November 1957, Box 6, Folder 1, Lorraine Hansberry Papers, Schomburg Center for Research in Black Culture, New York, NY.

2. Lisa Jones, "She Came with the Rodeo," in her *Bulletproof Diva: Tales of Race, Sex, and Hair* (New York: Doubleday, 1994), 128.

3. Ibid. 4. Ibid.

5. Lorraine Hansberry, *A Raisin in the Sun*, 1994, 47–48.

6. Lisa Jones, 128.

7. Brooks Atkinson, "The Theatre: A Raisin in the Sun," review of *A Raisin in the Sun*, by Lorraine Hansberry, *New York Times*, March 12, 1959, 27; Al Monroe, "The Sun Shines Brightly," review of *A Raisin in the Sun*, by Lorraine Hansberry, *Chicago Daily Defender*, February 21, 1959, 18; Rachelle S. Gold, "Education Has Spoiled Many a Good Plow Hand: How Beneatha's Knowledge Functions in *A Raisin in the Sun*," in *Reading Contemporary African American Drama: Fragments of History, Fragments of Self*. Edited by Trudier Harris and Jennifer Lawson, (New York: Peter Lang, 2007):11. Gold further argues that Beneatha uses her "knowledge for self-expression and self-promotion rather than for the family's gain" which distances her from her family (18). Yet in some instances, the ideas she shares with her family are ultimately embraced by them. For example, when she asserts that George Murchison is a fool, Lena supports her view.

8. In "From Center to Margin: Internationalism and the Origins of Black Feminism," Kevin Gaines argues that the African American Freedom Struggle's most significant legacy is the black feminist intervention in the Black Power movement's masculinist tendencies. Tracing that intervention's genealogies to a post–World War II "black radical culture of internationalism" in urban cities emerging from African independence and Civil Rights Movement activism, Gaines reads Gwendolyn Brooks's novel *Maud Martha* (1953), Alice Childress's novel *Like One of the Family* (1956), and Hansberry's *A Raisin in the Sun* as literary exemplars of those black feminist interventions. Clearly, the antecedents Gaines outlined informed Beneatha's characterization and my discussion of her draws on those genealogies, particularly the significance of racial uplift ideology within African American culture of the era. See Gaines, "From Center to Margin: Internationalism and the Origins of Black Feminism," in *Materializing Democracy: Toward a Revitalized Cultural Politics*, ed. Russ Castronovo and Dana D. Nelson (Durham, NC: Duke University Press, 2002).

9. Lisa Jones, 126; Ashe, 609–23. The question of naming this movement, structure of feeling, or collective has been debated since its debut. Bertram Ashe, Crystal Anderson, Mark Anthony Neal, Evie Shockley, and Alexander Weheliye, "These—Are –the 'Breaks': A Roundtable Discussion on Teaching The Post-Soul Aesthetic," in *Post-Soul Aesthetic*, ed. Bertram Ashe, special issue of *African American Review* 41, no. 4 (2007):787–803.

10. Lisa Jones, 134–35.

11. Trey Ellis, "Response to NBA Critiques," *Callaloo* 38, no. 1 (1989): 250–51.

12. Kevin K. Gaines, "Racial Uplift Ideology in the Era of 'the Negro Problem,'" Freedom's Story, TeacherServe©, National Humanities Center, http://nationalhumanitiescenter.org/tserve/freedom/1865-1917/essays/racialuplift.htm (accessed September 26, 2013).

13. Chappell, Hutchinson, and B. Ward, 69–100.

14. M. A. Neal, 9.

15. Ibid.

16. Lisa Jones, 126–28.

17. Ellis, "New Black Aesthetic," 239.

18. Thelma Golden, "Introduction," *Freestyle* (New York: Studio Museum of Harlem, 2001), 14–15. Exhibition catalog.

19. Discussed and informed by a range of critics and cultural producers including Lisa Jones, Thelma Golden, Greg Tate, Nelson George, Trey Ellis, and Touré, the NBA/PSA notes a shift in African American cultural production in the late 1980s through the late 1990s that makes it distinct from previous movements in cultural production.

20. Gregory Tate, *Flyboy in the Buttermilk: Essays on Contemporary America* (New York: Fireside, 1992), 206–7.

21. Ellis, "New Black Aesthetic," 239.

22. T. Golden, "Introduction," 14.

23. Thelma Golden, interview with Betsy Sussler, *Bomb Magazine*, Web., March 2004. http://bombmagazine.org/article/3588/thelma-golden (accessed September 24, 2013).

24. Ellis's essay elicited a response that comprised the entire issue of *Callaloo*. Bertram Ashe addressed the response from one critic to his call for papers on the post-soul era within his essay published in a special issue of *African American Review* and at least one critic taking part in a roundtable discussion of the Post-Soul Aesthetic also published in that issue was not entirely convinced of the post-soul "break" in representation from previous eras.

25. Ashe, 614.

26. Ibid., 614–15.

27. Ibid., 609.

28. DeKoven, 19.

29. Jack Kroll, "Theatre: Zapping Black Stereotypes," *Newsweek*, November 17, 1986, 85.

30. J. Charles Washington, "A Raisin in the Sun Revisited," *Black American Literature Forum*, Black Women Writers Issue, 22 no. 1 (1988) 109–24.

31. Harry J. Elam Jr. and Douglas A. Jones Jr., eds., *The Methuen Drama Book of Post-Black Plays* (London: Methuen, 2013), xii.

32. Hansberry, 35 (1994).

33. Ibid., 35.

34. Lorraine Hansberry Papers, Box 8, Folder 1, Letter to Peter Buitenhuis, February 3, 1959, Schomburg Center. New York, NY.

35. Hansberry, 23 (1994).

36. Ibid., 24.

37. Ibid.

38. Ibid.

39. José Esteban Muñoz. *Disidentifications: Queers of Color and the Performance of Politics* (Minneapolis: University of Minnesota Press, 1999) 28.

40. Ibid., 29.

41. Gaines, *Uplifting the Race*. 4.

42. Ibid., 2.

43. Ibid., 5.

44. Hansberry, 51 (1994).

45. Ibid.

46. Ibid.

47. Ibid., 52.

48. Ibid.

49. Ibid.

50. Ibid., 74.

51. Gaines, *Uplifting the Race*, 235.

52. Ibid.

53. Hansberry, 75 (1994).

54. Ibid., 94.

55. Michelle Gordon. "'Somewhat Like War': The Aesthetics of Segregation, Black Liberation and *A Raisin in the Sun*," *African American Review*: 42, no. 1 (2008): 121–33.

56. Hansberry, 49–50 (1994).

57. Gaines, *Uplifting the Race*, 16–17.

58. Hansberry, 79 (1994).

59. Ibid.

60. Ibid., 80.

61. Robert Nemiroff, Introduction, in *A Raisin in the Sun* (New York: Vintage, 1994), 6.

62. Ayana Byrd and Lori L. Tharps, *Hair Story: Untangling the Roots of Black Hair* (New York: St. Martin's Press, 2001), 54.

63. Robin D. G. Kelley, "Looking for the 'Real' Nigga: Social Scientists Construct the Ghetto," in his *Yo Mama's Dysfunktional!: Fighting the Culture Wars in Urban America* (Boston: Beacon Press, 1997), 25–27. Kelley argues that the Afro was a style that was primarily found in "the bourgeois high fashion circles in the late 1950s" and was often viewed as an affront to the cultural politics of uplift.

64. Hansberry, 80 (1994).

65. Ibid.

66. Ibid., 82.
67. Ibid.
68. Ibid., 81.
69. Ibid.
70. Ibid., 96.
71. Ibid., 96–97.
72. Ibid. A deleted scene between Beneatha and George further illustrates his investment in uplift and his anti-intellectual stance. When Beneatha asks him what he wants to do in life, he responds, "(*Easily*) Oh—I'll finish school and go into the business. What else? I'll get married. My father will retire. Simple." As she presses him further, he observes that one reason why she doesn't have a group of friends at their college is because she "moon[s] around too much." Telling her to stop it and speaking to its implications for racial uplift's project, George advises "People on campus aren't even used to that many colored girls yet—let alone the 'sensitive' kind. Let 'em get used to one thing at a time." Arguing here for the necessity of a monolithic black identity in uplift's project and pointing to the ways that Beneatha's "atmosphere" threatens it, George demands her compliance with uplift's gender roles. Hansberry, "A Raisin in the Sun," Original Play Script.
73. Ibid.
74. This point is further supported by one of the multiple deletions made in order keep the performance under three hours. Responding to his mocking of Walter, Ruth tells George, "One of these days, boy, I'm going to understand something you say and if it turns out you are insulting my husband as bad as I think you are your mother ain't going to recognize you." Hansberry, "A Raisin in the Sun," Original Play Script.
75. Hansberry, 102 (1994).
76. Ibid., 103.
77. Ibid., 104.
78. Ibid., 100.
79. Ibid.
80. Hansberry, 61 (1994).
81. Ibid., 62.
82. Ibid.
83. Ibid., 61–62.
84. Ibid., 62–63.
85. Hansberry, 137 (1994).
86. Ibid., 131.
87. Ibid.
88. Ibid.
89. Ibid.
90. Ibid.
91. Ibid., 136.

92. Ibid.

93. Ibid.

94. As Hansberry biographer Margaret Wilkerson and critics Stephen Carter, Michelle Gordon, and others have pointed out, one version of the play's final scene called for an armed Younger family huddled together in their living room waiting for a white mob to arrive at their new home. This scene drew from her family's experience with integrating a white Chicago neighborhood where the mob dispersed only after her mother brandished a shotgun.

95. Hansberry, 150 (1994).

96. Robin Bernstein, "Inventing a Fishbowl: White Supremacy and the Critical Reception of Lorraine Hansberry's A Raisin in the Sun," *Modern Drama*, 42, no. 1 (Spring 1999): 16–27.

97. Ibid., 22.

98. Atkinson, "The Theatre," 27; Monroe, 18.

99. Atkinson, "The Theatre," 27.

100. Frank Aston, review of *A Raisin in the Sun*, by Lorraine Hansberry, *New York World Telegram*, March 12, 1959, 20.

101. Lorraine Hansberry, interview by Eleanor Fisher, Box 3, Folder 8, Lorraine Hansberry Papers, Schomburg Center. New York, NY.

102. Atkinson, "The Theatre."

103. Brooks, "Raisin in the Sun: Vivid Drama about a Poor Negro Family," review of *A Raisin in the Sun*, by Lorraine Hansberry. *New York Times*, March 29, 1959, X1.

104. Ibid.

105. Lorraine Hansberry, "Willy Loman, Walter Younger, and He Who Must Live," *Village Voice*, August 12, 1959, 7–8.

106. Monroe, 18.

107. Darcy Demille, "Says Negro Playwright Is a Genius," review of *A Raisin in the Sun*, by Lorraine Hansberry, *Los Angeles Sentinel*, February 19, 1959, A7.

108. Walter Kerr, "First Night Report: *A Raisin in the Sun*," review of *A Raisin in the Sun*, by Lorraine Hansberry, *New York Herald-Tribune*, March 12, 1959, 18

109. Frank Aston, review of *A Raisin in the Sun*, by Lorraine Hansberry, *New York World Telegram*, March 12, 1959, 20.

110. Tom F. Driver, "Theatre," review of *A Raisin in the Sun*, by Lorraine Hansberry, *New Republic*, April 13, 1959, 21–22.

111. John McClain, "Theatre," review of *A Raisin in the Sun*, by Lorraine Hansberry, *New York Journal-American*, March 12, 1959, 35.

112. Karen Sánchez-Eppler, "Bodily Bonds: The Intersecting Rhetorics of Feminism and Abolitionism," in *The New American Studies: Essays from Representations*, ed. Philip Fisher (Berkeley: University of California Press, 1991): 235–36.

113. Ibid., 236.

114. Bernstein, 22.

115. Sánchez-Eppler, 235.

116. Dean Peerman, "A Raisin in the Sun: The Uncut Version," *Christian Century*, January 25, 1989, 71–73.

117. Driver, 21–22.

118. Margaret B. Wilkerson, "Lorraine Hansberry: The Complete Feminist," *Freedomways: A Quarterly Review of the Freedom Movement* 19 (1979): 237.

119. Ossie Davis, "The Significance of Lorraine Hansberry" in *Life Lit by Some Large Vision: Selected Speeches and Writings*, with editorial notes and a foreword by Ruby Dee. (New York: Atria Books, 2006): 99.

120. Wilkerson, 237.

121. Amiri Baraka, "A Critical Reevaluation: *A Raisin in the Sun*'s Enduring Passion," in *A Raisin in the Sun and the Sign in Sidney Brustein's Window*, by Lorraine Hansberry (New York: Vintage, 1995) 9–20.

122. Mike Wallace, interviews of Lorraine Hansberry, "Television Portraits of Colorful People," WNTA (Channel 13), n.d., Box 57, Folder 2, Lorraine Hansberry Papers, Schomburg Center, New York, NY.

Chapter 2

1. Touré, *Who's Afraid of Postblackness: What It Means to Be Black Now* (New York: Free Press, 2011), 48.

2. Rozalia Jovanovic, "Rashid Johnson on Staging LeRoi Jones in the Era of Amiri Baraka," BlouinArtInfo, November 8, 2013, http://www.blouinartinfo.com/news/story/982418/rashid-johnson-on-staging-leroi-jones-in-the-age-of-amiri (accessed November 11, 2013). Johnson told Jovanovic that his mother read *The Dead Lecturer* poems to him as a child and that his interest in staging *Dutchman* came in rereading the play several years ago and seeing its 2007 revival at the Cherry Lane Theatre, where it debuted in 1964. The staging in the baths came to mind because of stage direction suggestions of a hot steamy subway.

3. Harry Elam. "Introduction," in *The Methuen Drama Book of Post-Black Plays*, ed. Harry J. Elam Jr. and Douglas A. Jones Jr. (London: Methuen, 2012), xiv.

4. Jovanovic. In an interview with the *New York Times*'s Randy Kennedy, Johnson suggested that the bathhouse staging intensifies the play's content, saying that "it's a place where you can't take your phone, and there are no recording devices. People are disrobed. People are exposed to a degree that they never are in public, and so it's a place for really honest negotiations. I think of it as a very even playing field." Randy Kennedy, "A Play That's Sure to Make You Sweat: Baraka's 'Dutchman' to Be Staged in a Bathhouse," *New York Times*, November 10, 2013, D3.

5. "Backstage," *Ebony*, November 1963, 4, 8.

6. "It's Great to Be a Negro!!!," Ebony Photo-Editorial, *Ebony*, March 1964, 92.

7. Ibid.

8. Leroi Jones was born Everett Leroy Jones, but after he began studies at Howard University in 1952, he changed his name to Leroi Jones, and he published under it until 1967, when he changed his name to Imamu Ameer Baraka. In 1974 he changed it once again to Amiri Baraka. I have referenced him as LeRoi Jones when discussing him and the work he produced until 1967. In any references to him or his work after 1967, I have referenced him as Amiri Baraka.

9. Jovanovic; "Black Revolution and White Backlash: What Is the White Liberal's Role? A Report on the N.Y. Confrontation," *National Guardian* (United States), July 4, 1964, 9, Lorraine Hansberry Papers, Box 56, Folder 1, Schomburg Center. New York, NY.

10. Quoted in Willene P. Taylor, "The Fall of Man Theme in Imamu Amiri Baraka's (LeRoi Jones's) Dutchman," *Negro American Literature Forum* 7, no. 4 (Winter 1973): 128; Celia McGee. "A Return to Rage, Played Out in Black and White," *New York Times*, January 14, 2007, http://www.nytimes.com/2007/01/14/theater/14mcge.html?pagewanted=all&_r=0 (accessed November 14, 2013).

11. Joan W. Scott, "The Evidence of Experience," *Critical Inquiry* 17, no. 4 (Summer 1991): 773–97.

12. LeRoi Jones, 8–9.

13. Kevin Gaines. *Uplifting the Race: Black Leadership, Politics and Culture in the Twentieth Century* (Chapel Hill: University of North Carolina Press, 1995), 9

14. W. E. B. Du Bois, *The Souls of Black Folk* (New York: Penguin, 1989).

15. Lerone Bennett Jr., "The White Problem in America," *Ebony*, August 1965, 29–36.

16. Louis Lomax, "The White Liberal," *Ebony*, August 1965, 59–64.

17. Ibid., 60.

18. Ibid.

19. William Chafe, *Civilities and Civil Rights* (Oxford: Oxford University Press, 1981), 8–9

20. LeRoi Jones, 5.

21. Ibid., 17.

22. Ibid., 11.

23. Ibid., 16.

24. Chafe, 8.

25. Ibid., 9.

26. LeRoi Jones, 21.

27. Ibid.

28. Ibid., 32.

29. Ibid., 33.

30. Ibid.

31. Ibid., 34.

32. Scott, 776.

33. Darlene Clark Hine, "Rape and the Inner Lives of Black Women in the Middle West: Preliminary Thoughts on the Culture of Dissemblance," in *Unequal Sisters: A Multicultural Reader in U.S. Women's History*, ed. Ellen DuBois and Vicki L. Ruiz (New York: Routledge, 1990), 292–97.

34. Gaines, *Uplifting the Race*, 5–6.

35. Kimberly Nichelle Brown, *Writing the Black Revolutionary Diva: Women's Subjectivity and the Decolonizing Text* (Bloomington: Indiana University Press, 2010): 50.

36. LeRoi Jones, 35.

37. Ibid., 35–36.

38. Ibid., 38.

39. Ibid.

40. Ibid.

41. Ibid., 38.

42. Bernstein, 16–27.

43. Ibid., 22.

44. Ibid.

45. Ibid., 27.

46. Ibid.

47. Harry J. Elam and Michelle Elam, "Blood Debt: Reparations in Langston Hughes' Mulatto," *Theatre Journal* 61, no. 1 (March 2009): 85–103.

48. bell hooks, *Killing Rage: Ending Racism* (New York: Henry Holt, 1995), 26.

49. Edith Oliver, "Off Broadway over the Edge," review of *Dutchman*, by LeRoi Jones, *The New Yorker*, April 4, 1964, 23.

50. Philip Roth, "Channel X: Two Plays on the Race Conflict," *New York Times Review of Books*, May 28, 1964, 10–12.

51. Oliver, 23; Roth, 11.

52. Hoyt W. Fuller, "The Myth of White Backlash," *Negro Digest*, August 1964, 11–15.

53. Oliver, 23.

54. Ibid.

55. Roth, 11.

56. Ibid.

57. Ibid.

58. Ibid., 12.

59. Howard Taubman, "The Theatre: 'Dutchman' Opens on Triple Bill at the Cherry Lane," review of *Dutchman*, by LeRoi Jones, *New York Times*, March 25, 1964, 48.

60. Ibid.

61. Ibid.

62. Ibid.

63. Henry Popkin, "Dutchman a Furious Account," review of *Dutchman*, by LeRoi Jones, *Vogue*, July 1964, 32.

64. Ibid.

65. Ibid.

66. Ibid.

67. Ibid.

68. "Underground Fury," review of *Dutchman*, by LeRoi Jones, *Newsweek*, April 13, 1964, 60.

69. Celia McGee, "A Return to Rage, Played Out in Black and White," review of *Dutchman*, by Amiri Baraka, *New York Times*, January 14, 2007, http://www.nytimes.com/2007/01/14/theater/14mcge.html?pagewanted=all&_r=0 (accessed November 25, 2013).

70. Ibid.

71. Als Hilton, "The Theatre: In Black and White: Amiri Baraka's 'Dutchman,'" review of *Dutchman*, by Amiri Baraka, *The New Yorker*, February 5, 2007, http://www.newyorker.com/arts/critics/theater/2007/02/05/070205crth_theater_als?currentPage=1 (accessed November 20, 2013).

72. "Black Revolution and White Backlash," 5–9.

73. Amiri Baraka died on January 9, 2014, and in the wake of his death, the debate about his literary legacy continues. Parallel to the workings of cultural memory, which alternately remembers and forgets in the service of preserving a consensus narrative about the nation's history, obituaries for Baraka seemingly operated in the same vein. As critic Jennifer Ratner-Rosenhagen observed, while they offered a site of remembrance, "they are also testaments of our forgetting." While the obituaries acknowledged his literary contributions to both the Black Arts Movement and the New American Poetry, they also offered extended discussions of "Somebody Blew Up America," the controversial antisemitic poem he wrote in the wake of the September 11, 2001, attacks on the World Trade Center and the Pentagon, which ultimately ended his tenure as New Jersey's Poet Laureate, and of the antisemitism that also informed some of his other work. Jennifer Ratner-Rosenhagen, "Over Our Dead Bodies," *Dissent Magazine*, Winter 2014, http://www.dissentmagazine.org/article/over-our-dead-bodies.

Chapter 3

1. Zelizer, 379–87.

2. Rashid Johnson, Anderson Ranch Art Center Lecture, August 2012, http://vimeo.com/4815778 (accessed December 20, 2013).

3. Touré, 48.

4. Richard Shepard, "'Great White Hope' Author Avoided Strict History," *New York Times*, May 6, 1969, 35.

5. Ibid.

6. Several critics and writers observed a shift in African American cultural production in the late 1980s through the mid-1990s. Originally appearing in the *Village Voice* in 1986, Greg Tate's "Cult Nats Meet Freaky Deke" pointed to "a maturation of a postnationalist black arts movement, one more Afrocentric and cosmopolitan than anything that has come before" and featuring artists "for whom 'black culture' signifies a multicultural tradition of expressive practices" *Flyboy in the Buttermilk: Essays on Contemporary America.* (New York: Fireside Press, 1992) 206–207. Echoing Tate in his 1989 essay, "The New Black Aesthetic," Trey Ellis identifies himself and his NBA peers as cultural mulattos "educated by a multi-racial mix of cultures" who are committed to creating what philosopher Arthur Danto called "Disturbatory Art." Ellis, "New Black Aesthetic," 239. In *Buppies, B-Boys, Baps & Bohos: Notes on Post-Soul Black Culture* (New York: Da Capa, 2001), a collection of Nelson George's writing for the *Village Voice*, George traces the evolution of the post-soul era and argues that the four types outlined in its title mark an attempt to "capture the changes in the nature of African American life brought on by post–civil rights era reality" (xvi). Finally, in "She Came with the Rodeo," Lisa Jones recounts her work with eleven other women in the Rodeo Caldonia High-Fidelity Performance Theater, which provided an opportunity "to get out in public and act up; to toss off the expectations laid by our genitals, our melanin count, and our college degrees" (135). Citing both Tate's and Ellis's figuring of the NBA's "elastic view of 'black' art, ideas of integration and nationalism," she reflects on the Rodeo's performances from 1986 to 1988 as "trumpet[ing] the cultural explosion that followed" (135).

7. Ashe, 619–20.

8. The representational politics of the African American Freedom Struggle broadly and the Black Arts Aesthetic in particular are referenced throughout postblack discourse as both enabling and restricting post-soul representations. As an example, Trey Ellis writes in "The New Black Aesthetic" of the NBA's willingness to parody Black Arts Aesthetics and to "flout publicly the official, positivist black party line" but reiterates the NBA's indebtedness to Black Arts Aesthetics (236). Similarly, curator Thelma Golden argues in the introduction to the 2001 *Freestyle* catalogue that she "holds a certain degree of nostalgia for the passion and energy that created the nationalist/aesthetic dogma of the 1970s Black Arts Movement" (14). Yet she is compelled to exhibit the work of artists whose work speaks to "the quest to define ongoing changes in the evolution of African American art and ultimately to ongoing redefinition of blackness in contemporary culture" (14–15).

9. Kevin Everod Quashie. "The Problem of Blackness in Contemporary Criticism" (lecture, University of Sarajevo, Bosnia and Herzegovina, November 29, 2005).

10. Ibid.

11. Gerald Early. "Rebel of the Progressive Era," PBS.org., Public Broadcasting System, January 2005, Web., June 7, 2011, http://www.pbs.org/unforgivableblackness/rebel/. In the 1967 draft typescripts of the play, Sackler included exchanges between Jefferson and

reporters that pointed to the influence of Progressive Era anxieties about black male sexuality and the ubiquity of minstrel stereotypes in US racial discourse that were omitted from the final published script. In one example, after Jefferson tells the press corps he wants to get back to Chicago to enjoy his mother's "good home pot roast and spaghetti," one reporter asks "no fried chicken, Jack?" (79). In his dissembling response, which is directly addressed to the audience, Jefferson replies "**what he talking in, French?**"(80). However, in the published play, Jefferson's response to the same question is "Mmm mmh." Engaging stereotypes about black male sexuality, a reporter asks Jefferson, "Is it true that colored people can't take a punch to the stomach," to which Jefferson replies "I don't know nobody *like* one, Mister" (81). When the reporter presses further, asking "what about that yellow streak Brady talks about," Jefferson's signifying rejoinder as he moves to take off his robe is "yeah, you wanna see it?" (81). These and other such revisions undermined Sackler's construction of an aracial metaphor of struggle between man and the outside world because such a project necessitated revisions that deemphasized the significance of racial hierarchies and pervasive stereotypes in the Progressive Era. In effect, Sackler's efforts to evacuate race from the play's meaning hinged on the racial discourse and racial categories it attempts to set aside. Howard Sackler, "The Great White Hope," November 1, 1967, Typescript, Howard Sackler Manuscripts, Harry Ransom Humanities Research Center, University of Texas at Austin.

12. Michael Collins's compelling essay, "'Ali Even Motivates the Dead': The Pursuit of Sovereignty in Norman Mailer's *The Fight*," examined Mailer's "love-hate" balancing act between the "Noir" of his imagination and "the obstacle, a phenomenon" he calls "Black" embodied in the Black Power movement, Muhammad Ali, and Zairean dictator Mobutu Sese Seko (333). Tracing Mailer's swings from love to hate of "Black" to "fear of social death that sparks a jealous guarding of status and a thirst for . . . the high status of sovereignty in one's sphere," Collins argued that Mailer invested in both the rising sovereignty of "Black" while simultaneously enveloping himself in the rising anger of "White" (333). Sackler's limited discussion of the play's racial dynamics did not mirror Mailer's anxieties around race and representation; he clearly evaded the discussions about how the play's representations of racial identity signified in the current moment, particularly as it might potentially speak to the controversies surrounding Muhammad Ali. In maintaining that the play was simply about man and the outside world, Sackler sought to deemphasize how blackness signified in the play, even as it contributed to the play's plot and ultimately, its success. In effect, he invoked the imagined boundary between the universal and the particular to circumvent any discussion of race and how it signified in the play as well as in its critical reception. Michael Collins, "'Ali Even Motivates the Dead': The Pursuit of Sovereignty in Norman Mailer's *The Fight*," *PMLA* 128, no. 2 (March 2013): 322–36.

13. David Román, *Acts of Intervention: Performance, Gay Culture, and AIDS* (Bloomington: Indiana University Press, 1998), xxvi.

14. Mindful of Sackler's racial anxieties and evasions noted above, I offer the inclu-

sion of *The Great White Hope* in this study as a postblack gesture that, following Kevin Everod Quashie, neither echoes Sackler's "aracial" discussion of the play or that attempts to "police the quality of blackness" offered in Jefferson's representation. Elam and Jones, eds., xxviii.

15. Gaines, *Uplifting the Race*, 2.

16. Eversley, 51.

17. Chappell, 72–73.

18. Ibid.

19. Shepard, 35.

20. Nelson Pressley, "The Good Fight: Arena Stage Goes Another Round with the Heavyweight Drama That Changed All the Rules," *American Theatre*, October 2000, 28+; "Dr. Washington Asks Press to Fight Fighter," *Chicago Daily Tribune*, October 21, 1912, 3.

21. Zelizer, 379–87.

22. David Román, *Performance in America*, 297.

23. Geoffrey C. Ward, *Unforgivable Blackness: The Rise and Fall of Jack Johnson* (New York: Knopf, 2004), 369.

24. Thomas R. Hietala, "Ali and the Age of Bare Knuckle Politics," in *Muhammad Ali: The People's Champ*, ed. Elliot J. Gorn, 117–53 (Urbana: University of Illinois Press, 1995. Theatre and performance critic Harvey Young discussed Ali's identification and disidentification with Jack Johnson within a broader argument interpreting Ali's refusal to be inducted as a "performance of stillness" that empowered the black body in contrast to the "enforced stillness" alternately acceded to and imposed upon Johnson as well as boxers Tom Molineaux and Joe Louis. Harvey Young, "Between the Ropes: Staging the Black Body in American Boxing," in his *Embodying Black Experience: Stillness, Critical Memory, and the Black Body* (Ann Arbor: University of Michigan Press, 2010), 76–118.

25. Beyond the legal difficulties that Ali and Johnson shared, critics may have noted that Ali was the third African American to hold the heavyweight title during the 1960s and noted as well the renewed interest in Johnson's life concurrent with the play's debut and Broadway run. Finis Farr's *Black Champion: The Life and Times of Jack Johnson* was published in 1964, the same year that Ali defeated Sonny Liston for the title. Liston defeated Floyd Patterson in 1962, and Patterson regained the title in 1960 from Sweden's Ingemar Johansson. *The Great White Hope*'s Broadway performances from October 1968 to January 1970 and a national tour from September 1969 to February 1970 likely helped revive interest in Johnson's story. Following the play's initial production was the 1969 reissue of *Jack Johnson Is a Dandy: An Autobiography* and the appearance of other works, including Robert DeCoy's Johnson biography, *The Big Black Fire* (1969); Martin Ritt's film *The Great White Hope* (1970), for which Sackler wrote the screenplay; *Jack Johnson* (1971), a documentary directed by Jim Jacobs and scored by Miles Davis; Davis's own album *A Tribute to Jack Johnson* (1971); and finally, Al-Tony Gilmore's *Bad Nigger: The National Impact of Jack Johnson* (1975).

26. Randy Roberts, *Papa Jack: Jack Johnson and the Era of Great White Hopes* (New York: Free Press, 1983), 103.

27. "Dr. Washington," 3.

28. Jack Johnson, *Jack Johnson Is a Dandy: An Autobiography* (New York: Chelsea House, 1969), 329.

29. Howard Sackler. *The Great White Hope* (New York: Dial, 1968), 21.

30. Ibid.

31. Gaines, Uplifting the Race, 69.

32. Gates, 124.

33. Quashie.

34. Sackler, *Great White Hope*, 23–24.

35. Though Abraham Lincoln is often referenced as the Great Emancipator, his equivocating about the Emancipation Proclamation, slavery, and racial equality is well documented. As a presidential candidate, he argued that neither the president nor Congress had the power to interfere with slavery, and as president in a frequently cited meeting with a group of free blacks in August 1862, he posited that "not a single man of your race is made the equal of a single man of ours." H. W. Brands, "Hesitant Emancipator," *American History* 44, no. 2 (2009): 57.

36. Sackler, *Great White Hope*, 36.

37. Ibid., 38.

38. Ibid.

39. Ibid., 39.

40. My use of middle-class elites draws on Gaines's distinction in *Uplifting the Race* between the material conditions constituting class status and a "moral economy" of class. He writes, "Many blacks, or whites for that matter, were not middle class in any truly material or economic sense, but rather represented themselves as such, in a variety of complex ways" (17).

41. Gaines, Uplifting the Race, 58.

42. Sackler, *Great White Hope*, 130–31.

43. Gaines, Uplifting the Race, 88.

44. Gaines, 89.

45. Sackler, *Great White Hope*, 56.

46. Gaines, 88.

47. Ellis, "New Black Aesthetic," 235.

48. Sackler, *Great White Hope*, 199.

49. Ibid., 203.

50. Ibid., 238.

51. Ibid., 239.

52. Ibid.

53. Ibid.

54. Errol Hill and James V. Hatch, *A History of African American Theatre* (Cambridge: Cambridge University Press, 2003), 428.

55. Ibid., 393–95.

56. Stephen J. Bottoms, *Playing Underground: A Critical History of the 1960s Off-Off-Broadway Movement* (Ann Arbor: University of Michigan Press, 2004), 210; Anthony D. Hill and Douglas Q. Barnett, *Historical Dictionary of African American Theater* (Lanham, MD: Scarecrow, 2009), 212.

57. Hoyt W. Fuller, "A Report on Black Theatre in America: General Report," *Negro Digest*, April 1970: 34+.

58. Peter Bailey, "Report on Black Theater: New York," *Negro Digest*, April 1970, 20+.

59. Ibid., 23.

60. Pressley, 31.

61. Harry Golden, "Only in America," review of *The Great White Hope*, by Howard Sackler, *Chicago Daily Defender*, April 9, 1969, 15.

62. Ibid.

63. Toni Cade Bambara, "Thinking About 'The Great White Hope,'" *The Black Woman: An Anthology*, ed. Toni Cade Bambara, 237–43 (New York: Penguin, 1970).

64. Ibid., 240.

65. Ibid.

66. Riots in Newark and Detroit in July 1967 prompted President Lyndon Johnson to form an eleven-member National Advisory Commission on Civil Disorders, commonly known as the Kerner Commission, shortly afterward. Its report, issued on February 29, 1968, warned in a now frequently quoted phrase, that "the nation is moving toward two societies, one black, one white—separate and unequal" and held the mainstream media accountable for its passive escalation of racial tensions United States Kerner Commission. *Report of the National Advisory Commission on Civil Disorders*. (New York: Bantam, 1968), 1.

67. Clive Barnes, "Theater: 'White Hope' Tale of Modern Othello, Opens in Capital," review of *The Great White Hope*, by Howard Sackler, *New York Times*, December 14, 1967, 57.

68. Alan Bunce, "'White Hope' and Living Theater," review of *The Great White Hope*, by Howard Sackler, *Christian Science Monitor*, October 9, 1968, 10.

69. Julius Novick "Tragic Cakewalk," review of *The Great White Hope*, by Howard Sackler, *The Nation*, January 15, 1968, 93–94.

70. Ibid., 93.

71. Harold Clurman, "Theatre," review of *The Great White Hope*, by Howard Sackler, *The Nation*, October 28, 1968, 445–46; Cecil Smith, "'Great White Hope' a New Champion on Broadway," review of *The Great White Hope*, by Howard Sackler, *Los Angeles Times*, November 17, 1968, D30.

72. "The Theater: Feeling Good by Feeling Bad," review of *The Great White Hope*, by Howard Sackler, *Time*, October 11, 1968, 73.

73. Richard Gilman, "Not Quite Heavyweight," review of *The Great White Hope*, by Howard Sackler, *New Republic*, October 26, 1968, 36–38.

74. Clurman, 446.

75. Cathy Aldridge, "P.S.," *New York Amsterdam News*, November 9, 1968, 7.

76. Ashe, 609–23.

77. GeoffreyWard, 429.

Chapter 4

1. Lorna Simpson quoted in Touré, 23.

2. Clayton G. Holloway. "The Alembic of Genius: An Interview with Alice Childress," *Xavier Review* 17, no. 1: (1997): 9.

3. Alice Childress, "For a Strong Negro People's Theatre," *Daily Worker*, February 10, 1951, 11. Reprinted from *Masses and Mainstream* 4 (February 1951): 61–64.

4. Mary Helen Washington, James Smethurst, Cheryl Higashida, Kathlene McDonald, and Kevin Gaines, among other critics, detailed Childress's participation in what Washington calls a "Black Leftist cultural front" in the 1940s and 1950s that significantly informed her writing. Washington, Higashida, and McDonald restored her place in Left cultural historiography, while Gaines traced postwar black feminism's precursors to that era, enabling black women writers, including Childress, to take up gender concerns, and Smethurst mapped the Black Arts Movement's cultural genealogies, locating the Black Left as a crucial forebear to the Black Arts Movement. Clearly, the Black Left of the 1940s and 1950s shaped her oeuvre and therefore had implications for *Wine in the Wilderness*. As Gaines suggested about her column that began as "Like One of the Family" in Paul Robeson's newspaper, *Freedom*, and continued as "Here's Mildred" in the *Baltimore Afro-American*, *Wine in the Wilderness* provided Childress an opportunity to engage the intersections of race, gender, and representation through its protagonist, Mildred Johnson, within a black, urban social space. Gaines, "From Center to Margin," 294–314.

5. Touré, 153.

6. Ibid., 153–54.

7. Childress, *Wine*, 9.

8. Michael Eric Dyson. "Preface," in *Is Bill Cosby Right? Or Has The Black Middle Class Lost Its Mind?* New York: Basic Books, 2005, xiv–xv.

9. Ibid.

10. Ibid., xiv.

11. Ibid.," xv.

12. Alice Childress, *Wine in the Wilderness*, New York: Dramatist Play Service, 1969, 18–19.

13. Ibid., 8.

14. Ibid., 11.

15. Ibid., 5.

16. Ibid., 18–19.

17. Ibid., 19.

18. Lee Rainwater and William L. Yancey, *The Moynihan Report and the Politics of Controversy* (Cambridge, MA: MIT Press, 1967), 29–30.

19. Kelley, 27–28.

20. Ibid., 31.

21. While I read the play as a critique of masculinist tendencies within both the Black Power and Black Arts/Aesthetic Movements, I am aware that these movements did not univocally demonstrate the misogyny and homophobia that has become central to their discussion in cultural memory. The work of scholars including Peniel Joseph and Jeffrey O. G. Ogbar on the Black Power movement, as well as research on the Black Arts Movement by James Smethurst, Lisa Gail Collins, and Margo Natalie Crawford, intervened in this narrative. As Smethurst has argued, while gender bias and homophobia clearly had institutional and individual influence on them, they held no more authority in these movements than on any other aspect of American culture during that time. Further, their influence was contested by women and some men within, loosely affiliated with, and outside those movements, forcing them to rethink their positions and, in some cases, to renounce them altogether. Still, it remains that these impulses did influence cultural production and for writers like Childress, they warranted a response. See Joseph, *The Black Power Movement: Rethinking the Civil Rights-Black Power Era* (London: Routledge, 2006); Ogbar, *Black Power: Radical Politics and African American Identity* (Baltimore: Johns Hopkins University Press, 2004); Smethurst, *The Black Arts Movement: Literary Nationalism in the 1960s and 1970s* (Chapel Hill: University of North Carolina Press, 2005); and Collins and Crawford, *New Thoughts on the Black Arts Movement* (New Brunswick, NJ: Rutgers University Press, 2006).

22. Eldridge Cleaver, *Soul On Ice* (New York: Random House, 1968), 207.

23. Childress, *Wine*, 28.

24. Ibid., 34.

25. Ibid., 35.

26. Gaines. "Racial Uplift Ideology."

27. Childress, *Wine*, 35.

28. Touré, 153–54.

29. Childress, *Wine*, 9.

30. Ibid.

31. Ibid., 10.

32. Smethurst, 82.

33. Rainwater and Yancey, 29–30.

34. Ibid.

35. United States Kerner Commission, 362–63.

36. Ibid., 133.

37. Childress, *Wine*, 24–25.

38. Theda Skocpol, Ariane Liazos, and Marshall Ganz, *What a Mighty Power We Can Be: African American Fraternal Groups and the Struggle for Racial Equality* (Princeton, NJ: Princeton University Press, 2006), 178–88. Yet the appearance of black fraternal organizations in the play, particularly The Order of the Eastern Star and The Improved Benevolent Protective Order of Elks, organizations that took an anti-Communist stance, as Skocpol, Liaszos, and Ganz noted, suggested that while the play offers a model of black feminism through racial solidarity across class lines, it may also signal Childress's efforts toward what Mary Helen Washington has described as "erasing and disguising her Leftist past." Ibid., 185. Mary Helen Washington, "Alice Childress, Lorraine Hansberry and Claudia Jones: Black Women Write the Popular Front," in *Left of the Color Line: Race, Radicalism and Twentieth Century Literature*, ed. Bill V. Mullen and James Smethurst (Chapel Hill: University of North Carolina Press, 2003).

39. Childress, *Wine*, 28–29.

40. Joe William Trotter, "African American Fraternal Associations in American History: An Introduction," *Social Science History* 28, no. 3 (2004): 355–66.

41. Childress, *Wine*, 29.

42. Ibid., 37.

43. Ibid., 35.

44. Philip Brian Harper, *Are We Not Men?: Masculine Anxiety and the Problem of African American Identity* (New York: Oxford University Press, 1996), 48.

45. Childress, *Wine*, 36. Theatre and performance critic Soyica Diggs Colbert has argued that Tommy's first deployment of "nigger" in the play to describe the people who have destroyed her apartment introduces a class distinction between Tommy and the rioters and consequently reveals both her "assertion[s] of superiority" and an "overriding hypocrisy" that has escaped critics. Colbert, "A Pedagogical Approach to Understanding Childress' *Wine in the Wilderness*," *Theatre Topics* 19, no.1 (2009): 81. Yet put within the context of her multiple uses of it throughout the play, this initial deployment begins Tommy's demonstration of the word's multivalence and Bill's attempts to fix its meaning as pejorative. In other words, it marks the start of their struggle over narrative authority about the word "nigger" and its power that is central to black identity's discourse in the play. Her deployment in this instance singles out behavior as it adapts what legal scholar Randall Kennedy has called "abusive criticism to spur action that is intended to erase any factual predicate for the condemnation voiced." Kennedy, *Nigger: The Strange Career of a Troubling Word* (New York: Vintage, 2003), 38. Further, her observation that the rioters shout "whitey, whitey . . . but who they burn out? Me" offers a reading of their behavior that belies an assertion of superiority and interprets the behavior as not only misdirected,

but also as undermining the kind of community she envisions at the play's end. Childress, *Wine*, 14. Ultimately, there is a subtle but important distinction between an assertion of superiority and her repudiation of their actions, and in that sense her initial deployment of "nigger" does not univocally signify the subordination of the rioters. Colbert, 77–85.

46. Randall L. Kennedy, "Who Can Say 'Nigger'? And Other Considerations," *Journal of Blacks in Higher Education*, no. 26. (Winter 1999–2000): 86–96.

47. Ibid.

48. Colbert, 81.

49. Childress, *Wine*, 38.

50. WGBH-TV Boston Program Logs for "On Being Black," WGBH Archives, Boston, 1–15.

51. Robert Lewis Shayon, "Curiouser and Curiouser," *Saturday Review*, August 8, 1970, 43.

52. Ibid.

53. United States Kerner Commission, 383.

54. Ibid., 366.

55. Ibid.

56. Ibid., 389.

57. Taylor, 6.

58. Ibid.

59. Ibid.

60. Ibid.

61. Ibid.

62. Ibid.

63. Jack Gould, "TV Review: Social Ills Are Focus of 2 N.E.T Premieres," *New York Times*, October 7, 1969, 96.

64. Ibid.

65. Ibid.

66. Ibid.

67. Alan M. Kriegsman, "On Being Black," *Washington Post-Times Herald*, June 18, 1971, B13.

68. Ibid.

69. Ibid.

70. Ibid.

71. Ibid.

72. Ibid.

73. Ibid.

74. Ibid.

75. Ibid.

76. Ibid.

77. Lorraine Hansberry, *To Be Young, Gifted, and Black: Lorraine Hansberry in Her Own Words*, adapted by Robert Nemiroff (New York: Vintage, 1996), 228.

78. Alice Childress and Ruby Dee, interview by James Spruill, *Say Brother*, First Anniversary Program Number 36, July 10, 1969, WGBH Archives. Boston. DVD.

79. Vivian Robinson, "Opening Night Vibrations," *New York Amsterdam News*, November 14, 1970, 23.

80. "'On Being Black' in KCET Debut Saturday Night," *Los Angeles Sentinel*, October 2, 1969, E2.

81. "Theatre Wing: 'Wine in the Wilderness' Has Premiere at NIU," *Chicago Daily Defender*, December 15, 1970, 11.

82. United States Kerner Commission, "The Communications Media," 384.

83. Alice Childress. "For A Strong Negro People's Theatre," 61–64.

84. United States Kerner Commission, "The Communications Media," 383

Chapter 5

1. Paul Beatty, *The White Boy Shuffle: A Novel* (New York: Picador, 1996), 52.

2. Ibid.

3. Ibid.

4. Ibid., 122.

5. Madhu Dubey, "Postmodernism as Post-Nationalism?," *The Black Scholar* 33, no. 1 (2003): 2–18.

6. Ashe, 614.

7. Charles Gordone, "Legacy of a Seer: Doing it the Hard Way," *Gateway* 25, no. 2 (2004): 15–21.

8. Susan Kouyomijian Gordone, "Legacy of a Seer: The Second Sojourn," *Gateway* 25, no. 2 (2004): 12–14.

9. Ibid., 14.

10. C. Gordone 15; S. Gordone, 14; Susan Harris Smith, "An Interview with Charles Gordone," *Studies in American Drama 1945 to Present*, vol. 3 (1988): 123–32.

11. Bosworth, "From Nowhere."

12. C. Gordone, "Legacy of a Seer," 16.

13. Michael Eric Dyson, Foreword, "Tour(é)ing Blackness," in *Who's Afraid of Post-blackness: What It Means to Be Black Now*, by Touré (New York: Free Press, 2011), xiv.

14. Larry Neal, "The Black Arts Movement," *Drama Review* 12 (1968): 29–38.

15. Ibid., 38.

16. Quoted in Touré, 21–22.

17. Harry J. Elam Jr., "The Performance of Blackness and the Black Performer," *African American Performance and Theater History*, ed. Harry J. Elam, Jr. and David Krasner (New York: Cambridge University Press, 2003), 296.

18. Elam Jr., 297.

19. Charles Gordone, *No Place to Be Somebody: A Black Black Comedy in Three Acts* (Indianapolis, IN: Bobbs-Merrill, 1969), 3.

20. Elam Jr., 296–97.

21. Gordone's own involvement with direct action protest as a member, and briefly, the acting chair of the Committee for the Employment of Negro Performers (CENP) in 1961 and 1962, which originated as part of the Congress of Racial Equality (CORE), may inform Gabe's perspectives. It picketed theaters and television studios for casting discrimination against black performers as well as for the "distorted images" of African Americans on television, radio, and theater stages. The group, whose members included actors Godfrey Cambridge and Louis Gossett, also engaged in a letter-writing campaign to Federal Communications Commission (FCC) chair Newton Minnow to protest token integration in television and radio. The groups' protest of the production of *Subways Are for Sleeping* in March 1962 counted Ossie Davis, Charles Mingus, and Gordone among those in the picket line, which resulted in the hiring of African Americans to that production's staff. However, the organization had disbanded by the end of 1962 due to internal conflicts. Rosemary E. Reed, "The Committee for the Employment of Negro Performers. A Report on Group Action—An Attempt to Make Producers Present a Realistic Picture of American Life in the Area of Mass Communications," May 1962, Charles Gordone Collection, Box 1, Folder 6, Schomburg Center. New York, NY.

22. Jacqueline Dowd Hall, "The Long Civil Rights Movement and the Political Uses of the Past," *Journal of American History* 91, no. 4 (2005): 1233–63.

23. B. Ward, ed., *Media, Culture*, 8.

24. Hall, 1233–34.

25. Dyson, Foreword, "Tour(é)ing Blackness," *Who's Afraid of Postblackness: What It Means to Be Black Now*, by Touré (New York: Free Press, 2011), xiv.

26. C. Gordone, *No Place*, 13–14.

27. "The March on Washington for Jobs and Freedom," Civil Rights Movement Veterans Website, http://www.crmvet.org/tim/tim63b.htm#1963mow (accessed August 23, 2013).

28. Ibid.

29. Ibid.

30. C. Gordone, 14.

31. Ibid.

32. "The March on Washington."

33. Chappell, Hutchinson, and B. Ward, "'Dress modestly, neatly,'" 69–100.

34. "An Appeal by The March Leaders," Civil Rights Movement Veterans Website, http://www.crmvet.org/docs/mowprog.pdf (accessed August 23, 2013).

35. C. Gordone, 14.

36. Ibid.

37. Ibid., 15.
38. Ibid.
39. Ibid.
40. Ibid.
41. Ashe, 614–15.
42. Ibid., 619–20.
43. Martin Luther King Jr., "Remaining Awake Through a Great Revolution," in *A Knock at Midnight: Inspiration from the Great Sermons of Reverend Martin Luther King*, ed. Clayborne Carson and Peter Holloran (New York: Warner, 1998), 205–24. In this sermon, delivered on March 31, 1968, just three days before his assassination, King argued that the bootstraps ideology reduces the complex relationship between slavery and African American poverty to a pithy cliché. He contended that those subscribing to this ideology "never stop to realize that the nation made the black man's color a stigma. But beyond this they never stop to realize the debt that they owe a people who were kept in slavery two hundred and forty years." Pointing to the inherent hypocrisy of those supporting this view and who benefited from land and land grant colleges provided by the federal government, King contended that they are now "receiving millions of dollars in federal subsidies every year not to farm. And these are so often the very people who tell Negroes that they must lift themselves by their own bootstraps." Gordone's allusion to "the debt" then recognizes that compelling argument, but questions whether the March is an effective means of demanding its payment, particularly when the constituencies advocating bootstraps ideology fail to see their complicity with systems of oppression and the hypocrisy embedded in rejecting the federal government's involvement in civil rights. King's assertion in the sermon that "we must come to see that the roots of racism are very deep in our country, and there must be something positive and massive in order to get rid of all the effects of racism and the tragedies of racial injustice" suggests that Gordone's signifying on the sermon points to the inability to discover what the "something positive and massive" might be, and that further, African Americans would need to continue forward whether or not such a discovery came to pass.
44. "An Appeal by the March Leaders."
45. C. Gordone, 16.
46. "An Appeal by the March Leaders."
47. Quoted in Larry Neal, "The Black Arts Movement," *Drama Review* 12, no. 4 (Summer 1968): 29–38.
48. C. Gordone, 16.
49. Ibid.
50. Lawrence Spivak, Washington Bureau Chief of the *Nashville Banner*, Frank van der Linden, NBC News White House correspondent Robert MacNeil, Cowles Newspaper Publications' Richard Wilson interview of Roy Wilkins and Martin Luther King, Jr. August 25, 1963 http://www.nbcnews.com/video/meet-the-press/44233007#54693955.

51. The representational import of Gordone's reference to chitlins within his representation of the March on Washington should not be underestimated, as African American anxiety around "stereotypically black" foods continues in the current historical moment. In *Who's Afraid of Postblackness?: What It Means to Be Black Now*, the writer Touré acknowledged their representational, and perhaps psychological, power when he asked several of the black cultural producers he interviewed if they would be comfortable ordering those foods in a restaurant serving primarily white and a handful of black patrons. Touré himself offered that he "refuse[s] to live his life in fear of the white gaze," but the producer, music journalist, and musician Ahmir Thompson, better known as Questlove, said "I'll be the first to order fish instead of chicken. . . . I don't know why I still think that but it's just like that. I hate to say this, but no, I will not eat fried chicken in front of white people" (29). The Reverend Jesse Jackson has spoken to the cultural longevity of such stereotypes, reflecting that "Eating watermelon in public? We're not that free. 'Cause the stereotype was that deep. We're still overcoming the burden of a four-hundred-year journey and the beneficiaries of that journey must honor the integrity of that journey" (ibid.). Further, the numerous Photoshopped images of the nation's first African American president Barack Obama eating fried chicken, watermelon, or both have spoken to the continuing significance of such stereotypes and how they are still deployed to dehumanize and disempower African Americans. Thompson's and Jackson's responses illustrate the continuing cultural freight and meaning attached to such images in the twenty-first century. Gordone's deliberate reference to an African American foodway linked to slavery within a March meant to demonstrate African American progress and suitability for full citizenship since the Emancipation Proclamation, as well as to demonstrate African Americans' respectability, points to his refusal to capitulate to the stereotype and its implications. In effect, he has rejected both a black normative gaze and a white normative gaze around race and representation. As Cornel West has asserted, "Oftentimes the white supremacy inside of Black minds is so deep that the white normative gaze and the Black normative gaze are not that different" (ibid.). Gordone's play with representations within Gabe's recounting of the March anticipates West's assertion and defies the normative gaze. Touré.

52. C. Gordone, *No Place*, 21.

53. Ibid.

54. Martin Gottfried. "Is All Black Theater Beautiful? No." *New York Times*, 7 June 1970: 89.

55. Ibid.

56. bell hooks, *Killing Rage: Ending Racism* (New York: Henry Holt, 1995), 26.

57. C. Gordone, *No Place*, 3.

58. C. Gordone, *No Place*, 21.

59. Quoted in Touré, 21–22.

60. Elam Jr., 298.

61. C. Gordone, *No Place*, 45.

62. Ibid., 46–47.
63. Ibid., 80.
64. Elam Jr., 301.
65. Gordone, *No Place*, 81.
66. Ibid., 115.
67. Ibid.
68. Ibid.
69. Ibid. Sigmund Freud argues in "Mourning and Melancholia" that "mourning is regularly the reaction to the loss of a loved person, or to the loss of some abstraction which has taken the place of one, such as one's country, liberty, an ideal, and so on." Freud, *On Murder, Mourning and Melancholia* (New York: Penguin, 2007), 243. He further observes that while "mourning involves grave departures from the normal attitude toward life," it does not require intervention as melancholia does because mourning can be "overcome after a certain lapse of time" and any interference with it is "useless or even harmful." Ibid., 243–44. Though Gabe's mourning marks the loss of black subjectivity's framing within the limited social and political contexts of protest and struggle, Elam argued that he confirms male privilege and that the feminization which enables his mourning is "encoded with misogyny and male-centrism." (Elam Jr., 302). However, cross-dressing's inherent contingencies undermine Gabe's male privilege. As critic Marjorie Garber has suggested, cross-dressing facilitates "a mode of articulation, a way of describing a space of possibility" that "puts in question identities previously conceived as stable, unchallengeable, grounded and 'known.'" Marjorie Garber, *Cross-Dressing and Cultural Anxiety* (London: Routledge, 1992), 12–13. His performance, which includes a black shawl draped over his head, disrupts the gendered logic embedded in mourning, particularly in its allusion to the widely disseminated images of Coretta Scott King, Betty Shabazz, and Myrlie Evers all mourning the deaths of their husbands, as Elam points out. As Gabe signals those images of black female subjectivity, he highlights how even within the gendered logic of mourning that would enable black women's suffering to be heard, it is not. Thus, his female impersonation gestures toward a "space of possibility" that aligns with his previous solo performances' work in developing in black subjectivity's conceptual space. Instead of reinforcing patriarchal black masculinity's superiority, Gabe's breach of gendered boundaries draws attention to how that structure fails to acknowledge black women and attempts to overturn that erasure and render them visible. Still, that moment of visibility is staged within what is effectively a memorial service marking protest's death.

70. "Public Theater Presents Black Comedy," review of *No Place to Be Somebody: A Black Black Comedy in Three Acts*, by Charles Gordone, *New York Amsterdam News*, May 3, 1969, 24.

71. Walter Kerr, "Not Since Edward Albee . . . ," review of *No Place to Be Somebody: A Black Black Comedy in Three Acts*, by Charles Gordone, *New York Times*, May 18, 1969, D1.

72. Simon Anekwe, "No Place to Be Somebody Is Solid," review of *No Place to Be Somebody: A Black Black Comedy in Three Acts*, by Charles Gordone, *New York Amsterdam News*, February 7, 1970, 42.

73. Molly Haskell, "Theatre: No Place to Be Somebody," review of *No Place to Be Somebody: A Black Black Comedy in Three Acts*, by Charles Gordone, *Village Voice*, May 8, 1969: 40.

74. George Oppenheimer, "Play Attempts to Show Blacks Have 'No Place,'" review of *No Place to Be Somebody: A Black Black Comedy in Three Acts*, by Charles Gordone, *Newsday*, May 5, 1969. 32A; Clive Barnes, "Theatre: No Place to Be Somebody on Lafayette St.," review of *No Place to Be Somebody: A Black Black Comedy in Three Acts*, by Charles Gordone, *New York Times*, May 5, 1969, 53.

75. Mel Gussow, "Theatre: No Place to Be Somebody Opens," review of *No Place to Be Somebody: A Black Black Comedy in Three Acts*, by Charles Gordone, *New York Times*, December 31, 1969, 17.

76. Gottfried, 89.

77. Ibid.

78. Clayton Riley, "A Black View: O, Blacks Are We Damned Forever?," *New York Times*, May 18, 1969, 22.

79. Ibid.

80. Ibid.

81. Fuller, "A Report," 34+.

82. Ibid., 85.

83. Bailey, 25+.

84. Douglas Turner Ward, "American Theatre: For Whites Only?," *New York Times*, August 14, 1966, 93. Shortly after his essay appeared in the *New York Times*, the Ford Foundation solicited Ward to write a grant that it funded, establishing the NEC in 1967.

85. Bosworth, "From Nowhere."

86. D. Ward, 93.

87. Touré, 25.

Coda

1. Bob Abelman, "Review: High Hopes for Karamu Production Get Knocked Out," review of *The Great White Hope*, by Howard Sackler, *Cleveland News-Herald*, May 10, 2010, http://www.news-herald.com (accessed December 1, 2013).

2. Ted Hoover, "No Place to Be Somebody," review of *No Place to Be Somebody: A Black Black Comedy in Three Acts*, by Charles Gordone, *Pittsburgh City Paper*, November 6, 2008, http://www.pghcitypaper.com (accessed December 1, 2013).

3. Ed Siegel, "New York Stage Report: Bright But Not Sunny, the Sentimental Is Out

in a Crop of Smart Plays," review of *A Raisin in the Sun*, by Lorraine Hansberry, *Boston Globe*, May 30, 2004, N4.

4. Ibid.

5. James Baldwin, "Sweet Lorraine," in *The Price of the Ticket: Collected Nonfiction, 1948–1985*, by James Baldwin (New York: St. Martin's Press, 1985), 443–47.

6. Anna Deveare Smith, "Two Visions of Love, Family and Race across the Generations," *New York Times*, May 29, 2004, B9.

7. Ibid.

8. Ben Brantley, "No Rest for the Weary: *A Raisin in the Sun* Brings Denzel Washington Back to Broadway," *New York Times*, April 3, 2014, http://www.nytimes.com/2014/04/04/theater/raisin-in-the-sun-brings-denzel-washington-back-to-broadway.html?_r= (accessed July 28, 2014).

9. Ibid.

10. Ralph Ellison, "The World and the Jug," in *Shadow and Act*, by Ralph Ellison (New York: Random House, 1964), 107–43; Ellis, "New Black Aesthetic," 233–43.

11. Ashe, 609–23.

12. Ellison, "The World," 139.

13. Ibid. Emphasis in original.

BIBLIOGRAPHY

Abelman, Bob. "Review: High Hopes for Karamu Production Get Knocked Out," review of *The Great White Hope*, by Howard Sackler, *Cleveland News-Herald*, May 10, 2010, http://www.news-herald.com. Accessed December 1, 2013.

Aldridge, Cathy. "P.S." *New York Amsterdam News*. November 9, 1968, 7.

Als, Hilton. "The Theatre: In Black and White: Amiri Baraka's 'Dutchman.'" of *Dutchman*. By Amiri Baraka. *The New Yorker*. February 5, 2007. http://www.newyorker.com/arts/critics/theater/2007/02/05/070ED.205crth_theater_als?currentPage=1. Accessed November 20, 2013.

Anekwe, Simon. "No Place to Be Somebody Is Solid." Review of *No Place to Be Somebody: A Black Black Comedy in Three Acts*. By Charles Gordone. *New York Amsterdam News*, February 7, 1970, 42.

"An Appeal by the March Leaders." Civil Rights Movement Veterans Website. http://www.crmvet.org/docs/mowprog.pdf.

Ashe, Bertram. "Theorizing the Post-Soul Aesthetic: An Introduction." In *Post-Soul Aesthetic*. Ed. Bertram Ashe. Special issue of *African American Review* 41, no. 4 (2007): 609–23.

———. Crystal Anderson, Mark Anthony Neal, Evie Shockley, and Alexander Weheliye. "These—Are –the 'Breaks': A Roundtable Discussion on Teaching the Post-Soul Aesthetic." In *Post-Soul Aesthetic*, ed. Bertram Ashe, special issue of *African American Review* 41, no. 4 (2007):787–803

Aston, Frank. Review of *A Raisin in the Sun*. By Lorraine Hansberry. *New York World Telegram*, March 12, 1959, 20.

Atkinson, Brooks. "Raisin in the Sun: Vivid Drama about a Poor Negro Family." Review of *A Raisin in the Sun*. By Lorraine Hansberry. *New York Times*, March 29, 1959, X1.

———. "The Theatre: A Raisin in the Sun." Review of *A Raisin in the Sun*. By Lorraine Hansberry. *New York Times*, March 12, 1959.

Backstage. *Ebony*, November 1963, 4.

———. *Ebony*, August 1947, 8.

Bailey, Peter. "Report on Black Theater: New York." *Negro Digest*, April 1970, 20+.

Baldwin, James. "Sweet Lorraine." In *The Price of the Ticket: Collected Nonfiction, 1948–1985*, by James Baldwin, 443–47 (New York: St. Martin's Press, 1985).

Bambara, Toni Cade. "Thinking About 'The Great White Hope.'" In *The Black Woman: An Anthology*. Ed. Toni Cade Bambara. New York: Penguin, 1970.
Baraka, Amiri (LeRoi Jones). "A Critical Reevaluation: A Raisin in the Sun's Enduring Passion." In *A Raisin in the Sun and the Sign in Sidney Brustein's Window*. By Lorraine Hansberry. New York: Vintage, 1995.
Barnes, Clive. "Theatre: Howard Sackler's 'Great White Hope,' Edwin Sherin Staged Cheated Hero's Story." Review of *The Great White Hope*. By Howard Sackler. *New York Times*, October 4, 1968, 40.
———. "Theater: 'White Hope' Tale of Modern Othello, Opens in Capital." Review of *The Great White Hope*. By Howard Sackler. *New York Times*, December 14, 1967, 57.
———."Theatre: No Place to Be Somebody on Lafayette St." Review of *No Place to Be Somebody: A Black Black Comedy in Three Acts*. By Charles Gordone. *New York Times*, May 5, 1969, 53.
Beatty, Paul. *The White Boy Shuffle: A Novel*. New York: Picador, 1996.
Bennett, Lerone, Jr. "The White Problem in America." *Ebony*, August 1965, 29–36.
Bernstein, Robin. "Inventing a Fishbowl: White Supremacy and the Critical Reception of Lorraine Hansberry's *A Raisin in the Sun*." *Modern Drama* 42, no.1 (Spring 1999): 16–27.
"Black Revolution and White Backlash: What Is the White Liberal's Role? A Report on the N.Y. Confrontation." *National Guardian* (United States), July 4, 1964, 5–9. Lorraine Hansberry Papers. Box 56, Folder 1. Schomburg Center for Research in Black Culture. New York, NY.
Bosworth, Patricia. "From Nowhere to 'No Place.'" *New York Times*, June 8, 1969, D1.
Bottoms, Stephen J. *Playing Underground: A Critical History of the 1960s Off-Off-Broadway Movement*. Ann Arbor: University of Michigan Press, 2004.
Brands, H. W. "Hesitant Emancipator." *American History* 44, no. 2 (2009): 54–59.
Brantley, Ben. "No Rest for the Weary: *A Raisin in the Sun* Brings Denzel Washington Back to Broadway." *New York Times*, April 3, 2014. http://www.nytimes.com/2014/04/04/theater/raisin-in-the-sun-brings-denzel-washington-back-to-broadway.html?_r=0. Accessed July 28, 2014.
Bunce, Alan. "'White Hope' and Living Theater." Review of *The Great White Hope*. By Howard Sackler. *Christian Science Monitor*, October 9, 1968, 10.
Byrd, Ayana, and Lori L. Tharps. *Hair Story: Untangling the Roots of Black Hair*. New York: St. Martin's, 2001.
Carson, Clayborne, and Peter Holloran. *A Knock at Midnight: Inspiration from the Great Sermons of Reverend Martin Luther King, Jr*. New York: Warner Books, 1998.
Chafe, William. *Civilities and Civil Rights*. Oxford: Oxford University Press, 1981.
Chappell, Marisa, Jenny Hutchinson, and Brian Ward. "'Dress modestly, neatly . . . as if you were going to church': Respectability, Class, and Gender in the Montgomery Bus Boycott and the Early Civil Rights Movement." In *Gender and the Civil Rights Move-*

ment. Ed. Peter J. Ling and Sharon Monteith. New Brunswick, NJ: Rutgers University Press, 2004.

Childress, Alice. *Wine in the Wilderness*. New York: Dramatist Play Service, 1969.

———. "For A Strong Negro People's Theatre." *Daily Worker*, February 10, 1951, 11. Reprinted from *Masses and Mainstream*, 4 (February 1951): 61–64.

———, and Ruby Dee. Interview by James Spruill. "Say Brother" First Anniversary Program no. 36, July 10, 1969. WGBH Archives.

Cleaver, Eldridge. *Soul On Ice*. New York: Random House, 1968.

Clurman, Harold. "Theatre." Review of *The Great White Hope*. By Howard Sackler. *The Nation*, October 28, 1968, 445–46.

Colbert, Soyica Diggs. "A Pedagogical Approach to Understanding Childress' *Wine in the Wilderness*." *Theatre Topics* 19, no. 1 (2009): 77–85.

Davis, Miles. *A Tribute to Jack Johnson*. Recording, Feb. 18, 1970. Columbia, 1992. CD.

DeCoy, Robert H. *The Big Black Fire*. Los Angeles: Holloway House, 1969.

DeKoven, Marianne. *Utopia Limited: The Sixties and the Emergence of the Postmodern*. Durham, NC: Duke University Press, 2004.

Demille, Darcy. "Says Negro Playwright is a Genius." Review of *A Raisin in the Sun*. *Los Angeles Sentinel*, February 19, 1959, A7.

"Dr. Washington Asks Press to Fight Fighter." *Chicago Daily Tribune*, October 21 1912, 3.

"Dr. Washington Raps Jack Johnson." *Baltimore Afro-American*, October 26, 1912, 4.

Driver, Tom F. "Theatre." Review of *A Raisin in the Sun*. By Lorraine Hansberry. *New Republic*, April 13, 1959, 21–22.

Du Bois, W. E. B. *The Souls of Black Folk*. New York: Penguin, 1989.

Dubey, Madhu. "Postmodernism as Post-nationalism?" *The Black Scholar* 33, no. 1 (2003): 2–18.

Dyson, Michael Eric. *Is Bill Cosby Right? Or Has the Black Middle Class Lost Its Mind?* New York: Basic Books, 2005.

———. Foreword. "Tour(é)ing Blackness." In *Who's Afraid of Postblackness: What It Means to Be Black Now*. By Touré. New York: Free Press, 2011.

Early, Gerald. "Rebel of the Progressive Era." PBS.org. Public Broadcasting System. January 2005. Web. June 7, 2011. http://www.pbs.org/unforgivableblackness/rebel/.

Elam, Harry J., Jr. "The Performance of Blackness and the Black Performer." In *African American Performance and Theater History*. Ed. Harry J. Elam Jr. and David Krasner. New York: Cambridge, 2003.

———, and Douglas A. Jones Jr., eds. *The Methuen Drama Book of Post-Black Plays*. London: Methuen, 2012.

———, and Michelle Elam. "Blood Debt: Reparations in Langston Hughes' *Mulatto*." *Theatre Journal* 61, no. 1 (March 2009): 85–103.

Ellis, Trey. "The New Black Aesthetic." *Callaloo* 12, no. 1 (1989): 233–43.

———. "Response to NBA Critiques." *Callaloo* 12, no. 1 (1989): 250–51.

Ellison, Ralph. *Invisible Man*. New York: Vintage, 1995.

———. "The World and the Jug." In *Shadow and Act*, by Ralph Ellison, 107–43 (New York: Random House, 1964).

Eversley, Shelly. *The Real Negro: The Question of Authenticity in Twentieth-Century African American Literature*. New York: Routledge, 2004.

Farr, Finis. *Black Champion: The Life and Times of Jack Johnson*. New York: Scribner, 1964.

Fleetwood, Nicole R. *Troubling Vision: Performance, Visuality, and Blackness*. Chicago: University of Chicago Press, 2011.

Fuller, Hoyt W. "The Myth of White Backlash." *Negro Digest*, August 1964, 11–15.

———. "A Report on Black Theatre in America: General Report." *Negro Digest*, April 1970: 34+.

Gaines, Kevin. "From Center to Margin: Internationalism and the Origins of Black Feminism." In *Materializing Democracy: Toward a Revitalized Cultural Politics*. Ed. Russ Castronovo and Dana D. Nelson. Durham, NC: Duke University Press, 2002.

———. "Racial Uplift Ideology in the Era of 'the Negro Problem.'" Freedom's Story, TeacherServe©. National Humanities Center. Accessed September 26, 2013. http://nationalhumanitiescenter.org/tserve/freedom/1865-1917/essays/racialuplift.htm.

———,*Uplifting the Race: Black Leadership, Politics, and Culture in the Twentieth Century*. Chapel Hill: University of North Carolina Press, 1996.

Gates, Henry Louis. *The Signifying Monkey: A Theory of African-American Literary Criticism*. New York: Oxford University Press, 1988.

George, Nelson. *Buppies, B-Boys, Baps & Bohos: Notes on Post-Soul Black Culture*. New York: Da Capa, 2001.

Gilman, Richard. "Not Quite Heavyweight." Review of *The Great White Hope*. By Howard Sackler. *New Republic*, October 1968, 36–38.

Gilmore, Al-Tony. *Bad Nigger: The National Impact of Jack Johnson*. Port Washington, NY: Kennikat, 1975.

Golden, Harry. "Only in America." Review of *The Great White Hope*. By Howard Sackler. *Chicago Daily Defender*, April 9, 1969, 15.

Golden, Thelma. Interview with Betsy Sussler. *Bomb Magazine*. March 2004. http://bombmagazine.org/article/3588/thelma-golden. Accessed September 24, 2013.

———. "Introduction." *Freestyle*. New York: Studio Museum in Harlem, 2001. Exhibition Catalog.

Gordon, Michelle. "'Somewhat Like War': The Aesthetics of Segregation, Black Liberation and A Raisin in the Sun." *African American Review* 42, no. 1 (2008): 121–33.

Gordone, Charles. "Legacy of a Seer: Doing It the Hard Way." *Gateway* 25, no. 2 (2004): 15–21.

———. *No Place to Be Somebody: A Black Black Comedy in Three Acts*. Indianapolis, IN: Bobbs-Merrill, 1969.

Gordone, Susan Kouyomijian. "Legacy of a Seer: The Second Sojourn." *Gateway* 25, no. 2 (2004): 12–14.

Gottfried, Martin. "Is All Black Theater Beautiful? No." *New York Times*, June 7, 1970: 89.

Gould, Jack. "TV Review: Social Ills Are Focus of 2 N.E.T Premieres." *New York Times*, October 7, 1969: 96.

The Great White Hope. Dir. Martin Ritt. Perf. James Earl Jones and Jane Alexander. Screenplay by Howard Sackler. 1970. Twentieth Century Fox, 2006. DVD.

Gussow, Mel. "Theatre: No Place to Be Somebody Opens." Review of *No Place to Be Somebody: A Black Black Comedy in Three Acts*. By Charles Gordone. *New York Times*, December 31, 1969, 17.

Hall, Jacqueline Dowd. "The Long Civil Rights Movement and the Political Uses of the Past." *Journal of American History* 91, no. 4 (2005): 1233–63.

Hansberry, Lorraine. Interview with Eleanor Fisher. Box 3, Folder 8. Lorraine Hansberry Papers. Schomburg Center for Research in Black Culture. New York, NY.

———. Interview with Mike Wallace. "Television Portraits of Colorful People." WNTA (Channel 13), n.d. Box 57, Folder 2. Lorraine Hansberry Papers. Schomburg Center for Research in Black Culture. New York, NY.

———. Letter to Peter Buitenhuis. Lorraine Hansberry Papers. Box 8, Folder 1. February 3, 1959. Schomburg Center for Research in Black Culture. New York, NY.

———. *A Raisin in the Sun*. New York: Vintage, 1994.

———. "A Raisin in the Sun." Original Play Script with Annotations. November 1957. Box 6, Folder 1. Lorraine Hansberry Papers. Schomburg Center for Research in Black Culture. New York, NY.

———. *To Be Young, Gifted, and Black: Lorraine Hansberry in Her Own Words*. Adapted by Robert Nemiroff. New York: Vintage, 1996.

———. "Willy Loman, Walter Younger, and He Who Must Live." *Village Voice*, August 12, 1959, 7–8.

Harper, Philip Brian. *Are We Not Men?: Masculine Anxiety and the Problem of African American Identity*. New York: Oxford University Press, 1996.

Haskell, Molly. "Theatre: No Place to Be Somebody." Review of *No Place to Be Somebody: A Black Black Comedy in Three Acts*. By Charles Gordone. *Village Voice*, May 8, 1969: 40.

Hietala, Thomas R. "Ali and the Age of Bare Knuckle Politics." In *Muhammad Ali: The People's Champ*. Ed. Elliot J. Gorn. Urbana: Illinois University Press, 1995.

Hill, Anthony D., and Douglas Q. Barnett. *Historical Dictionary of African American Theater*. Lanham, MD: Scarecrow Press, 2009.

Hill, Errol, and James V. Hatch. *A History of African American Theatre*. Cambridge: Cambridge University Press, 2003.

Hine, Darlene Clark. "Rape and the Inner Lives of Black Women in the Middle West: Preliminary Thoughts on the Culture of Dissemblance." In *Unequal Sisters: A Multicul-*

tural Reader in U.S. Women's History. Ed. Ellen DuBois and Vicki L. Ruiz. New York: Routledge, 1990.

Holloway, Clayton G. "The Alembic of Genius: An Interview with Alice Childress." *Xavier Review* 17, no. 1 (1997): 5–22.

"Honoring the Legacy of Rosa Parks." Mitch McConnell Speech at Rosa Parks Statue Dedication on February 27, 2013. http://uneditedpolitics.com/mitch-mcconnell-speech-at-rosa-parks-statue-dedication-22713. Accessed September 3, 2013.

hooks, bell. *Killing Rage: Ending Racism*. New York: Henry Holt, 1995.

———. "Postmodern Blackness." In her *Yearning: Race, Gender, and Cultural Politics*. Boston, MA: South End Press, 1990.

Hoover, Ted. "No Place to Be Somebody. Review of *No Place to Be Somebody: A Black Black Comedy in Three Acts*. By Charles Gordone. *Pittsburgh City Paper*, November 6, 2008. http://www.pghcitypaper.com. Accessed December 1, 2013.

"It's Great to be a Negro!!!" Ebony Photo-Editorial. *Ebony*, March 1964, 92.

Jack Johnson. Dir. Jim Jacobs. Perf. Jack Johnson, Miles Davis, Brock Peters. Big Fights, 1970. Film.

Johnson, Jack. *Jack Johnson Is a Dandy: An Autobiography*. New York: Chelsea House, 1969.

Johnson, Rashid. Anderson Ranch Art Center Lecture. August 2012. http://vimeo.com/4815778. Accessed December 20, 2013.

Jones, LeRoi (Amiri Baraka). *Dutchman and the Slave*. New York: Morrow, 1964. Print.

Jones, Lisa. "She Came with the Rodeo." In her *Bulletproof Diva: Tales of Race, Sex, and Hair*. New York: Doubleday, 1994.

Jovanovic, Rozalia. "Rashid Johnson on Staging LeRoi Jones in the Era of Amiri Baraka." BlouinArtInfo, November 8, 2013. http://www.blouinartinfo.com/news/story/982418/rashid-johnson-on-staging-leroi-jones-in-the-age-of-amiri. Accessed September 3, 2013.

Kelley, Robin D. G. "Looking for the 'Real' Nigga: Social Scientists Construct the Ghetto." In his *Yo Mama's Dysfunktional!: Fighting the Culture Wars in Urban America*. Boston: Beacon Press, 1997.

Kennedy, Randall L. *Nigger: The Strange Career of a Troublesome Word*. New York: Vintage, 2003.

———. "Who Can Say "Nigger"? And Other Considerations." *Journal of Blacks in Higher Education* 26 (Winter 1999–2000): 86–96.

Kennedy, Randy. "A Play That's Sure to Make You Sweat: Baraka's 'Dutchman' to Be Staged in a Bathhouse." *New York Times*, November 10, 2013, D3.

Kerr, Walter. "First Night Report: A Raisin in the Sun." Review of *A Raisin in the Sun*. By Lorraine Hansberry. *New York Herald-Tribune*, March 12, 1959, 18.

———. "Not Since Edward Albee . . ." Review of *No Place to Be Somebody: A Black Black Comedy in Three Acts*. By Charles Gordone. *New York Times*, May 18, 1969, D1.

Kriegsman, Alan M. "On Being Black." *Washington Post-Times Herald*, June 18, 1971, B13.
Kroll, Jack. "Theatre: Zapping Black Stereotypes." *Newsweek*, November 17, 1986, 85.
Lomax, Louis. "The White Liberal." *Ebony*, August 1965, 59–64.
"The March on Washington for Jobs and Freedom." Civil Rights Movement Veterans Website. http://www.crmvet.org/tim/tim63b.htm#1963mow.
McClain, John. "Theatre." Review of *A Raisin in the Sun*. By Lorraine Hansberry. *New York Journal-American*, March 12, 1959, 35.
McGee, Celia. "A Return to Rage, Played Out in Black and White." *New York Times*, January 14, 2007.
Monroe, Al. "The Sun Shines Brightly" Review of *A Raisin in the Sun*. By Lorraine Hansberry. *Chicago Daily Defender*, February 21, 1959.
Muñoz, José Esteban. *Disidentifications: Queers of Color and the Performance of Politics*. Minneapolis: University of Minnesota Press, 1999.
Neal, Larry. "The Black Arts Movement." *Drama Review* 12, no. 4 (Summer 1968): 29–38.
Neal, Mark Anthony. *Soul Babies: Black Popular Culture and the Post-Soul Aesthetic*. New York: Routledge, 2002.
Novick, Julius. "Tragic Cakewalk." Review of *The Great White Hope*. By Howard Sackler. *The Nation*, January 15, 1968, 93–94.
Oliver, Edith. "Off Broadway over the Edge." Review of *Dutchman*. By LeRoi Jones (Amiri Baraka). *The New Yorker*, April 4, 1964, 23.
"'On Being Black' in KCET Debut Saturday Night." *Los Angeles Sentinel*, October 2, 1969: E2.
Oppenheimer, George. "Play Attempts to Show Blacks Have 'No Place.'" Review of *No Place to Be Somebody: A Black Black Comedy in Three Acts*. By Charles Gordone. *Newsday*, May 5, 1969, 32A.
Peerman, Dean. "A Raisin in the Sun: The Uncut Version." *Christian Century*, January 25, 1989, 71–73.
Popkin, Henry. "Dutchman a Furious Account." Review of *Dutchman*. By LeRoi Jones (Amiri Baraka). *Vogue*, July 1964, 32.
Pressley, Nelson. "The Good Fight: Arena Stage Goes Another Round with the Heavyweight Drama That Changed All the Rules." *American Theatre*, October 2000: 28+.
"Public Theater Presents Black Black Comedy." Review of *No Place to Be Somebody: A Black Black Comedy in Three Acts*. By Charles Gordone. *New York Amsterdam News*, May 3, 1969, 24.
Quashie, Kevin Everod. "The Problem of Blackness in Contemporary Criticism." Lecture, University of Sarajevo, Bosnia and Herzegovina, November 29, 2005.
Rainwater, Lee, and William L. Yancey. *The Moynihan Report and the Politics of Controversy*. Cambridge, MA: MIT Press, 1967.
Reed, Rosemary E. "The Committee for the Employment of Negro Performers. A Report on Group Action—An Attempt to Make Producers Present a Realistic Picture of

American Life in the Area of Mass Communications," May 1962. Charles Gordone Collection. Box 1, Folder 6. Schomburg Center for Research in Black Culture. New York, NY.

Report of the National Advisory Commission on Civil Disorders. Washington, DC: Government Printing Office, 1968.

Riley, Clayton. "A Black View: O, Blacks Are We Damned Forever?" *New York Times*, May 18, 1969, 22.

Roberts, Randy. *Papa Jack: Jack Johnson and the Era of Great White Hopes*. New York: Free Press, 1983.

Robinson, Vivian. "Opening Night Vibrations." *New York Amsterdam News*, November 14, 1970, 23.

Román, David. *Acts of Intervention: Performance, Gay Culture and AIDS*. Bloomington: Indiana University Press, 1998.

———. *Performance in America: Contemporary U.S. Culture and the Performing Arts*. Durham, NC: Duke University Press, 2005.

Roth, Philip. "Channel X: Two Plays on the Race Conflict." *New York Times Review of Books*, May 28, 1964, 10–12.

Sackler, Howard. *The Great White Hope*. New York: Dial, 1968.

———. "The Great White Hope." November 1, 1967. Typescript. Howard Sackler Manuscripts. Harry Ransom Humanities Research Center. University of Texas at Austin.

Sánchez-Eppler, Karen. "Bodily Bonds: The Intersecting Rhetorics of Feminism and Abolitionism." In *The New American Studies: Essays from Representations*. Ed. Philip Fisher. Berkeley: University of California Press, 1991, 235–36.

Scott, Joan W. "The Evidence of Experience." *Critical Inquiry* 17, no. 4 (Summer 1991): 773–97.

Shayon, Robert Lewis. "Curiouser and Curiouser." *Saturday Review*, August 8, 1970, 43.

Shepard, Richard. "'Great White Hope' Author Avoided Strict History." *New York Times*, May 6, 1969, 35.

Siegel, Ed. "New York Stage Report: Bright But Not Sunny, the Sentimental Is Out in a Crop of Smart Plays." Review of *A Raisin in the Sun*. By Lorraine Hansberry. *Boston Globe*, May 30, 2004, N4.

Skocpol, Theda, Ariane Liazos, and Marshall Ganz. *What a Mighty Power We Can Be: African American Fraternal Groups and the Struggle for Racial Equality*. Princeton, NJ: Princeton University Press, 2006.

Smethurst, James. *The Black Arts Movement: Literary Nationalism in the 1960s and 1970s*. Chapel Hill: University of North Carolina Press, 2005.

Smith, Anna Deveare. "Two Visions of Love, Family and Race across the Generations." *New York Times*, May 29, 2004, B9.

Smith, Cecil. "'Great White Hope' a New Champion on Broadway." Review of *The Great White Hope*. By Howard Sackler. *Los Angeles Times*, November 17, 1968, D30.

Smith, Susan Harris. "An Interview with Charles Gordone." *Studies in American Drama.* Vol. 3. *1945 to Present* (Erie, PA: P. C. Kolin and C. H. Kullman, 1988): 123–32.

Southall, Ashley. "Statue of Rosa Parks Is Unveiled at Capitol." *New York Times*, February 27, 2013. http://mobile.nytimes.com/2013/02/28/us/politics/statue-of-rosa-parks-is-unveiled-at-the-capitol.html. Accessed 30 June 2013.

Spelman, Elizabeth. *The Fruits of Sorrow: Framing Our Attention to Suffering.* Boston: Beacon Press, 1998.

Tate, Gregory. *Flyboy in the Buttermilk: Essays on Contemporary America.* New York: Fireside Press, 1992.

Taubman, Howard. "The Theatre: 'Dutchman' Opens on Triple Bill at the Cherry Lane." Review of *Dutchman*. By LeRoi Jones. *New York Times*, March 25, 1964, 48.

Taylor, Willene P. "The Fall of Man Theme in Imamu Amiri Baraka's (LeRoi Jones') Dutchman." *Negro American Literature Forum* 7, no. 4 (Winter 1973): 127–31.

"The Theater: Feeling Good by Feeling Bad." Review of *The Great White Hope*. By Howard Sackler. *Time*, October 11, 1968, 73.

"Theatre Wing: 'Wine in the Wilderness' Has Premiere at NIU." Review of *Wine in the Wilderness*. By Alice Childress. *Chicago Daily Defender*, December 15, 1970, 11.

Theoharis, Jeanne. *The Rebellious Life of Mrs. Rosa Parks.* Boston: Beacon Press, 2013.

Touré. *Who's Afraid of Postblackness: What It Means to Be Black Now.* New York: Free Press, 2011.

Trotter, Joe William. "African American Fraternal Associations in American History: An Introduction." *Social Science History* 28, no. 3 (2004): 355–66.

"Underground Fury." Review of *Dutchman*. By LeRoi Jones. *Newsweek*, April 13, 1964, 60.

United States Kerner Commission. *Report of the National Advisory Commission on Civil Disorders.* New York: Bantam, 1968.

Wanzo, Rebecca. *The Suffering Will Not Be Televised: African American Women and Sentimental Political Storytelling.* Albany, NY: SUNY Press, 2009.

Ward, Brian. *Media, Culture, and the African American Freedom Struggle of the 1960s.* Tallahassee: University of Florida Press, 2001.

Ward, Douglas Turner. "American Theatre: For Whites Only?" *New York Times*, August 14, 1966, 93.

Ward, Geoffrey C. *Unforgivable Blackness: The Rise and Fall of Jack Johnson.* New York: Knopf, 2004.

Washington, J. Charles. "A Raisin in the Sun Revisited." *Black American Literature Forum.* Black Women Writers Issue, 22, no. 1 (1988): 109–24.

Washington, Mary Helen. "Alice Childress, Lorraine Hansberry and Claudia Jones: Black Women Write the Popular Front." In *Left of the Color Line: Race, Radicalism and Twentieth Century Literature.* Ed. Bill V. Mullen and James Smethurst. Chapel Hill: University of North Carolina Press, 2003.

WGBH-TV Boston Program Logs for "On Being Black." WGBH Archives, 1–15. Boston.

Wilkerson, Margaret B. "Lorraine Hansberry: The Complete Feminist." *Freedomways: A Quarterly Review of the Freedom Movement* 19, no. 4 (1979): 235–55.

Young, Harvey. "Between the Ropes: Staging the Black Body in American Boxing." In his *Embodying Black Experience: Stillness, Critical Memory, and the Black Body*. Ann Arbor: University of Michigan Press, 2010.

Zelizer, Barbie. "Journalism's Memory Work." In *Cultural Memory Studies: An International and Interdisciplinary Handbook*. Ed. Astrid Erll and Ansgar Nünning. Berlin: Walter de Gruyter, 2008.

INDEX

Abelman, Bob, 157
ACT Theatre (Seattle), 156
Advocates, The (NET), 124
AETC. *See* Alabama Educational Television Commission
Affirmative action, 13
African American fraternal organizations. *See* black fraternal organizations
African American Freedom Struggle, 7–21, 23–24, 29, 33, 45, 57–58, 60, 73, 79–80, 82, 86–88, 100, 102–3, 106, 116, 123, 128, 132, 137–40, 142, 155, 157–60, 163, 174
African Americans: in American West, 131; audiences, 100, 157–58; critics, 14, 18, 55, 100–101, 127–28, 152–54, 157, 160; foodways, 186
African culture, 45–48
"Afristocracy," 108
Afro, 111–12, 167
Ailey, Alvin, 123
Alabama Educational Television Commission, 123–24
Albee, Edward, 75
Aldridge, Cathy, 102
Alexander, Jane, 100
Ali, Muhammad, 19, 82, 87–88, 101, 103, 175–76
Allusion-disruption strategy, 12–13, 15, 28, 34, 43–45, 47, 84, 106, 134, 158–59
Als, Hilton, 79
Alton Flipped (James), 123

Alvin Ailey Dance Theater, 123
Alvin Theatre (New York), 82
American National Theatre and Academy, 152
American Negro Theatre, 105–6
American Stage Theater, 132
Anabiosis (Gordone), 130
Anderson, Marian, 143
Anekwe, Simon, 152
anger. *See* rage
ANTA. *See* American National Theatre and Academy
aracial universality, 50–54, 84–85, 103, 175–76
Arena Stage (Washington, DC), 82
Asagai, Joseph (*A Raisin in the Sun*), 16, 32, 34, 40, 44–49
Ashe, Bertram, 12, 13, 28–29, 34, 61, 84, 87, 142, 155–56
Assimilation, 40–42, 45–47
Aston, Frank, 50, 52
Atkinson, Brooks, 50–52

Bachman, Eleanor (*The Great White Hope*), 93, 97, 100
Bailey, Peter, 100, 153–54
Bakke case. *See Regents of the University of California vs. Bakke*
Baldwin, James, 76–78, 157
Bambara, Toni Cade, 101
Baraka, Amiri, 17–18, 55, 57–80, 106, 132, 147, 154, 160, 171, 173
Barnes, Clive, 101, 152

BARTS. *See* Black Arts Repertory Theatre and School
Basis of Need (Riley), 123
Beatty, Paul, *The White Boy Shuffle*, 129, 132
Beatty, Talley, 123
Beauty standards, 45–47
Beckwourth, James P., 131
Belafonte, Harry, 106
Bennett, Lerone, Jr., 64
Bernstein, Robin, 50, 53, 73–74
Big Black Fire, The (DeCoy), 176
Black Aesthetic Movement, 132, 135, 137, 144, 163, 180
Black aestheticians, 20, 100, 104, 106, 132–33
Black Arts Movement, 7, 9–10, 17, 19–20, 45, 57, 100, 106, 111, 113–14, 119, 122, 126, 132–35, 137, 144, 147–48, 150, 163, 173–74, 180
"Black Arts Movement, The" (L. Neal), 133, 136
Black Arts Repertory Theatre and School, 154
Black Belt (T. Beatty), 123
Black Champion: The Life and Times of Jack Johnson (Farr), 176
Black bohemianism, 68–69
Black femininity, 22–56, 106, 108, 111–15, 118–23, 127, 150
Black feminism, 22–24, 26, 30–36, 40–43, 49, 55–56, 108–20, 165, 181
black fraternal organizations, 20, 116–18, 181; Improved Benevolent Order of the Elks of the World, 20, 106, 116–18, 181; Order of the Eastern Star, 116, 181; Prince Hall Masons, 116, 181
Black Girl (Franklin), 123
Black hair, 41, 45–47, 110–12, 167. *See also* Afro
Black History Month, 29–30
Black Lady in Mourning (*No Place to Be Somebody*), 150

Black masculinity, 38, 58, 61–64, 81, 110–11, 114, 175, 187
Black media, 58–61, 76, 88, 127–28
Black middle class, 25, 34, 39, 70, 95–96, 107–12, 120–21, 177. *See also* Class
Black No More (Schuyler), 143
Black Panther Party for Self-Defense, 20, 111
Black Power Movement, 8, 9–10, 17, 19–20, 45, 106, 111, 115–16, 126, 137, 165, 175, 180
Black subjectivity, 16–18, 22–23, 28–29, 32, 37–50, 187
Black Theatre Workshop (Northern Illinois University), 127
Black working class, 115–16, 120–21
Blackface minstrelsy, 85–86, 90, 96, 175
Blackness, as performance, 17–18
"Blackness of Blackness" (*Invisible Man*), 150
"Black-on-black emancipation proclamations," 158–59
"Blaxploration," 28, 84, 130
Blood Knot (Fugard), 100
Blues for Mr. Charlie (Baldwin), 77–78
Boehner, John, 5
Bootstrap philosophy, 143
Bourgeois morality, 25, 35–38, 86–89, 96
Brantley, Ben, 157–58
Bromberg, Conrad, 123
Brooks, Gwendolyn, 165
Brotherhood of Sleeping Car Porters, 137
Brown, Drew "Bundini," 103
Brown, John, 113, 117
Brown, Kimberly N., 71
Brown vs. Board of Education, 10, 136
Bullins, Ed, 100, 147, 154
Bunce, Alan, 101

Caldwell, Ben, 133
Candidate, The (Hayes), 123
Cap'n Dan (*The Great White Hope*), 94
Carmella & King Kong (Lisa Jones), 22, 24

Carmichael, Stokely, 10, 137
Carpio, Glenda, 79
Carter, Dan, 76
Cell Block Theater (Bordentown, New Jersey), 21
Chafe, William, 65, 68
Chappell, Marissa, and Jenny Hutchinson and Brian Ward, 86, 139
Cherry Lane Theatre (New York), 73, 78–79
Chicago Daily Defender, 52, 101
Chickenbones and Watermelon Seeds: The African American Experience as Abstract Art (R. Johnson), 57
Childress, Alice, 19–20, 104–28, 165
Christian Science Monitor, 101, 124–25
Christianity, 16, 33, 35–38
City Players of St. Louis, 130
Civil Rights Act (1964), 137, 145; white backlash, 75–76
Civil Rights Movement, 3–13, 24, 29–30, 58, 73, 84, 130, 135–47, 155, 163; civility and respectability, 12, 19, 25, 33, 67–68, 70, 86–88, 91, 95–96, 139, 141–42, 144, 146–47, 162; counternarrative, 10, 19, 70, 93–96, 106, 110–11, 113, 115–16, 137, 142–45; Heroic Era, 3–13, 106, 116, 136, 146–47; inspirational fable, 3–13; master narrative, 3–12, 20–21, 136–37, 158–59, 161–62; narrative messiness, 8, 159. *See also* African American Freedom Struggle
Clark, Kenneth B., 64
Class, 19–20, 25, 36–43, 74, 86, 95, 106–13, 116, 120–21, 128, 137–44, 162, 177; consciousness, 117–18; mobility, 16, 25, 37–39, 54, 88; stratification, 25; warfare, 108, 110, 112. *See also* Black middle class; Black working class; Classism
Classism, 43, 86, 95, 109–12, 116–17, 120–21, 181–82

Clay (*Dutchman*), 17–18, 58–80, 106–7, 147
Clay, Cassius. *See* Ali, Muhammad
Cleaver, Eldridge, 111
Clurman, Harold, 102
Colbert, Soyica Diggs, 121
Colbert, Stephen, 162–63
Color-blind casting, 131
Colored Museum, The (Wolfe), 29
Colvin, Claudette, 25, 161–62
Combination Skin (Lisa Jones), 22, 24
Combs, Sean, 157
Committee for the Employment of Negro Performers (CENP), 21, 155, 184
Congress of Racial Equality, 137, 155, 184
Cora (*No Place to Be Somebody*), 137
CORE. *See* Congress of Racial Equality
Cornell, Ted, 152
Crane, Sweets (*No Place to Be Somebody*), 135
Critical generosity, 85
Cross-dressing. *See* Drag
Crouch, Stanley, 79
Cultural memory, 3–12, 14–15, 20–21, 23, 29, 73, 80–81, 83, 87, 103–28, 139, 146, 158, 160, 163, 173, 180
"Cultural mulatto," 18, 21, 27–28, 84, 97, 129–30, 132, 134, 155, 174
Cultural nationalism, 20, 147–48, 160
Cynthia (*Wine in the Wilderness*), 19, 108–28

Daily Worker, 106
Danger Zone (Elder), 123
Danto, Arthur, 27
Davis, Benjamin O., 143
Davis, Miles, 176
Davis, Ossie, 55, 184
Davis, Sammy, Jr., 143
Dead Lecturer: Laboratory, Dojo and Performance Space, The (R. Johnson), 57
Dead Lecturer, The (LeRoi Jones), 57, 170
Dean, Phillip Hayes, 123

Decoy, Robert, 176
DeKoven, Marianne, 11, 29
Demille, Darcy, 52
Disidentification, 34, 44
Disturbatory art, 27, 174
Dixon, Ivan, 52
Dixon, Jim (*The Great White Hope*), 93–95, 97
Double consciousness, 61, 63–64, 71–72, 75, 156
Douglas, Frederick, 113
Dostoyevsky, Fyodor, 158
Drag, 150, 187
Driver, Tom F., 53–54
Du Bois, W. E. B., 26, 28, 61
Dubey, Madhu, 130
Dutchman (LeRoi Jones), 13, 17–18, 57–80, 106, 112, 156, 160
Dyson, Michael Eric, 108, 132

"Easy to Remember" (Simpson), 104–5
Ebony Magazine, 58–61, 64
Elam, Harry J., Jr., 57–58, 135, 149, 187; and Douglas A. Jones, 85–86
Elder, Lonnie, III, 123
Eliot, T. S., 158
Elks. *See* black fraternal organizations: Improved Benevolent Order of the Elks of the World
Ellis, Trey, 13, 15, 21, 24–27, 84, 97, 104, 159
Ellison, Ralph, 149, 156, 158–59
Emancipation Proclamation, 141
Ensemble Theatre (Cleveland), 156
Eppler, Karen Sanchez. *See* Sanchez-Eppler, Karen
Exceptionalism, 61, 73–74, 91, 94

Face in the Mirror, The (Bromberg), 123
Factor, Ben, 131
Farr, Finis, 176
Farrakhan, Louis, 8

Faulkner, William, 158
Federal Bureau of Investigation, 106
Feminism. *See* Black feminism
"57/09" (Simpson), 104
Florence (Childress), 105
"For a Strong Negro People's Theater" (Childress), 106–7, 127
Ford, Bill, 123
Foster, Paul, 124
Franklin, J. E., 123
Freedom Struggle. *See* African American Freedom Struggle
Freeman, Al, Jr., 123
Freestyle, 26–28, 57
Freud, Sigmund, 187
Fugard, Athol, 100
Fugitive, The (Gordone), 131
Fuller, Hoyt W., 76, 100, 153
Funnyhouse of a Negro (A. Kennedy), 76

Gabriel, Gabe (*No Place to Be Somebody*), 20–21, 129, 132–55
Gaines, Kevin, 34–35, 37, 39, 71, 86, 177
Garber, Marjorie, 187
Garrett, Jimmy, 133
Gender, 16, 19–20, 22, 33–43, 45–46, 58, 61–64, 86, 106, 108–23, 127, 150, 161–63, 168, 175, 179, 187. *See also* Black femininity
Genuine realism, 127
George, Nathan, 153
George, Nelson, 13
"Ghettocracy," 108
Gilman, Richard, 102
Gilmore, Al-Tony, 176
Golden, Harry, 101
Golden, Thelma, 26–28
Gordon, Michelle, 38
Gordone, Charles, *No Place to Be Somebody:*

A Black Black Comedy, 20–21, 100, 129–55, 184
Gordone Is a Muthah (Gordone), 130
Gossett, Lou, Jr., 123
Gottfried, Martin, 147–48, 152
Gould, Jack, 125–26
Great Migration, 25, 36–38, 93–96
Great White Hope, The (film), 176
Great White Hope, The (play), 13, 18–19, 81–103, 156–57, 160, 174–75
Gregory, Dick, 123
Gunn, Moses, 123
Gussow, Mel, 152

Hair (Rado and Ragni), 100
Hall, Jacqueline Dowd, 137
Hansberry, Lorraine, 16, 22–56, 127, 168–69
Harlem Civil Disturbance of 1965, 19, 108, 115–16
Harlem Renaissance, 12, 133
Harper, Phillip Brian, 119
Harriman, Averell, 68
Harris, Moses "Black," 131
Haskell, Molly, 152
Hayes, Rose Jourdain, 123
Heimskringla or the Stoned Angels (Foster), 124
Hemingway, Ernest, 158
Hero Ain't Nothin' but a Sandwich, A (Childress), 105
Heroic Era. *See* Civil Rights Movement: Heroic Era
Heteronormative black family. *See* Patriarchal family
Heyward, Dubose, 85
Hill, Abram, 105
Homophobia, 180
hooks, bell, 75, 147–48
Hooks, Robert, 154
Hoover, Ted, 157

Howe, Irving, 158, 160
Hughes, Langston, 158
Humphrey, Hubert, 145
Hutchinson, Jenny. *See* Chappell, Marissa

"I Have a Dream" (King), 137
Improved Benevolent Order of the Elks of the World. *See* Black fraternal organizations: Improved Benevolent Order of the Elks of the World
In the Wine Time (Bullins), 100
Intellectual freedom, 16, 22–56
Invisible Man (Ellison), 149

Jack Johnson (documentary), 176
Jack Johnson Is a Dandy: An Autobiography (J. Johnson), 176
Jackson, Jesse, 186
James, Luther, 123, 126
Jameson, Bill (*Wine in the Wilderness*), 19, 107–28, 181–82
Jefferson, Jack (*The Great White Hope*), 18–19, 82–103, 174–76
Jim Crow, 3, 5, 12, 37–38, 43–44, 95. *See also* Segregation
Johnny Ghost (Dean), 123
Johnson, Jack, 81–103, 176
Johnson, Lyndon B., 3, 7, 115, 145, 178
Johnson, Mrs. (*A Raisin in the Sun*), 16, 43–44
Johnson, Rashid, 57–58, 61, 73, 80–82, 160, 170
Johnson Publishing Company, 58–59
Jones, Douglas A., and Harry J. Elam Jr., 85–86
Jones, James Earl, 88, 101
Jones, LeRoi, 57–80, 171. *See also* Baraka, Amiri
Jones, Lisa, 13, 15, 22–24, 26

Karamu House (Cleveland), 156
Kauffman, Gunnar (*The White Boy Shuffle*), 129–30, 132
Kelley, Robin D. G., 41, 111
Kennedy, Adrienne, 76
Kennedy, John F., 137–38, 145
Kennedy, Randall, 120
Kerner Commission Report (Report of the National Advisory Commission on Civil Disorders), 19–20, 106, 115–16, 123–25, 127, 178
Kerr, Walter, 52, 152
Kid, The (*The Great White Hope*), 97–99
King, Martin Luther, 8, 9, 113, 137, 139–45, 162–63, 185
Knight, Ethridge, 144–45, 148
Kongi's Harvest (Soyinka), 100
Kouyomijian, Susan, 131
Kriegsman, Alan, 125–26, 128
Kumar, Nita, 17

Laughing to Keep from Crying, 123
"Last Mama on the Couch Play, The" (Wolfe), 29, 35
Leon, Kenny, 158
Lewis, John, 138, 145
Ligon, Glenn, 27
Like One of the Family (Childress), 165
Lincoln, Abbey, 41, 123–24, 126
Lincoln, Abraham, 91, 177
Lindner, Karl (*A Raisin in the Sun*), 49
Lomax, Louis, 64–65, 68
Lorna Simpson: Gathered, 104–5, 128
Los Angeles Sentinel, 127
Lubiano, Wahneema, 133, 148, 152
Lula (*Dutchman*), 17–18, 58–80, 106–7

Mabley, Moms, 123
Macbeth, Robert, 154
Mailer, Norman, 175

Malcolm X, 8, 9, 113
Mann Act, 18, 87–88, 93–95, 97
March on Washington for Jobs and Freedom (1963), 3, 20, 58, 60, 73, 79, 132, 134, 136–37, 139–48
Marriage, 33–43, 49
Masses and Mainstream, 106
Master Narrative of Civil Rights Movement. *See* Civil Rights Movement: master narrative
Matriarchal family, 35–39, 109–10, 114, 116
Matthews, Edmond "Oldtimer" (*Wine in the Wilderness*), 108–28
Maud Martha (Brooks), 165
McClain, John, 53
McConnell, Mitch, 5–6
McDonald, Audra, 157
McNeil, Claudia, 51
Men Are Not Made of Steel (Russell), 123
Methuen Drama Book of Post-Black Plays, The, 85–86
Militant Preacher (Caldwell), 133
Million Man March, 8
Milner, Ron, 100, 133
Mingus, Charles, 184
Minstrel imagery, 37
Minstrelsy. *See* Blackface minstrelsy
Miscegenation, 93
Monroe, Al, 52
Montgomery Bus Boycott, 3–13, 25, 140, 161–62
Mojo (Childress), 127
Mother Africa trope, 114
Motherhood, 33, 35–36
"Mourning and Melancholia" (Freud), 187
Moynihan, Daniel Patrick, 110
Moynihan Report. *See Negro Family, The*
Mr. Roger's Neighborhood, 124
Muñoz, Jose Esteban, 34

Murchison, George (*A Raisin in the Sun*), 16, 22, 34, 38–43, 168

NAACP. *See* National Association for the Advancement of Colored People
NAB. *See* National Black Theatre
Narrative messiness. *See* Civil Rights Movement: narrative messiness
Nation, The, 101–2
Nation of Islam, 8
National Advisory Committee on Civil Disorders. *See* Kerner Commission Report
National African American Leadership Summit, 8
National Association for the Advancement of Colored People, 8, 20, 137–38, 161–63
National Black Theatre (NBT), 154
National Educational Television (NET), 19, 122–25
National redemption narrative, 5–6
National Urban League, 137
Natural hair. *See* Black Hair
NBA. *See* New Black Aesthetic
Neal, Larry, 17, 133, 136, 147–48
Neal, Mark Anthony, 13, 15, 25–26
Negro Digest, 153
Negro Ensemble Company (NEC), 100, 147, 154
Negro Family: The Case for National Action, The (Moynihan Report), 106, 110, 112, 114, 116
Negro Question, 23, 54–55, 73–75, 77
Nemiroff, Robert, 41
Neo-African essentialism, 17
NET. *See* National Educational Television
NET Journal, 125
New Black Aesthetic, 15, 24–28, 104, 174. *See also* Post-soul aesthetic
New Heritage Repository Theater (Harlem), 127

New Lafayette Theatre (New York), 100, 154
New Leader, 158
New Republic, 102
New York Amsterdam News, 102, 127, 152
New York Daily News, 50, 52
New York Shakespeare Festival's Public Theater, 152
New York Times, 50–52, 125–26, 152
New York Times Book Review, 75
NLT. *See* New Lafayette Theatre
No Place to Be Somebody: A Black Black Comedy (Gordone), 13, 19–20, 100, 129–57, 160
Non-African American playwrights, 84–85
Novick, Julius, 101

Obama, Barack, 5, 186
O'Boyle, Patrick, 138
Odetta, 41
"Oldtimer." *See* Matthews, Edmond "Oldtimer"
Oliver, Edith, 75–77
On Being Black (NET), 19, 123–26
O'Neal, Frederick, 105
O'Neal, Ron, 153
O'Neill, Eugene, 85
Oppenheimer, George, 152
Order of the Eastern Star. *See* Black fraternal organizations: Order of the Eastern Star
Oser, Jennifer Lynn, and Theda Skopcol, 117

Papp, Joseph, 152–54
Parker, Charlie, 71
Parks, Rosa, 3–9, 25, 161–63
Parks, Suzan-Lori, 79
Patriarchal family, 16, 38–43, 114
Patriarchy, 16–17, 38–43
Pavilion Theatre (Penn State University), 156
Peerman, Dean, 54
Performa, 13, 58, 61, 79, 156

Pierce, Jim, 131
Pivot texts, 29
"Please remind me of who I am" (Simpson), 104–5
Poitier, Sidney, 51, 106, 143
Pop (*The Great White Hope*), 94
Popkin, Henry, 78–79
Postcolonialism, 45–48
Post-modernism, 29
Post-soul aesthetic (PSA), 12–13, 15, 18, 24–29, 34, 43–44, 47, 61, 83–84, 97, 142, 174. *See also* New Black Aesthetic
Powell, Adam Clayton, 101, 113
Prayer Meeting, or the First Militant Minister (Caldwell), 133
"Presentist," 14
Prince Hall Masons. *See* Black Fraternal Organizations: Prince Hall Masons
Profanity, 77–78, 123
Progressive Era, 18, 25, 81, 83–86, 88, 90–91, 93, 95–99, 103, 174–75
Progressive mystique, 65, 67, 70
PSA. *See* Post-soul aesthetic
Public Theater, 100, 152
Pulitzer Prize for Drama, 82

Quashie, Kevin Everod, 84–85, 176
Quasi-postblack Texts, 12
Questlove (Ahmir Thompson), 186

Race man archetype, 84, 91–95
Race neutral universality, 50–51, 82
Race riots, 19, 115, 149, 178
Race treason, 20–21, 153
Racial common sense, 18, 84–85, 88, 96–98, 100, 103
Racial segregation. *See* Jim Crow; Segregation: racial
Racial uplift ideology, 10, 16–18, 20, 22–62, 64, 67, 70–72, 83, 86, 89, 91–93, 95–99, 101, 112, 133, 160, 165, 167–68
Rage, 18, 74–80, 147–48, 150
Raisin in the Sun, A, 13, 16–17, 22–56, 73–74, 82, 102, 156–57, 160, 165, 168–69
Randolph, A. Philip, 137
Rashad, Phylicia, 157
Record Is 21 Minutes, The (Riley), 123
Red Square Russian and Turkish Baths (Chicago), 156
Regents of the University of California vs. Bakke, 13
"Remaining Awake through a Great Revolution" (King), 143, 184
Revelations (Ailey), 123
Riley, Clayton, 123, 132, 153
Roan Browne & Cherry (Gordone), 131
Roberts, John, 7
Robinson, Vivian, 127
Rodeo Caldonia High-Fidelity Performance Theater, 22–25
Román, David, 12–14, 15; and critical generosity, 85
Rose, Edward, 131
Roth, Phillip, 75–77
Rowan, Carl T., 64
Russell, Charlie, 123
Russian & Turkish Baths (New York), 58, 80, 156, 170
Rustin, Bayard, 137

Sackler, Howard, 18–19, 81–103, 174–76
Sanchez-Eppler, Karen, 53–54
Sands, Diana, 41, 52
"Santa Clausification," 8, 162–63
Say Brother, 127
Say It Out Loud (Ford), 123
Scalia, Antonin, 162
Schuyler, George, 143

SCLC. *See* Southern Christian Leadership Conference
Segregation, racial, 3–4, 25, 27, 38–39, 43–44, 139. *See also* Jim Crow
Self Portrait Laying on Jack Johnson's Grave (R. Johnson), 81
Sentimentality, 52–54
Sesame Street, 124–25
Sexism, 30–36, 40–43, 150, 165, 180, 187
Sexual content, 77–78, 123
Shelby County v. Holder, 7, 162
Sheridan Square Playhouse, 100, 152
Simone, Nina, 41
Simpson, Lorna, 104, 118
Skopcol, Theda, and Jennifer Lynn Oser, 117
Smethurst, James, 114
Smith, Anna Deveare, 157–58
Smith, Bessie, 71
Smith, Cecil, 102
Smith, Howard W., 145
Smith, Mary Louise, 161–62
Smitherman, Geneva, 120
SNCC. *See* Student Nonviolent Coordinating Committee
"Somebody Blew Up America" (Baraka), 173
Songs of the Lusitanian Bogey (Weiss), 100
Sonny-Man (*Wine in the Wilderness*), 19, 108–28
Soul on Ice (Cleaver), 111
Southern Christian Leadership Conference, 8, 20, 137
Soyinka, Wole, 100
"Speak Out on Drugs" (NET), 25
"Spiritual bellhop," 5
Spivak, Lawrence, 146
Street, Joe, 9
Student Nonviolent Coordinating Committee, 10, 137–38, 141, 145
Studio Museum (Harlem), 57
"Structure of feeling," 12–13

Subways Are for Sleeping (Betty Comden and Adolph Green), 184

Tate, Greg, 13, 15, 27, 84
Taubman, Howard, 78
Taylor, Nora E., 124–25
Teer, Barbara Ann, 154
"Texts out of time," 12
Theatre America (NET), 124
Theoharis, Jeanne, 3–4, 5
"Theorizing the Post-Soul Aesthetic: An Introduction," 156
Thompson, Ahmir. *See* Questlove
Tomorrow Marie "Tommy" (*Wine in the Wilderness*), 19, 107–28, 181–82
Touré, 57, 82, 107, 186
Tribute to Jack Johnson, A (M. Davis), 176
Trotter, Joe, 118
Trotter, Monroe, 113

Uncle Tom, 112
Universal/particular paradox, 18, 29, 40, 50–55, 73–74, 78, 82, 85, 87
Uplift ideology. *See* Racial uplift ideology
Us, 20

Village Voice, 152
Visibility, 17, 69–72, 150, 187
Voting Rights Act (1965), 3, 7, 10, 58, 60, 136, 162

Wallace, George, 75–76
Washington, Booker T., 16, 43–44, 89, 96
Washington, Denzel, 156
Washington Post, 125–26, 128
Wanzo, Rebecca, 8
Ward, Brian, 9. *See also* Chappell, Marissa
Ward, Douglas Turner, 154
Waterbearer, The (Simpson), 104
WBIQ, 123

We Own the Night (Garrett), 133
Weathervane Community Playhouse (Akron, Ohio), 156
Weiss, Peter, 100
Welcome to the Black Aesthetic (Rodeo Caldonia High-Fidelity Performance Theater), 24
West, Cornell, 186
West, Jennifer, 79
WGBH TV, 19, 123, 127
White audiences, 53–54, 100, 102
White backlash. *See* Civil Rights Movement: white backlash
White Boy Shuffle, The (P. Beatty), 129
White characters, objections about, 78–79, 154–55
White critics, 74–77, 124–26
White identity, 64–65
White liberals, 17, 64–65, 67–68, 76, 85, 100–101
"White Problem in America, The" (*Ebony Magazine*), 64
"Whiter Than Snow," 148
Who's Got His Own (Milner), 100, 133
Wilkerson, Margaret, 55
Wilkins, Roy, 137–38
Willard, Jess, 88
Williams, Billy Dee, 123
Williams, Johnny (*No Place to Be Somebody*), 135, 150, 153–54
Williams, Raymond, 12
Wine in the Wilderness, 13, 19–20, 104–28, 160
Wolfe, George, 29, 35
"World and the Jug, The" (Ellison), 156, 158
Wright, Richard, 156, 158

Younger, Beneatha (*A Raisin in the Sun*), 16, 22–56, 111, 165, 168
Younger, Lena (*A Raisin in the Sun*), 16, 22, 29, 32–33, 35–39, 50–52, 157
Younger, Ruth (*A Raisin in the Sun*), 16, 22, 32–37, 157, 168
Younger, Travis (*A Raisin in the Sun*), 22, 49
Younger, Walter Lee (*A Raisin in the Sun*), 16, 22, 29–32, 37–39, 47–52, 156–57, 168

Zoo Story, The (Albee), 75

York, 131
Young, Harvey, 176
Young, Whitney, 64, 137

www.ingramcontent.com/pod-product-compliance
Lightning Source LLC
Chambersburg PA
CBHW022019220426
43663CB00007B/1134